CO

The
CH SPURGEON
collection

Volume 1   COMFORT AND ASSURANCE

Volume 2   EVANGELISM

Volume 3   MIRACLES

Volume 4   PARABLES

Volume 5   PRAYER

Volume 6   PSALMS

Volume 7   REVIVAL

The
CH SPURGEON
collection

Comfort and Assurance

EMERALD HOUSE

BELFAST **GREENVILLE**
NORTHERN IRELAND **SOUTH CAROLINA**

The CH Spurgeon Collection
VOLUME 1: COMFORT AND ASSURANCE

Copyright © 1998 Emerald House Group

Published by

Emerald House Group, Inc.

1 Chick Springs Road, Suite 206
Greenville, SC 29609 USA

and

Ambassador Productions
16 Hillview Avenue
Belfast, Northern Ireland
BT5 6JR

Cover design and illustration by Matt Donovan

Handwriting in background on cover from actual sermon notes written by C.H.
Spurgeon. Used by permission. Courtesy of the Bob Jones University Mack Library.

CONTENTS

I. A NEW YEAR'S WISH 7
(*Phil. 4:19*)

II. GOOD CHEER FROM CHRIST'S VICTORY
OVER THE WORLD 17
(*John 16:33*)

III. THE CHRISTIAN'S HEAVINESS AND REJOICING . . . 28
(*I Peter 1:6*)

IV. FOR THE TROUBLED. 38
(*Psalm 88:7*)

V. "JESUS WEPT" 51
(*John 11:35*)

VI. "LET NOT YOUR HEART BE TROUBLED". 63
(*John 14:1-4*)

VII. "OUR LIGHT AFFLICTION" 76
(*2 Cor. 4:17*)

VIII. GOOD NEWS FOR OUTCASTS 86
(*Psalm 147:2*)

IX. THE JOY OF REDEMPTION. 99
(*Isaiah 44:23*)

X. HOPE FOR THE WORST BACKSLIDERS. 108
(*Jeremiah 3:22, 23*)

XI. BEAUTY FOR ASHES 120
(*Isaiah 61:3*)

XII. AN ENCOURAGING WORD IN TROUBLOUS TIMES. 134
(*Acts 27:25*)

XIII. THE DRAWINGS OF LOVE. 147
(*Jeremiah 31:3*)

XIV. THE BEST STRENGTHENING MEDICINE 158
(*Hebrews 11:34*)

XV. LIGHT AT EVENING TIME. 171
(*Zechariah 14:6, 7*)

XVI. SERMONS FROM SAINTLY DEATH-BEDS 182
(*Genesis 49:33*)

XVII. LIFE IN CHRIST 196
       (John 14:19)
XVIII. LIFE MORE ABUNDANT 209
       (John 10:10)

I

A NEW YEAR'S WISH

"But my God shall supply all your need, according to his riches in glory by Christ Jesus."—Phil. 4: 19.

THE Philippians had several times sent presents to Paul, to supply his necessities. Though they were not themselves rich, yet they made a contribution, and sent Epaphroditus with it, "an odour of a sweet smell, a sacrifice acceptable, well pleasing to God." Paul felt very grateful: he thanked God, but he did not forget also to thank the donors; he wished them every blessing, and he did as good as say, "You have supplied my need, and my God shall supply yours. You have supplied my need of temporal food and raiment out of your poverty ; my God shall supply all your need out of his riches in glory." "As," he says, in the eighteenth verse, "I have all and abound: I am full," "so," he adds, "'my God shall supply all your need.' You have sent what you gave me by the hand of a beloved brother, but God will send a better messenger to you, for he will supply all your need 'by Christ Jesus.'" Every single word sounds as if he had thought it over, and the Spirit of God had guided him in his meditation, so that he should to the fullest extent wish them back a blessing similar to that which they had sent to him, only of a richer and more enduring kind.

This verse is particularly sweet to me, for, when we were building the Orphanage, I foresaw that, if we had no voting, and no collecting of annual subscriptions, but depended upon the goodness of God, and the voluntary offerings of his people, we should have times of trial, and therefore I ordered the masons to place upon the first columns of the Orphanage entrance these words, "My God shall supply all your need, according to his riches in glory by Christ Jesus." The text therefore is cut in stone upon the right hand and upon the left of the great archway. There stands this declaration of our

7

confidence in God; and as long as God lives, we shall never need to remove it, for he will certainly supply the needs of his own work. While we serve him, he will furnish our tables for us.

The text might suggest to us a field of gloomy thought, if we wished to indulge the melancholy vein, for it speaks of "all your need." So, first, behold A GREAT NECESSITY: *"all your need."* What a gulf! What an abyss! *"All your need."* I do not know how many believers made up the church at Philippi, but the need of one saint is great enough; what must many need? It would not be possible to tell the number of God's children on earth, but the text comprehends the need of the whole chosen family, *"all your need."* We will not ask you to reckon up the wonderful draught upon the divine exchequer which must be made by all the needs of all the saints who are yet on earth: but please think of your own need; that will be more within the compass of your experience and the range of your meditation. May the Lord supply your need and *all* your need!

There is *our temporal need,* and that is no little matter. If we have food and raiment, we should be therewith content; but there are many of God's people to whom the mere getting of food and raiment is a wearisome toil; and what with household cares, family trials, sickness of body, losses in business, and sometimes the impossibility of obtaining suitable labour, many of God's saints are as hard put to it as Elijah was when he sat by the brook Cherith. If God did not send them their bread and meat in a remarkable manner, they would surely starve; but their bread shall be given them, and their water shall be sure. "My God shall supply all your need." You have, perhaps, a large family, and your needs are therefore greatly increased, but the declaration of the text includes the whole of your needs personal and relative.

After all, our temporal needs are very small compared with *our spiritual needs.* A man may, with the blessing of God, pretty readily provide for the wants of the body, but who shall provide for the requirements of the soul? There is need of perpetual pardon, for we are always sinning; and Jesus Christ's blood is always pleading for us, and cleansing us from sin. Every day there is need of fresh strength to battle against inward sin; and, blessed be God, it is daily supplied, so that our youth is renewed like the eagle's. As good soldiers of Jesus Christ, we need armour from head to foot, and even then we do not know how to wear the armour, or how to wield the sword, unless he who gave us these sacred implements shall be always with us. Warring saint, God will supply all your need by his presence and Spirit.

But we are not merely warriors, we are also workers. We are called, many of us, to important spheres of labour, (and, indeed, let no man think his sphere unimportant,) but here also our hands shall be sufficient for us, and we shall accomplish our life-work. You have need to be helped to do the right thing, at the right time, in the right spirit, and in the right manner; your need, as a Sunday-school teacher, as an open-air preacher, and especially as a minister of the Gospel, will be very great; but the text meets all your requirements, "My God shall supply all your need." Then comes our need in suffering, for many of us are called to take our turn in the Lord's prison-house. Here we need patience under pain, and hope under depression of spirit. Who is sufficient for furnace-work? Our God will supply us with those choice graces and consolations which shall strengthen us to glorify his name even in the fires. He will either make the burden lighter, or the back stronger; he will diminish the need, or increase the supply.

Beloved, it is impossible for me to mention all the forms of our spiritual need. We need to be daily converted from some sin or other, which, perhaps, we have scarcely known to be sin. We need to be instructed in the things of God, we need to be illuminated as to the mind of Christ, we need to be comforted by the promises, we need to be quickened by the precepts, we need to be strengthened by the doctrines. We need, oh, what do we *not* need? We are just a bag of wants, and a heap of infirmities. If any one of us were to keep a *want-book,* as I have seen tradesmen do, what a huge folio it would need to be; and it might be written within and without, crossed and re-crossed, for we are full of wants from the first of January to the end of December; but here is the mercy, "My God shall supply all your need."

"Are you put in high places? Have you many comforts? Do you enjoy wealth? What need you have to be kept from loving the world, to be preserved from wantonness and pride, and the follies and fashions of this present evil world. My God will supply your need in that respect. Are you very poor? Then the temptation is to envy, to bitterness of spirit, to rebellion against God. "My God shall supply all your need." Are you alone in the world? Then you need the Lord Jesus to be your Companion; and your Companion he will be. Have you many around you? Then you have need of grace to set them a good example, to bring up your children and manage your household in the fear of God. "My God shall supply all your need." You have need, in times of joy, to be kept sober and steady; you have need, in times of sorrow, to be strong and quit yourselves like men; you have needs in living, and you will have needs in dying, but your last need shall be supplied as surely as your first. "My God shall supply *all* your need."

That first thought, which I said might be a gloomy one, has all the dreariness taken out of it by four others equally true, but each of them full of good cheer.

So, second, for our enormous wants here is A GREAT HELPER: "*My God* shall supply all your need."

Whose God is that? Why, Paul's God. That is one of the matters in which the greatest saints are no better off than the very least, for though Paul called the Lord "My God," he is my God too. My dear old friend who sits yonder, and has nothing but a few pence in all the world, can also say, "and he is my God too. He is my God, and he is as much my God if I am the meanest, most obscure, and weakest of his people, as he would be my God if I were able, like Paul, to evangelize the nations." It is, to me, delightful to think that *my God is Paul's God*, because, you see, Paul intended this; he meant to say, "You see, dear brethren, my God has supplied all my wants; and as he is your God, he will supply yours." I have been in the Roman dungeon in which Paul is said to have been confined, and a comfortless prison indeed it is. First of all you descend into a vaulted chamber, into which no light ever comes except through a little round hole in the roof; and then, in the middle of the floor of that den, there is another opening, through which the prisoner was let down into a second and lower dungeon, in which no fresh air or light could possibly come to him. Paul was probably confined there. The dungeon of the

Prætorium in which he was certainly immured is not much better. Paul would have been left well nigh to starve there, but for those good people at Philippi. I should not wonder but what Lydia was at the bottom of this kind movement, or else the jailor. They said, "We must not let the good apostle starve"; and so they made up a contribution, and sent him what he wanted; and when Paul received it he said, "My God has taken care of me. I cannot make tents here in this dark place so as to earn my own living, but my Master still supplies my need; and even so, when you are in straits, will he supply you."

"*My* God." It has often been sweet to me, when I have thought of my orphan children, and money has not come in, to remember Mr. Müller's God, and how he always supplies the children at Bristol. His God is my God, and I rest upon him. When you turn over the pages of Scripture, and read of men who were in sore trouble, and were helped, you may say, "Here is Abraham, he was blessed in all things, and Abraham's God will supply all my need, for he is *my* God. I read of Elijah, that the ravens fed him; I have Elijah's God, and he can command the ravens to feed me if he pleases." The God of the prophets, the God of the apostles, the God of all the saints that have gone before us, "this God is our God for ever and ever." It seems to be thought by some that God will not work now as he used to do. "Oh, if we had lived in miraculous times," they say, "then we could have trusted him! Then there was manifest evidence of God's existence, for he pushed aside the laws of nature, and wrought for the fulfilment of his promises to his people." Yet that was a rather coarser mode of working than the present one, for now the Lord produces the same results without the violation of the laws of nature. It is a great fact that, without the disturbance of a single law of nature, prayer becomes effectual with God; and God being enquired of by his people to do it for them, does fulfil his promise, and supply their needs. Using means of various kinds, he still gives his people all things necessary for this life and godliness. Without a miracle, he works great wonders of loving care, and he will continue so to do.

Beloved, *is the God of Paul your God?* Do you regard him as such? It is not every man who worships Paul's God. It is not every professing Christian who really knows the Lord at all, for some invent a deity such as they fancy God ought to be. The God of Paul is the God of the Old and New Testament,— such a God as we find there. Do you trust such a God? Can you rest upon him? "There are such severe judgments mentioned in Scripture." Yes, do you quarrel with them? Then you cast him off; but if, instead thereof, you feel, "I cannot understand thee, O my God, nor do I think I ever shall, but it is not for me, a child, to measure the infinite God, or to arraign thee at my bar, and say to thee, 'Thus shouldst thou have done, and thus oughtest thou not to have done.' Thou sayest, 'Such am I,' and I answer, 'Such as thou art, I love thee, and I cast myself upon thee, the God of Abraham, of Isaac, and of Jacob, the God of thy servant Paul. Thou art my God, and I will rest upon thee.'" Very well, then, he will "supply all your need, according to his riches in glory by Christ Jesus." Just think of that for a minute.

If *he* will supply you, you will be supplied indeed, for God is infinite in capacity. He is infinitely wise as to the manner of his actions; and infinitely powerful as to the acts themselves. He never sleeps nor tires; he is never absent from any place, but is always ready to help. Your needs come, perhaps, at very unexpected times; they may occur in the midnight of despondency or in the noonday of delight, but God is ever near to supply the surprising need. He is everywhere present and everywhere omnipotent, and he can supply all your need, in every place, at every time, to the fullest degree. "Remember that Omnipotence has servants everywhere"; and that, whenever God wishes to send you aid, he can do it without pausing to ask, "How shall it be done?" He has but to will it, and all the powers of heaven and earth are subservient to your necessity. With such a Helper, what case have you to doubt?

The next point in the text is, A GREAT SUPPLY. "My God shall *supply* all your need."

Sometimes, we lose a good deal of the meaning of Scripture through the translation; in fact, nothing ever does gain by translation except a Bishop! The present passage might be rendered thus, "My God will fill to the full all your need." The illustration which will best explain the meaning is that of the woman whose children were to be sold by her creditor to pay the debts of her late husband. She had nothing to call her own

except some empty oil-jars, and the prophet bade her set these
in order, and bring the little oil which still remained in the
cruse. She did so, and he then said to her, "Go among your
neighbours, and borrow empty vessels, not a few." She went
from one to another till she had filled her room full of these
empty vessels, and then the prophet said, "Pour out." She
began to pour out from her almost empty cruse; and, to her
surprise, it filled her largest oil-jar. She went to another, and
filled that, and then another and another. She kept on filling
all the oil-jars, till at last she said to the prophet, "there is not
a vessel more." Then the oil stayed, but not till then. So will
it be with your needs. You were frightened at having so many
needs just now, were you not? But now be pleased to think
you have them, for they are just so many empty vessels to be
filled. If the woman had borrowed only a few jars, she could
not have received much oil; but the more empty vessels she
had, the more oil she obtained. "So, the more wants and the
more needs you have, if you bring them to God, so much the
better, for he will fill them all to the brim, and you may be
thankful that there are so many to be filled. When you have
no more wants, (but oh, when will that be?) then the supply
will be stayed, but not till then.

How gloriously God gives to his people! We wanted pardon
once: he washed us, and he made us whiter than snow. We
wanted clothing, for we were naked. What did he do? Give
us some rough dress or other? Oh, no! but he said, "Bring
forth the best robe, and put it on him." It was a fortunate
thing for the prodigal that his clothes were all in rags, for then
he needed raiment, and the best robe was brought forth. It is
a grand thing to be sensible of spiritual needs, for they will all
be supplied. A conscious want in the sight of God,—what is it
but a prevalent request for a new mercy? We have sometimes
asked him to comfort us, for we were very low; but when the
Lord has comforted us, he has so filled us with delight that we
have been inclined to cry with the old Scotch divine, "Hold,
Lord, hold! It is enough. I cannot bear more joy. Remember
I am only an earthen vessel." We, in relieving the poor, generally give no more than we can help, but our God does not stop
to count his favours, he gives like a king. He pours water upon
him that is thirsty, and floods upon the dry ground.

We must pass on to the next thought, and consider for a minute or two THE GREAT RESOURCES out of which this supply is to come: "My God shall supply all your need, *according to his riches in glory.*" The preacher may sit down now, for he cannot compass this part of the text. God's riches in glory are beyond all thought.

Consider *the riches of God in Nature;* who shall count his treasures? Get away into the forests; travel on league after league among the trees which cast their ample shade for no man's pleasure, but only for the Lord. Mark on lone mountain-side and far-reaching plain the myriads of flowers whose perfume is for God alone. What wealth each spring and summer is created in the boundless estates of the great King! Observe the vast amount of animal and insect life which crowds the land with the riches of divine wisdom, for "the earth is the Lord's, and the fulness thereof." Look towards the sea; think of those shoals of fish, so countless that, when only the fringe of them is touched by our fishermen, they find enough food to supply a nation. Mark, too, the sunken treasures of the ocean, which no hand gathereth but that of the Eternal. If you would see the wealth of the Creator, cast your eye to the stars; tell ye their numbers if ye can. Astronomy has enlarged our vision, and made us look upon this world as a mere speck compared with innumerable other worlds that God has made; and it has told us that, probably, all the myriads of worlds that we can see with the telescope are a mere fraction of the countless orbs which tenant infinite space. Vast are God's riches in nature. It needs a Milton to sing, as he sang in *Paradise Lost,* the riches of the creating God.

The riches of God in Providence are equally without bound. He saith to this creature, "Go," and he goeth, and to another, "Do this," and he doeth it, for all things do his bidding. Think of *the wealth of God in grace.* There nature and providence stand eclipsed, for we have the fountain of eternal love, the gift of an infinite sacrifice, the pouring out of the blood of his own dear Son, and the covenant of grace in which the smallest blessing is infinite in value. The riches of his grace! "God is rich in mercy,"—rich in patience, love, power, kindness, rich beyond all conception.

Now your needs shall be supplied according to the riches of

Nature, and the riches of Providence, and the riches of Grace; but this is not all; the apostle chooses a higher style, and writes "according to *his riches in glory.*" Ah, we have never seen God in glory! That were a sight our eyes could not at present behold. Christ in his glory, when transfigured upon earth, was too resplendent a spectacle even for the tutored eyes of Peter, and James, and John. "At the too-transporting light," darkness rushed upon them, and they were as men that slept. What God is in his glory do ye know, ye angels? Does he not veil his face even from you lest, in the excessive brightness of his essence, even you should be consumed? Who amongst all his creatures can tell the riches of his glory, when even the heavens are not pure in his sight, and he charges his angels with folly?

"His riches in Glory." It means not only the riches of what he has done, but the riches of what he could do; for if he has made hosts of worlds, he could make as many myriads more, and then have but begun. The possibilities of God omnipotent, who shall reckon? But the Lord shall supply all your need according to such glorious possibilities. When a great king gives according to his riches, then he does not measure out stinted alms to beggars, but he gives *like a king,* as we say; and if it be some grand festival day, and the king is in his state array, his largesse is on a noble scale. Now, when God is in his glory, bethink you, if you can, what must be the largesse that he distributes,—what the treasures that he brings forth for his own beloved! Now, "according to his riches in glory," he will supply all your needs. After that, dare you despond? O soul, what insanity is unbelief! What flagrant blasphemy is doubt of the love of God! He must bless us; and, blessed by him, we must be blest indeed. If he is to supply our needs "according to his riches in glory," they will be supplied to the full.

Now let us close our meditation by considering THE GLORIOUS CHANNEL by which these needs are to be supplied: "According to his riches in glory *by Christ Jesus.*"

You shall have all your soul's wants satisfied, but you must go to Christ for everything. "By Christ Jesus." That is the fountain-head where the living waters well up. You are not to keep your wants supplied by your own care and fretfulness. "Consider the lilies, how they grow." You are to be enriched "by Christ Jesus." You are not to have your spiritual wants supplied by going to Moses, and working and toiling as if you were your own saviour, but by faith in Christ Jesus. Those who will not go to Christ Jesus must go without grace, for God will give them nothing in the way of grace except through his Son. Those who go to Jesus the most shall oftenest taste of his abundance, for through him all blessings come. My advice to myself and to you is that we abide in him; for, since that is the way by which the blessing comes, we had better abide in it. We read of Ishmael that he was sent into the wilderness with a bottle, but Isaac dwelt by the well Lahai-roi, and it is wise for us to dwell by the well Christ Jesus, and never trust to the bottles of our own strength. If you wander from Christ Jesus, brother, you depart from the centre of bliss.

All this year I pray that you may abide by the well of this text. Draw from it. Are you very thirsty? Draw from it, for it is full and when you plead this promise, the Lord will supply all your need. Do not cease receiving from God for a minute. Let not your unbelief hinder the Lord's bounty, but cling to this promise, "My God shall supply all your need, according to his riches in glory by Christ Jesus." I know not how to wish you a greater blessing.

II

GOOD CHEER FROM CHRIST'S VICTORY
OVER THE WORLD

"These things I have spoken unto you, that in me ye might
have peace. In the world ye shall have tribulation: but be of
good cheer; I have overcome the world."—John 16: 33.

THE believer is in two places, and he lives two lives. In the
text are two places spoken of, "in me," and "in the world."
The saint's noblest life is "hid with Christ in God"; this is his
new life, his spiritual life, his incorruptible life, his everlasting
life. Rejoice, beloved, if you are in Christ, and enjoy the
privilege which belongs to that condition: "that in me ye might
have peace." Do not be satisfied without it; it is your right
through your relationship to the Prince of peace. Because you
are in Christ, your life of lives is always safe, and should be
always restful. Your greatest interests are all secure, for they
are guaranteed by the covenant of which Jesus is the Surety.
Your treasure, your eternal portion, is laid up with him in
heaven where neither rust nor robber can enter. Therefore, be
of good cheer.

You are sorrowfully conscious that you also live another life,
for you dwell in the midst of evil men, or, as the text puts it,
you are "in the world." I need not enlarge upon that fact; for
probably every time you go out to business or to daily labour,
you find by the ungodly speeches of graceless men that you are
in the world which lieth in the wicked one. Even while you
dwell in the sweet seclusion of domestic life, though your family
has been graciously visited, and your dear ones are all believers, yet even there matters occur which make you feel that
you are "in the world,"—a world of sin and sorrow. You are
not in heaven yet; do not dream that you are. It would be a
pity for a sailor to expect the sea to be as stable as the land,
for the sea will be the sea to the end; and the world will be the
world to you as long as you are in it.

The Saviour warns his people, "In the world ye shall have tribulation"; that is to say, your condition will at times be as unpleasant as that of wheat under the flail; for the Latin word "tribulation" signifies threshing. Many blows of the flail are needed to separate your chaff from your wheat, and therefore, while you are in this world, you are on the threshing-floor. The Greek word which Jesus used is not quite of the same import as our English-Latin word, but it means pressing grief and searching trial. You must at times experience trial while you are in the world, though not always to the same degree; for God gives some of his people much rest even while here below; but this does not arise out of the world, it is his own special gift. "In the world ye shall have tribulation" is as sure a fact as that in Christ you shall have peace.

WHAT IS THIS TRIBULATION IN THE WORLD AT WHICH THE SAVIOUR'S WORDS OF COMFORT ARE AIMED?

It includes *the afflictions which come upon us because we are men living among men,* and not yet at home among angels and glorified saints. We dwell among beings who are born to trouble as the sparks fly upward. Between us and other men there are many points of difference; but we share with them in the common infirmities, labours, sicknesses, bereavements, and necessities of our fallen race. We are outside of Eden's gate with the rest of Adam's family. We may be greatly beloved of God and yet be poor. God's love to Lazarus did not prevent his lying at the rich man's gate, nor hinder the dogs from licking his sores. Saints may be sick as well as other men; Job and David and Hezekiah felt sore diseases. Saints go into the hospital as well as sinners, for their bodies are liable to the same accidents and ailments. Such diseases as men bring upon themselves by vice the godly escape, and therefore, as a rule, God's people have a great advantage over the reckless and reprobate in point of health; but, still, in this respect the best of men are only men, and it will often be said, "Lord, he whom thou lovest is sick." Upon the bodies of the godly the elements have the same power as upon others; upon them the hot sirocco blows, or through their garments the cold penetrates; the sun scorches them in the fierceness of his summer heat, or chilling damps threaten the flame of life; in this respect, one event happeneth unto all, though not without mysterious and blessed differences. No screen is set around the godly to protect them from physical suffering; they are not living in the land of Goshen so that light cheers their dwellings while the dense fog hangs over the rest of the land.

Nor may we forget that we endure a second set of tribulations *because we are Christian men.* Ishmael was not mocked, but Isaac was, for he was born after the promise. Esau's posterity never suffered bondage in Egypt, but Israel must be trained by hard service. Persecution is for the righteous, wicked men are in honour among their ungodly associates. Slander shoots her poisoned arrows, not at the vicious, but at the virtuous. Birds do not peck at sour fruit, but they wage war upon the sweet and ripe. Holy men must expect to be misrepresented, misinterpreted, and often wilfully maligned, while hypocrites have their reward in undeserved homage. Carry what load you choose upon your shoulders, and no one will notice it, unless indeed they obey the good old rule, and "respect the burden"; but if you take up Christ's cross, and bravely bear it, few will respect the burden, or praise the bearer. Graceless men will add weight to your load, for the offence of the cross has not ceased. It is the nature of the wicked to hate the righteous, even as the wolf rages against the sheep. This world cannot be the friend of the friend of God, unless, indeed, Belial can have concord with Christ, and this we know is impossible. In one form or another, the Egyptian will oppress the Israelite till the day of the bringing out with a high hand and an outstretched arm. If to-day the enmity is restrained in its manifestation, it is because the law of the land, by the good providence of God, does not now allow of the rack, the stake, or the dungeon. Our Lord said to his first disciples, "In the world ye shall have tribulation," and he explained it to mean that men would put them out of the synagogues; yea, that the time would come when those that killed them would think that they did God service. "All that will live godly in Christ Jesus shall suffer persecution."

Nor is the opposition of the world confined to persecution, but it sometimes takes the far more dangerous form of flattery, —pleasing baits are held out, and allurements are used to decoy the believer from his Lord. Many have been grievously wounded by the world when it has met them with the kiss of

Judas on its lip and a dagger in its right hand wherewith to slay the soul. Woe unto those who are ignorant of its devices. This is a sore trouble under the sun, that men are false; their words are softer than butter, but inwardly they are drawn swords. This has often surprised young Christians. They imagined that, since the godly were charmed at the sight of their early graces, all others would be equally pleased; they are stumbled when they find that their good is evil spoken of. Is any hearer of mine one of these raw recruits? Let him learn that to be a soldier of the cross means real war, and not a sham fight. He is in an enemy's country, and the time will yet come when, as a veteran warrior, he will be surprised if he lives a day without a conflict, or is able for an hour to sheathe his sword.

> *"Must I be carried to the skies,*
> *On flowery beds of ease;*
> *While others fought to win the prize*
> *And sail' d through bloody seas?"*

Certain tender hearts are not only surprised, but they are daunted and grieved, by the world's opposition. Gentle, loving spirits, who would not oppose anybody if they could help it, keenly feel the wanton assaults of those whom they would rather please than provoke. The sensitiveness of love renders the choicest characters the most susceptible to pain under cruel opposition, especially when it comes from beloved kinsfolk. To those who love God and man, it is at times an agony to be compelled to appear as the cause of strife, even for Christ's sake.

We are sent forth as sheep among wolves, and this jars upon our gentleness, which loves far better to lie down in the green pastures near the Shepherd, and in the midst of his flock. We are most of all grieved to think that men should not love Christ. It makes us deeply sorrowful that they should not see the beauties of the Man of sorrows. In our inmost hearts we are wounded when they wound our Well-beloved. That they oppose *us* is little; but that they stumble at the great foundation stone, upon which they will surely be broken, is terrible to perceive. They sin against light and love; they sin against their own souls; and this is a tribulation which bruises every holy heart, and causes every loving spirit to bleed.

This calls for constant watchfulness, since our very love to men might become, unless salted by the grace of God, a cause of decay to our purity. Some spirits love fighting, and are never more happy than when they can denounce, resist, secede, and contend. These are members of the church militant in another than the best sense. When the grace of God enters their hearts, and consecrates their obstinacy into firmness, they make fine men in a way; but if we measure them by the scale of love, and that, I take it, is the standard of the sanctuary— for he is most like God who loves most, and he has come nearest to the image of Christ whose heart is fullest of tenderness— these rougher spirits turn out to be rather dwarfs than giants in the Kingdom of God. We must have backbone, and must be prepared to contend earnestly for the faith; but yet, the more love we exhibit the better, and hence the more pain it will cost us to be continually at war with unloving spirits. This is a part of the tribulation which we must endure; and the more bravely we face it, the more thoroughly shall we win the battles of peace and purity.

Let us now consider WHAT THE COMFORT IS WHICH JESUS GRACIOUSLY OFFERS US. "Be of good cheer," he says, "I have overcome the world." This is a glorious sentence, spoken by the greatest conqueror that ever lived, in whom all his people shall yet be "more than conquerors."

Here let us view our Lord in his blessed person, for there is much of good cheer in the contemplation. Remember, first, that *our blessed Lord was a man.* Believe all that this means, for many are apt to think that, because he was God as well as man, therefore he was not so fully a man. The tendency is to separate him from the race, and so from ourselves; but I pray you to reflect that Jesus was in some respects more a man than any one of us.

There are some points in which no one man is all that manhood is; but Jesus was the summary of all manhood. I might almost venture to say that he had about him the whole nature of mankind, as it respects the mental conformation of both man and woman, for he was as tender as woman though as strong as man. Holy women, as much as godly men, find in

Jesus all that is in their own souls. There is nothing effeminate in him, and yet all the loveliness which is feminine; read his life-story, and see. He was man in the broadest sense of the term, taking up into one the whole genus. Men are of certain ranks and grades, but Christ is without limit, save only that in him was no sin. Though a Jew, he bore no special national peculiarity, for Gentiles find in him their next of kin. You apply no descriptive word to the Son of man, except it be that you call him "the Man of sorrows." He was a man who greatly suffered in body and in mind, and displayed his manhood by the bravery of his endurance; a man joying in man's joy, depressed in man's grief; a man who ran up the entire scale of humanity, from its deepest to its highest tone. Now, if a typical man has overcome the world, then man has done it, and man can be enabled to do it again. This inspires courage and banishes despair. It was the mighty power of the Holy Ghost dwelling in him by which Jesus overcame the world; and that same quiet power, if it dwells in us, will make us win the like victory by faith. The arch enemy has been conquered by man, and our hearts may be comforted by the conviction that, by God working in us, we, too, shall bruise Satan under our feet shortly.

It is cheering to remember that, wherein our Lord's was a special case, it is to our comfort; for he, as man, entered into the conflict under serious disadvantages, which we cannot labour under. He was weighted with a care unique and unexampled. Be our charge what it may, it cannot be comparable to his heavy burden as the Shepherd of souls. We think ourselves overweighted, and speak of life as though it were rendered too stern a conflict by the load of our cares and responsibilities; but what comparison is there between our load and that of Jesus? A pastor with a great flock is not without his hourly anxieties; but what are those to the cares of the Chief Shepherd? He watched over the great multitude which no man can number, who were committed to him by the Father, and for these he carried all their griefs; here was a burden such as you and I, dear friend, cannot even imagine; and yet, without laying aside the weight, he fought the world, and overcame it. Let his name be praised, and let his victory be the comfort of all that labour and are heavy laden.

Recollect, next, that he was loaded with substitutionary sorrows which he bore for us. These are not ours. He came into the world to suffer griefs that were not his own. He had human guilt laid upon him to bear, and, because of that, he was exceeding sorrowful even unto death. Some seem to think we are to imitate Christ in being men of sorrows as he was. No, no, the argument is the other way. Because Jesus took our sorrows, we may leave them all with him, rolling our burden upon the Lord. Because he was grieved for me and in my stead, it is my privilege to rejoice with joy unspeakable in full redemption. No weight of sin remains to press us to the dust. Christ has carried it all away, and in his sepulchre he has buried it for ever. Yet never let us forget what an inconceivable pressure our sin put upon him; for, remembering this, it becomes the more a comfort to us that, notwithstanding all, he could say, "I have overcome the world."

Recollect, again, that our Lord in the battle with the world was the centre of the attack. When the whole host marches to the fight, we each one take our place in the ranks, and the war goes on against us all; but where, think you, did the arrows fly most thickly? Where were the javelins hurled one after the other, thick as hail? "The standard-bearer among ten thousand" was the chief target. It seems to me as if the prince of darkness had said to his armies, "Fight neither with small nor great, save only with the King of Israel"; for he was tempted in all points like as we are. You and I encounter some temptations, but he endureth them all. I have mine and you have yours, but he had mine and yours, and such as are common to all his saints; and yet, standing in the thick of the fray, he remained unwounded, and cried aloud, "I have overcome the world." Grace, then, can clothe us also with triumph, for against us no such supreme charges of hosts upon hosts will ever be led.

Remember again, that the Redeemer was, in many respects, a lonely man. If we want spiritual succour, we know someone to whom we can go. If we need converse with a superior mind, we can find such an one among our brethren; but our blessed Master could scarcely find a kindred spirit, and never an adviser. Like some lone mountain top which towers above all surrounding heights, he stood alone where winter's snowstorms beat full upon him, spending all their fury on his unshielded height. We are but valley dwellers, and rise not to his loftiness. To whom could he tell his secret griefs? To Peter, James, John? As well might a mother whisper to her babe the throes that rend her heart. He did once in deep distress resort to the three noblest spirits among the twelve Apostles; but they slept for sorrow, and could not watch with him one hour. O lonely Christ, if thou didst overcome the world alone, how surely shall thy warrior brethren overcome it, when they stand shoulder to shoulder, cheering each man his fellow, and, above all, when thou thyself art in the field communicating thy victorious valour to the whole host!

I beg you to notice that there were possibilities about our Lord that were never ours. A man who does not know his letters is little tempted to be proud of his learning, and the man who lives from hand to mouth, and never has a penny to lay by, can hardly be tempted to be purse-proud. We poor creatures could not be tempted to the same degree as our great Lord. The multitude would have taken him by force, and made him a king; nay, more, all the kingdoms of the earth were proffered him, and instead of suffering poverty and yielding himself up to death he might have pushed Cæsar from his throne. The world with all its honours, the cattle on a thousand hills, and secret mines, and rocks of gold and silver, were all his, and he might have left his life-work to be the greatest, richest, mightiest monarch that ever reigned—had he not been Jesus, to whom such things were as dirt beneath his feet. But none of us have such great offers and brilliant opportunities, and therefore we have not such a battle to fight as he had. Shall we not, by his help, overcome the lesser temptations, since he went on to victory over the greatest that can be imagined?

Recollect, too, that the intense zeal that burned in his spirit, had he been capable of ever yielding to a temptation, might have suggested to him, in a hundred ways, a turning aside from his own chosen line of action by which he had resolved to conquer the world. He came to vanquish evil by the force of love and truth, through his Spirit. If some of his followers had been girt with his power, they would not have kept to his order of battle. I stood in Rome, one day, at the bottom of the Santa Scala, and watched the poor votaries of superstition creeping up those so-called sacred steps upon their knees, imagining them to be the very stairs which our Lord descended when Pilate said, "Behold the man." As I saw certain priests watching their dupes, I longed for a thunderbolt or two with which to make a clearance of Pope, cardinals, and priests. But the spirit of our Lord Jesus was not so hot; for when James and John asked, "Lord, wilt thou that we command fire to come down from heaven, and consume them?" their Lord replied, "Ye know not what manner of spirit ye are of."

We may never have been tempted to ask fire from heaven, because we knew that we could not get it; but our Lord had only to ask his Father, and he would presently have sent him legions of angels. See with grief what a part of the church has done; certain professors easily fell into the snare which their Lord avoided. Suppose the Lord Jesus had been made a king, and had marshalled an army, he might have set up an established Church, and have maintained it by the power and wealth of the State. A temple might have been built in every parish in the Roman empire, and the heathen might have been compelled to pay tithes for the support of the ministry and the apostleship. By the help of imperial prestige and patronage, nominal professors of the faith would have been multiplied by millions, and, outwardly, religion would have prevailed. Would it not have been as great a blessing as our established Church is to us? But the Lord Jesus Christ did not choose this method, for his Kingdom is not to be set up by other force than by that of truth and love. It was his purpose to die for men, but not to lift the mailed hand of power, or even the jewelled finger of rank to bring them into subjection. Jesus *loves* men to himself; love and truth are his battle-axe and weapons of war. Thus he overcame the world in that most insidious form of worldliness—the suggestion to make alliance with it, and set up a mongrel society, a kingdom at once earthly and heavenly, a state church, a society loyal both to God and Mammon, fearing the Lord and serving the High Court of Parliament. It might have appeared to us to be the readiest means to bless the world; but it was not his Father's way, nor the way of holiness, and therefore he would not follow it, but overcame the world.

Let us now observe that the main point of the comfort lies in the fact that not only did our Lord overcome the world as an individual, but *he vanquished it as the representative man.* Clear a space! Clear a space! A deadly fight is to be fought. Here comes into the lists, stalking along, a monster man, towering high above his fellows. He is for Philistia! Here comes the champion of Israel, a youth and ruddy. These two are to decide the day. Anxious eyes are turned towards the field of duel. Philistia, look to thy champion! Israel, watch thy stripling with beating heart! O maids of Judah, lift up your prayers for the son of Jesse, that he may play the man this day! As we watch that fight, and see the stone sink into the champion's brow, and behold the youth taking off the giant's head, and bringing it to the camp, we are ready to join in the dances of the jubilant women, for David has won the victory. See the result of his deed—the victory of David is the triumph of every man in Israel's land. It was a representative conflict—Israel against Philistia, and when Philistia's hero fell, Israel was the conqueror. Up to the spoil, O sons of Jacob! The uncircumcised are utterly routed! They fly! Pursue them, and scatter them as dust before the whirlwind! Even so, when Christ overcame the world, the victory was won on the behalf of all his people, and to-day we face a vanquished foe. Up, and spoil the enemy! Let your infirmities become the subject of your glorying. Let your tribulations become the themes of your thanksgivings; and if you are persecuted for righteousness' sake, do not whine and whimper as though some dread calamity had come upon you; but rejoice that ye are made participators of the honours of prophets and saints, and of your great Leader who won the battle as your Champion.

Let us remember that here we have not merely representation, but also *union.* "I have overcome the world," means more than, "I overcame in your name." All believers have virtually overcome the world, for they are one with Christ. Did my hand win the victory? Then my foot triumphs. Did my head achieve the conquest? Then my heart shares the honour. The sole of my foot is victorious when my head is crowned. When Jesus Christ, the Head of the Church, was victorious over the foe, every member of his mystical body, even the most uncomely, was, virtually, a conqueror in the conquering Head. So let us shout the victory, and wave the palm branch, for we are more than conquerors through him that hath loved us.

III

THE CHRISTIAN'S HEAVINESS AND
REJOICING

"Wherein ye greatly rejoice, though now for a season, if need be, ye are in heaviness through manifold temptations."— 1 Pet. 1: 6.

THIS verse to a worldly man looks amazingly like a contradiction; and even to a Christian man, when he understands it best, it will still be a paradox. "Ye greatly rejoice," and yet "ye are in heaviness." Is that possible? Can there be in the same heart great rejoicing, and yet a temporary heaviness? Most assuredly. This paradox has been known and felt by many of the Lord's children, and it is far from being the greatest paradox of the Christian life. Men who live within themselves, and mark their own feelings as Christians, will often stand and wonder at themselves. Of all riddles, the greatest riddle is a Christian man. As to his pedigree, what a riddle he is! He is a child of the first Adam, "an heir of wrath, even as others." He is a child of the second Adam: he was born free; there is therefore now no condemnation unto him. He is a riddle in his own existence. "As dying, and behold we live; as chastened, and not killed." He is a riddle as to the component parts of his own spiritual frame. He finds that which makes him akin to the devil—depravity, corruption, binding him still to the earth, and causing him to cry out, "O wretched man that I am"; and yet he finds that he has within himself that which exalts him, not merely to the rank of an angel, but higher still—a something which raises him up together, and makes him "sit together with Christ Jesus in heavenly places." He finds that he has that within him which must ripen into heaven, and yet that about him which would inevitably ripen into hell, if grace did not forbid. What wonder, then, beloved, if the Christian man be a paradox himself, that his condition should be a paradox too? Why marvel ye, when

ye see a creature corrupt and yet purified, mortal and yet immortal, fallen but yet exalted far above principalities and
powers—why marvel ye, that ye should find that creature
also possessed of mingled experience, greatly rejoicing, and
yet at the same time, "in heaviness through manifold temptations."

I would have you look first of all at THE CHRISTIAN'S
HEAVINESS: he is "in heaviness through manifold temptations."
This is one of the most unfortunate texts in the Bible. I have
heard it quoted ten thousand times for my own comfort, but
I never understood it till a day or two ago. On referring to most
of the commentaries in my possession, I cannot find that they
have a right idea of the meaning of this text. You will notice
that your friends often say to you when you are in trouble,
"There is a needs be for this affliction"; there is a needs be,
say they, "for all these trials and troubles that befall you."
That is a very correct and Scriptural sentiment; but that sentiment is not in the text at all. And yet, whenever this text is
quoted in my hearing, this is what I am always told, that the
great temptations, the great trials which befall us, have a needs
be for them. But it does not say so here: it says something
better; not only that there is a needs be for our temptations,
but that there is a needs be for our heaviness under the temptation. Now, let me show you the difference. There is a man of
God, full of faith—strong; he is about to do his Master's work,
and he does it. God is with him, and gives him great success.
The enemy begins to slander him; all manner of evil is spoken
against him falsely for Christ's name's sake. You say, there is
a needs be for that, and you are quite correct: but look at the
man. How gallantly he behaves himself! He lifts his head
above his accusers, and unmoved amidst them all, he stands
like a rock in the midst of a roaring tempest, never moved
from the firm basis on which it rests.

The scene changes, and instead of calamity, perhaps he is
called to endure persecution, as in Apostolic times. We imagine
the man driven out from house and home, separated from all
his kindred, made to wander in the pathless snows of the
mountains; and what a brave and mighty man he appears,
when you see him enduring all this! His spirits never sink.
"All this can I do," says he, "and I can greatly rejoice in it,

for Christ's name's sake ; for I can practise the text which says, 'Rejoice ye in that day and leap for joy' "; and you will tell that man there is a needs be for his persecution ; he says, "Yes, I know it, and I fear not all I have to endure ; I am not cowed by it." At last imagine the man taken before the Inquisition and condemned to die. You still comfort him with the fact that there is a needs be that he shall die—that the blood of the martyrs must be the seed of the Church—that the world can never be overcome by Christ's Gospel, except through the sufferings and death of his followers—that Christ stooped to conquer, and the Church must do the same—that through death and blood must be the road to the Church's victory. And what a noble sight it is, to see that man going to the stake, and kissing it—looking upon his iron chains with as much esteem as if they had been chains of gold. Now tell him there is a needs be for all this, and he will thank you for the promise ; and you admire the man ; you wonder at him.

Ah ! but there is another class of persons that get no such honour as this. There is another sort of Christian for whom this promise really was intended, who do not get the comfort of it. I do admire the man I have pictured to you: may God long preserve such men in the midst of the Church ; I would stimulate every one of you to imitate him. Seek for great faith and great love to your Master, that you may be able to endure, being "stedfast, immovable, always abounding in the work of the Lord." But remember, that this text has not in it comfort for such persons ; there are other texts for them ; this text has been perverted for such a use as that. This is meant for another and a feebler grade of Christians, who are often overlooked and sometimes despised.

I was lying upon my couch during this last week, and my spirits were sunken so low that I could weep by the hour like a child, and yet I knew not what I wept for—but a very slight thing will move me to tears just now—and a kind friend was telling me of some poor old soul living near, who was suffering very great pain, and yet she was full of joy and rejoicing. I was so distressed by the hearing of that story, and felt so ashamed of myself, that I did not know what to do ; wondering why I should be in such a state as this ; while this poor woman, who had a terrible cancer, and was in the most frightful agony, could nevertheless "rejoice with joy unspeakable, and full of glory." And in a moment this text flashed upon my mind, with its real meaning. I am sure it is its real meaning. Read it over and over again, and you will see I am not wrong. "Though now for a season, if need be, ye are in heaviness." It does not say, "Though now for a season ye are suffering pain, though now for a season you are poor; but you are 'in heaviness'"; your spirits are taken away from you; you are made to weep; you cannot bear your pain; you are brought to the very dust of death, and wish that you might die. Your faith itself seems as if it would fail you. That is the thing for which there is a needs be. That is what my text declares, that there is an absolute needs be that sometimes the Christian should not endure his sufferings with a gallant and a joyous heart; there is a needs be that sometimes his spirits should sink within him, and that he should become even as a little child smitten beneath the hand of God.

Ah! beloved, we sometimes talk about the rod, but it is one thing to see the rod, and it is another thing to feel it; and many a time have we said within ourselves, "If I did not feel so low spirited as I now do, I should not mind this affliction"; and what is that but saying, "If I did not *feel* the rod I should not mind it"? It is just how you feel, that is, after all, the pith and marrow of your affliction. It is that breaking down of the spirit, that pulling down of the strong man, that is the very fester of the soreness of God's scourging—"the blueness of the wound, whereby the soul is made better." I think this one idea has been enough to be food for me many a day; and there may be some child of God here to whom it may bring some slight portion of comfort. We will yet again dwell upon it. "Though now for a season, if need be, ye are in heaviness through manifold temptations."

And here let me for a moment or two try to explain why it is that there is an absolute needs be, not merely for temptations and troubles, but likewise for our being in heaviness under them. In the first place, *if we were not in heaviness during our troubles we should not be like our Covenant Head—Christ Jesus.* It is a rule of the Kingdom that all the members must be like the Head. They are to be like the Head in that day when he shall appear. "We shall be like him, for we shall see

him as he is." But we must be like the Head also in his humiliation, or else we cannot be like him in his glory. Now, you will
observe that our Lord and Saviour Jesus Christ very often
passed through much of trouble, without any heaviness. When
he said, "Foxes have holes, and the birds of the air have nests,
but the Son of Man hath not where to lay his head," I observe
no heaviness. I do not think he sighed over that. And when
athirst he sat upon the well, and said, "Give me to drink,"
there was no heaviness in all his thirst. I believe that through
the first years of his ministry, although he might have suffered
some heaviness, he usually passed over his troubles like a ship
floating over the waves of the sea. But you will remember that
at last the waves of swelling grief came into the vessel; at last
the Saviour himself, though full of patience, was obliged to
say "My soul is exceeding sorrowful, even unto death"; and
one of the evangelists tells us that the Saviour "began to be
very heavy." What means that, but that his spirits began to
sink? There is a more terrible meaning yet, which I cannot
enter into this morning; but still I may say that the surface
meaning of it is that all his spirits sank within him. He had
no longer his wonted courage, and though he had strength to
say, "Nevertheless, not my will, but thine be done" ; still the
weakness did prevail, when he said, "If it be possible let this
cup pass from me." The Saviour passed through the brook,
but he "drank of the brook by the way"; and we who pass
through the brook of suffering must drink of it too. He had to
bear the burden, not with his shoulders omnipotent, but with
shoulders that were bending to the earth beneath a load. And
you and I must not always expect a giant faith that can remove
mountains: sometimes even to us the grasshopper must be a
burden, that we may in all things be like unto our head.

Yet again; *if the Christian did not sometimes suffer heaviness he would begin to grow too proud,* and think too much of
himself, and become too great in his own esteem. Those of us
who are of elastic spirit, and who in our health are full of
everything that can make life happy, are too apt to forget the
Most High God. Lest we should be satisfied from ourselves,
and forget that all our own springs must be in him, the Lord
sometimes seems to sap the springs of life, to drain the heart of
all its spirits, and to leave us without soul or strength for

mirth, so that the noise of tabret and of viol would be unto us as but the funeral dirge, without joy or gladness. Then it is that we discover what we are made of, and out of the depths we cry unto God, humbled by our adversities.

Another reason for this discipline is, I think, that *in heaviness we often learn lessons that we never could attain elsewhere.* Do you know that God has beauties for every part of the world; and he has beauties for every place of experience? There are views to be seen from the tops of the Alps that you can never see elsewhere. Ay, but there are beauties to be seen in the depths of the dell that ye could never see on the tops of the mountains; there are glories to be seen on Pisgah, wondrous sights to be beheld when by faith we stand on Tabor; but there are also beauties to be seen in our Gethsemanes, and some marvellously sweet flowers are to be culled by the edge of the dens of the leopards. Men will never become great in divinity until they become great in suffering. "Ah!" said Luther, "affliction is the best book in my library"; and let me add, the best leaf in the book of affliction is that blackest of all the leaves, the leaf called heaviness, when the spirit sinks within us, and we cannot endure as we could wish.

And yet again; *this heaviness is of essential use to a Christian, if he would do good to others.* Ah! there are a great many Christian people that I was going to say I should like to see afflicted—but I will not say so much as that; I should like to see them heavy in spirit; if it were the Lord's will that they should be bowed down greatly, I would not express a word of regret; for a little more sympathy would do them good; a little more power to sympathize would be a precious boon to them, and even if it were purchased by a short journey through a burning, fiery furnace, they might not rue the day afterwards in which they had been called to pass through the flame. There are none so tender as those who have been skinned themselves. Those who have been in the chamber of affliction know how to comfort those who are there. Do not believe that any man will become a physician unless he walks the hospitals; and I am sure that no one will become a divine, or become a comforter, unless he lies in the hospital as well as walks through it, and has to suffer himself. God cannot make ministers—and I speak with reverence of his Holy Name—he cannot make a

Barnabas except in the fire. It is there, and there alone, that
he can make his sons of consolation; he may make his sons of
thunder anywhere; but his sons of consolation he must make
in the fire, and there alone. Who shall speak to those whose
hearts are broken, who shall bind up their wounds, but those
whose hearts have been broken also, and whose wounds have
long run with the sore of grief?

And now to the second part of the text. Here we have something far more joyous and comfortable than the first. "WHERE-
IN YE GREATLY REJOICE." And can a Christian greatly rejoice
while he is in heaviness? Yes, most assuredly he can. Mariners
tell us that there are some parts of the sea where there is a
strong current upon the surface going one way, but that down
in the depths there is a strong current running the other way.
Two seas do not meet and interfere with one another; but one
stream of water on the surface is running in one direction, and
another below in an opposite direction. Now, the Christian is
like that. On the surface there is a stream of heaviness rolling
with dark waves; but down in the depths there is a strong
under-current of great rejoicing that is always flowing there.
Do you ask me what is the cause of this great rejoicing? The
Apostle tells us, "*Wherein* ye greatly rejoice." What does he
mean? You must refer to his own writings, and then you will
see. He is writing "to the strangers scattered throughout
Pontus," and so forth. The first thing that he says to them is,
that they are "elect according to the foreknowledge of God";
"wherein we greatly rejoice." Ah! even when the Christian
is most "in heaviness through manifold temptations," what a
mercy it is that he can know that he is still elect of God! Any
man who is assured that God has "chosen him from before the
foundation of the world," may well say, "Wherein we greatly
rejoice." Let me be lying upon a bed of sickness, and just
revel in that one thought. Before God made the heavens and
the earth, and laid the pillars of the firmament in their golden
sockets, he set his love upon me; upon the breast of the great
High Priest he wrote my name, and in his everlasting book it
stands, never to be erased—"elect according to the foreknowledge of God." Why, this may make a man's soul leap
within him, and all the heaviness that the infirmities of the flesh
may lay upon him shall be but as nothing; for this tremendous

current of his overflowing joy shall sweep away the mill-dam of his grief. Bursting and overleaping every obstacle, it shall overflood all his sorrows till they are drowned and covered up, and shall not be mentioned any more for ever. "Wherein we greatly rejoice." Come, thou Christian! thou art depressed and cast down. Think for a moment. Thou art chosen of God and precious.

Again, you will see another reason. The Apostle says that we are "*elect through sanctification of the Spirit unto obedience and sprinkling of the blood of Jesus Christ,*"—"wherein we greatly rejoice." Is the obedience of the Lord Jesus Christ girt about my loins, to be my beauty and my glorious dress; and is the blood of Jesus sprinkled upon me, to take away all my guilt and all my sin; and shall I not in this greatly rejoice? What shall there be in all the depressions of spirits that can possibly come upon me that shall make me break my harp, even though I should for a moment hang it upon the willows? Do I not expect that yet again my songs shall mount to heaven; and even now through the thick darkness do not the sparks of my joy appear, when I remember that I have still upon me the blood of Jesus, and still about me the glorious righteousness of the Messiah?

But the great and cheering comfort of the Apostle is, that *we are elect unto an inheritance incorruptible, and undefiled, and that fadeth not away, reserved in heaven for us.* And here, brethren, is the grand comfort of the Christian. When the child of God is sore-stricken and much depressed, the sweet hope, that living or dying, there is an inheritance incorruptible, reserved in heaven for him, may indeed make him greatly rejoice. He is drawing near the gates of death, and his spirit is in heaven, for he has to leave behind him all his family and all that life holds dear. Besides, his sickness brings upon him naturally a depression of spirit. But you sit by his bedside, and you begin to talk to him of the "Sweet fields beyond the swelling flood, arrayed in living green." You tell him of Canaan on the other side the Jordan—of the land that floweth with milk and honey—of the Lamb in the midst of the throne, and of all the glories which God hath prepared for them that love him; and you see his dull leaden eye light up with seraphic brightness, he shakes off his heaviness, and he begins to sing,

"On Jordan's stormy banks I stand,
And cast a wishful eye,
To Canaan's fair and happy land,
Where my possessions lie."

This makes him greatly rejoice; and if to that you add that possibly before he has passed the gates of death his Master may appear—if you tell him that the Lord Jesus Christ is coming in the clouds of heaven, and though we have not seen him yet believing in him we rejoice with joy unspeakable and full of glory, expecting the second advent—if he has grace to believe in that sublime doctrine, he will be ready to clap his hands upon his bed of weariness and cry, "Even so, Lord Jesus, come quickly! come quickly!"

There is one more doctrine that will always cheer a Christian, and I think that this perhaps is the one chiefly intended here in the text. Look at the end of the 15th verse; "Reserved in heaven for you who are kept by the power of God through faith unto salvation." This perhaps will be one of the greatest cordials to a Christian in heaviness, that he is not kept by his own power, but by the power of God, and that he is not left in his own keeping, but he is kept by the Most High. "When flesh and heart faileth, God is the strength of my life, and my portion for ever." "I know whom I have believed, and I am persuaded that he is able to keep that which I have committed unto him against that day." But take away that doctrine of the Saviour's keeping his people, and where is my hope? What is there in the Gospel worth my preaching, or worth your receiving? I know that he hath said, "I give unto my sheep eternal life, and they shall never perish, neither shall any man pluck them out of *my* hand." What, Lord, but suppose they should grow faint—that they should begin to murmur in their affliction. Shall they not perish then? No, they shall never perish. But suppose the pain should grow so hot that their faith should fail: shall they not perish then? No, "they shall not perish, neither shall any man pluck them out of my hand." But suppose their sense should seem to wander, and some should try to pervert them from the faith: shall they not be perverted? No; "they shall never perish." But suppose in some hour of their extremity hell and the world and their own fears should all beset them, and they should have no power to stand—no power whatever to resist the fierce onslaughts of the enemy, shall they not perish then? No, they are "kept by the power of God through faith unto salvation, ready to be revealed," "and they shall never perish, neither shall any man pluck them out of my hand." Ah! this is the doctrine, the cheering assurance "wherein we greatly rejoice, though now for a season, if needs be, we are in heaviness through manifold temptations."

IV

FOR THE TROUBLED

"Thy wrath lieth hard upon me, and thou hast afflicted me
with all thy waves."—Psalm 88: 7.

IT is the business of a shepherd not only to look after the
happy ones among the sheep, but to seek after the sick of
the flock, and to lay himself out right earnestly for their comfort
and succour. I feel, therefore, that I do rightly when I make it
my special business to speak to such as are in trouble. Those
of you who are happy and rejoicing in God, full of faith and
assurance, can very well spare a discourse for your weaker
brethren; you can be even glad and thankful to go without
your portion, that those who are depressed in spirit may receive
a double measure of the wine of consolation.

It is clear to all those who read the narratives of Scripture,
or are acquainted with good men, that the best of God's servants may be brought into the very lowest estate. There is no
promise of present prosperity appointed to true religion, so as
to exclude adversity from believers' lives. As men, the people
of God share the common lot of men, and what is that but
trouble? Yea, there are some sorrows which are peculiar to
Christians, some extra griefs of which they partake because
they are believers, though these are something more than
balanced by those peculiar and bitter troubles which belong
to the ungodly, and are engendered by their transgressions,
from which the Christian is delivered. From the passage which
is open before us, we learn that sons of God may be brought
so low as to write and sing psalms which are sorrowful throughout, and have no fitting accompaniment but sighs and groans.
They do not often do so; their songs are generally like those
of David, which if they begin in the dust mount into the clear
heavens before long; but sometimes, I say, saints are forced
to sing such dolorous ditties that from beginning to end there
is not one note of joy. Yet even in their dreariest winter night,

the saints have an aurora in their sky, and in this Eighty-eighth Psalm, the dreariest of all psalms, there is a faint gleam in the first verse, like a star-ray falling upon its threshold—"O Jehovah, God of my salvation." Heman retained his hold upon his God. It is not all darkness in a heart which can cry, "My God"; and the child of God, however low he may sink, still keeps hold upon his God. "Though he slay me, yet will I trust in him," is the resolution of his soul. Jehovah smites me, but he is my God. Even when he leaves me I will cry, "My God, my God, why hast thou forsaken me?"

Moreover, the believer in his worst time still continues to pray, and prays, perhaps, the more vigorously because of his sorrows. This psalm is full of prayer, it is as much sweetened with supplication as it is salted with sorrow. It weeps like Niobe, but it is on bended knees, and from uplifted eyes. Now, while a man can pray he is never far from light; he is at the window, though, perhaps, as yet the curtains are not drawn aside. The man who can pray has the clue in his hand by which to escape from the labyrinth of affliction. A man must have true and eternal life within him while he can continue still to pray, and while there is such life there is assured hope.

I will endeavour, in a few observations, to EXPOUND THE TEXT.

In the first place, its strong language suggests the remark that *tried saints are very prone to overrate their afflictions.* I believe we all err in that direction, and are far too apt to say, "I am the man that hath seen affliction." The inspired man of God, who wrote our text, was touched with this common infirmity, for he overstates his case. Read his words, "Thy wrath lieth hard upon me." I have no doubt Heman meant wrath in its worst sense. He believed that God was really angry with him, and wrathful with him, even as he is with the ungodly; but that was not true. As we shall have to show by-and-by, there is a very grave difference between the anger of God with his children and the anger of God with his enemies; and we do not think Heman sufficiently discerned that difference, even as we are afraid that many of God's children even now forget it, and therefore fear that the Lord is punishing them according to strict justice, and smiting them as though he were their executioner. Ah, if poor bewildered believers could but see it, they would learn that the very thing which they call wrath is only love, in its own wise manner, seeking their highest good. Besides, the Psalmist saith, "Thy wrath *lieth hard upon me.*" Ah, if Heman had known what it was to have God's wrath lie hard on him, he would have withdrawn that word, for all the wrath that any man ever feels in this life is but as a laying on of God's little finger.

All God's waves have broken over no man, save only the Son of Man. There are still some troubles which we have been spared, some woes to us unknown. Have we suffered all the diseases which flesh is heir to? Are there not modes of pain from which our bodies have escaped? Are there not also some mental pangs which have not wrung our spirit? And what if we seem to have traversed the entire circle of bodily and mental misery, yet in our homes, households, or friendships we have surely some comfort left, and therefore from some rough billow we are screened. All God's waves had not gone over thee, O Heman, the woes of Job and Jeremiah were not thine. Among the living none can literally know what *all* God's waves would be. They know, who are condemned to feel the blasts of his indignation, they know in the land of darkness and of everlasting hurricane ; they know what all God's waves and billows are ; but we know not. The metaphor is good and admirable, and correct enough poetically, but as a statement of fact it is strained. We are all apt to aggravate our grief: I say this here as a general fact, which you who are happy can bear to be told, but I would not vex the sick man with it while he is enduring the weight of his affliction. If he can calmly accept the suggestion of his own accord, it may do him good, but it would be cruel to throw it at him. True as it is, I should not like to whisper it in any sufferer's ear, because it would not console but grieve him.

I have often marvelled at the strange comfort persons offer you when they say, "Ah, there are others who suffer more than you do." Am I a demon then? Am I expected to rejoice at the news of other people's miseries? Far otherwise, I am pained to think there should be sharper smarts than mine, my sympathy increases my own woe. I can conceive of a fiend in torment finding solace in the belief that others are tortured with a yet fiercer flame, but surely such diabolical comfort should not be offered to Christian men. There is, however, a form of comfort akin to it, but of far more legitimate origin, a consolation honourable and divine. There was ONE upon whom God's wrath pressed very sorely. ONE who was in truth afflicted with all God's waves, and that One is our brother, a man like ourselves, the dearest lover of our souls; and because he has known and suffered all this, he can enter into sympathy with us this morning whatever tribulation may beat upon us. His passion is all over now, but not his compassion. He has borne the indignation of God, and turned it all away from us: the waves have lost their fury, and spent their force on him, and now he sitteth above the floods, yea, he sitteth King for ever and ever. As we think of him, the Crucified, our souls may not only derive consolation from his sympathy and powerful succour, but we may learn to look upon our trials with a calmer eye, and judge them more according to the true standard. In the presence of Christ's cross our own crosses are less colossal.

But, secondly, let us remark that *saints do well to trace all their trials to their God.* Heman did so in the text: *"Thy* wrath lieth hard upon me, *thou* hast afflicted me with all *thy* waves." He traces all his adversity to the Lord his God. It is God's wrath, they are God's waves that afflict him, and God makes them afflict him. Child of God, never forget this; all that thou art suffering of any sort, or kind, comes to thee from the divine hand. Truly, thou sayest, "my affliction arises from wicked men," yet remember that there is a predestination which, without soiling the fingers of the Infinitely Holy, nevertheless rules the motions of evil men as well as of holy angels. It were a dreary thing for us if there were no appointments of God's providence which concerned the ungodly; then the great mass of mankind would be entirely left to chance, and the godly might be crushed by them without hope. The Lord, without interfering with the freedom of their wills, rules and over-rules, so that the ungodly are as a rod in his hand, with which he wisely scourges his children.

Perhaps you will say that your trials have arisen not from the sins of others, but from your own sin. Even then I would have you penitently trace them still to God. What though the trouble spring out of the sin, yet it is God that hath appointed the sorrow to follow the transgression, to act as a remedial

agency for your spirit. Look not at the second cause, or, looking at it with deep regret, turn your eye chiefly to your heavenly
Father, and "hear ye the rod and who hath appointed it." The
Lord sends upon us the evil as well as the good of this mortal
life; his is the sun that cheers and the frost that chills; his the
deep calm and his the fierce tornado. To dwell on second
causes is frequently frivolous, a sort of solemn trifling. Men
say of each affliction, "It might have been prevented *if* so and
so had occurred." Perhaps if another physician had been
called in, the dear child's life had still been spared; possibly
if I had moved in such a direction in business I might not have
been a loser. Who is to judge of what might have been? In
endless conjectures we are lost, and, cruel to ourselves, we
gather material for unnecessary griefs. Matters happened not
so; then why conjecture what would have been had things been
different? It is folly. You did your best, and it did not answer:
why rebel? To fix the eye upon the second cause will irritate
the mind. We grow indignant with the more immediate agent
of our grief, and so fail to submit ourselves to God. As long as
I trace my pain to accident, my bereavement to mistake, my
loss to another's wrong, my discomfort to an enemy, and so
on, I am of the earth earthy; but when I rise to my God and
see his hand at work, I grow calm, I have not a word of re-
pining, "I open not my mouth because thou didst it." "Cast
thy burden on the Lord" is a precept which it will be easy to
practise when you see that the burden came originally from
God.

But now, thirdly, *afflicted children of God do well to have
a keen eye to the wrath that mingles with their troubles.* "Thy
wrath lieth hard upon me." There is Heman's first point. He
does not mention the waves of affliction till he has first spoken
of the wrath. We should labour to discover what the Lord
means by smiting us; what he purposes by the chastisement,
and how far we can answer that purpose. We must use a keen
eye clearly *to distinguish* things. There is an anger and an
anger, a wrath and a wrath. God is never angry with his
children in one sense, but he is in another. As men, we have
all of us disobeyed the laws of God, and God stands in relationship to all of us as a judge. As a judge, he must execute upon
us the penalties of his law, and he must, from the necessity of

his nature, be angry with us for having broken that law. That concerns all the human race. But the moment a man believes in the Lord Jesus Christ his offences are his offences no longer; they are laid upon Christ Jesus, the substitute, and the anger goes with the sin. The anger of God towards the sins of believers has spent itself upon Christ. Christ has been punished in their stead; the punishment due to their sin has been borne by Jesus Christ. God forbid that the Judge of all the earth should ever be unjust, it were not just for God to punish a believer for a sin which has been already laid upon Jesus Christ. Hence the believer is altogether free from all liability to suffer the judicial anger of God, and all risk of receiving a punitive sentence from the Most High. The man is absolved—shall he be judged again? The man has paid the debt—shall he be brought a second time before the judge, as though he were still a debtor? Christ has stood for him in his place and stead, and therefore he boldly asks, "Who shall lay anything to the charge of God's elect? It is God that justifieth. Who is he that condemneth? It is Christ that died, yea rather, that is risen again, who is even the right hand of God, who also maketh intercession for us."

Now, then, the Christian man takes up another position; he is adopted into the family of God: he has become God's child. He is under the law of God's house. There is in every house an economy, a law by which the children and servants are ruled. If the child of God breaks the law of the house the Father will visit his offence with fatherly stripes—a very different kind of visitation from that of a judge. Wide as the poles asunder are the anger of a judge and the anger of a father. The father loves the child while he is angry, and is mainly angry for that very reason; if it were not his child he would probably take no notice of its fault, but because it is his own boy who has spoken an untruth or committed an act of disobedience he feels he must chastise him, because he loves him. This needs no further explanation. There is a righteous anger in God's heart towards guilty impenitent men; he feels none of that towards his people. Now, child of God, if you are suffering to-day in any way whatever, whether from the ills of poverty or bodily sickness, or depression of spirits, recollect there is not a drop of the judicial anger of God in it all. You are not being punished for your sins as a judge punishes a culprit;—never believe such false doctrine, it is clean contrary to the truth as it is in Jesus.

But we must use the eye of our judgment in looking at our present affliction to *see and confess* how richly, as children, we deserve the rod. Go back to the time since you were converted, dear brother and sister, and consider—do you wonder that God has chastened you? Speaking for myself, I wonder that I have ever escaped the rod at any time. If I had been compelled to say "All day long have I been plagued, and chastened every morning," I should not have marvelled, for my shortcomings are many. How ungrateful have we been, how unloving, and how unlovable, how false to our holiest vows, how unfaithful to our most sacred consecrations. Is there a single ordinance over which we have not sinned? Did we ever rise from our knees without having offended while at prayer? Did we ever get through a hymn without some wandering of mind or cold-ness of heart? Did we ever read a chapter which we might not have wept over, because we did not receive the truth in the love of it into our soul as we ought to have done? O, good Father, if we smart, richly do we deserve that we should yet smart again.

When you have confessed your ill-desert, let me exhort you to use those same eyes zealously to *search out the particular sin* which has caused the present chastisement. "Oh," says one, "I do not think I should ever find it out." You might. Perhaps it lies at the very door. I do not wonder that some Christians suffer: I should wonder if they did not. I have seen them, for instance, neglect family prayer and other household duties; and their sons have grown up to dishonour them. If they cry out, "What an affliction," we would not like to *say*, "Ah, but you might have expected it; you were the cause of it"; but such a saying would be true. When children have left the parental roof, and gone into sin, we have not been surprised when the father has been harsh, sour, and crabbed in temper. We did not expect to gather figs of thorns, or grapes of thistles. We have seen men whose whole thought was "Get money, get money," and yet they have professed to be Christians. Such persons have been fretful and unhappy, but we have not been astonished. No, if they walk frowardly with him, he will show himself froward to them.

But sometimes the cause of the chastisement lies further off. Every surgeon will tell you that there are diseases which become troublesome in the prime of life, or in old age, which may have been occasioned in youth by some wrong doing, or by accident, and the evil may have lain latent all those years. So may the sins of our youth bring upon us the sorrows of our riper years, and faults and omissions of twenty years ago may scourge us to-day. I know it is so. If the fault may be of so great an age, it should lead us to more thorough search, and more frequent prayer. Bunyan tells us that Christian met with Apollyon, and had such a dark journey through the Valley of the Shadow of Death, because of slips he made when going down the hill into the Valley of Humiliation. It may be so with us. Perhaps when you were young you were very untender towards persons of a sorrowful spirit; you are such yourself now—your harshness is visited upon you. It may be that, when in better circumstances, you were wont to look down upon the poor and despise the needy; your pride is chastened now. We have seen men who could ride the high horse among their fellow-creatures, and speak very loftily, and when they have been brought very, very low, we have understood the riddle. God will visit his children's transgressions. He will frequently let common sinners go on throughout life unrebuked; but not so his children. If you were going home to-day, and saw a number of boys throwing stones and breaking windows, you might not interfere with them, but if you saw your own lad among them, I will be bound you would fetch him out, and make him repent of it.

Perhaps the chastisement may be sent by reason of a sin as yet undeveloped, some latent proneness to evil. The grief may be meant to unearth the sin, that you may hunt it down. Have you any idea of what a devil you are by nature? None of us know what we are capable of if left by grace. We think we have a sweet temper, an amiable disposition! We shall see!! We fall into provoking company, and are so teased and insulted, and so cleverly touched in our raw places, that we become mad with wrath, and our fine amiable temper vanishes in smoke, not without leaving blacks behind. Is it not a dreadful thing to be so stirred up? Yes it is, but if our hearts were pure no sort of stirring would pollute them. Stir pure water as long as you like and no mud will rise. The evil is bad when seen, but it was quite as bad when not seen. It may be a great gain to a man to know what sin is in him, for then he will humble himself before his God, and begin to combat his propensities. If he had never seen the filth he would never have swept the house; if he had never felt the pain the disease would have lurked within, but now that he feels the pain he will fly to the remedy. Sometimes, therefore, trial may be sent that we may discern the sin which dwelleth in us, and may seek its destruction.

When you have so done let me give one word of caution before I leave this point. Do not let us expect when we are in the trouble to perceive any immediate benefit resulting from it. I have tried myself when under sharp pain to see whether I have grown a bit more resigned or more earnest in prayer, or more rapt in fellowship with God, and I confess I have never been able to see the slightest trace of improvement at such times, for pain distracts and scatters the thoughts. Remember that word, "Nevertheless, *afterward* it yieldeth the peaceable fruit of righteousness." The gardener takes his knife and prunes the fruit trees to make them bring forth more fruit; his little child comes trudging at his heels and cries, "Father, I do not see that the fruit comes on the trees after you have cut them." No, dear child, it is not likely you would, but come round in a few months when the season of fruit has come, and then shall you see the golden apples which thank the knife. Graces which are meant to endure require time for their production, and are not thrust forth and ripened in a night.

Now, I want to give a very short EXPOSITION OF THE BENEFITS OF TROUBLE. This is a great subject. Many a volume has been written upon it.

Severe trouble in a true believer has the effect of loosening the roots of his soul earthward and tightening the anchor-hold of his heart heavenward. How can he love the world which has become so drear to him? Why should he seek after grapes so bitter to his taste? Should he not now ask for the wings of a dove that he may fly away to his own dear country, and be at rest for ever? Every mariner on the sea of life knows that when the soft zephyrs blow men tempt the open sea with outspread sails, but when the black tempest comes howling from its den they hurry with all speed to the haven. Afflictions clip our wings with regard to earthly things, so that we cannot fly away from our dear Master's hand, but sit there and sing to him; but the same afflictions make our wings grow with regard to heavenly things, we are feathered like eagles, we catch the soaring spirit, a thorn is in our nest, and we spread our pinions towards the sun.

Affliction frequently open truths to us, and opens us to the truth—I know not which of these two is the more difficult. Experience unlocks truths which else were closed against us; many passages of Scripture will never be made clear by the commentator; they must be expounded by experience. Many a text is written in a secret ink which must be held to the fire of adversity to make it visible. I have heard that you see stars in a well when none are visible above ground, and I am sure you can discern many a starry truth when you are down in the deeps of trouble which would not be visible to you elsewhere. Besides, I said it opened us to the truth as well as the truth to us. We are superficial in our beliefs: we are often drenched with truth, and yet it runs off from us like water from a marble slab; but affliction, as it were, ploughs us and sub-soils us, and opens up our hearts, so that into our innermost nature the truth penetrates and soaks like rain into ploughed land. Blessed is that man who receives the truth of God into his inmost self; he shall never lose it, but it shall be the life of his spirit.

Affliction, when sanctified by the Holy Spirit, brings much glory to God out of Christians, through their experience of the Lord's faithfulness to them. I delight to hear an aged Christian giving his own personal testimony of the Lord's goodness. Vividly upon my mind flashes an event of some twenty-five years ago; it is before me as if it had occurred yesterday, when I saw a venerable man of eighty, grey and blind with age, and heard him in simple accents, simple as the language of a child, tell how the Lord had led him, and had dealt well with him, so that no good thing had failed of all that God had promised. He spoke as though he were a prophet, his years lending force to his words. But suppose he had never known a trial, what testimony could he have borne? Had he been lapped in luxury and never endured suffering, he might have stood there dumb and have been as useful as if he had spoken.

Again, affliction gives us through grace the inestimable privilege of conformity to the Lord Jesus. We pray to be like Christ, but how can we be if we are not men of sorrows at all, and never become the acquaintance of grief? Like Christ, and yet never traverse through the vale of tears! Like Christ, and yet have all that heart could wish, and never bear the contradiction of sinners against thyself, and never say, "My soul is exceeding sorrowful, even unto death!" O, sir, thou knowest not what thou dost ask. Hast thou said, "Let me sit on thy right hand in thy Kingdom"? It cannot be granted to thee unless thou wilt also drink of his cup and be baptised with his baptism. A share of his sorrow must precede a share of his glory.

Once more, our sufferings are of great service to us when God blesses them, for they help us to be useful to others. It must be a terrible thing for a man never to have suffered physical pain. You say, "I should like to be the man." Ah, unless you had extraordinary grace, you would grow hard and cold, you would get to be a sort of cast-iron man, breaking other people with your touch. No; let my heart be tender, even be soft, if it must be softened by pain, for I would fain know how to bind up my fellow's wound. Let mine eye have a tear ready for my brother's sorrows even if in order to that, I should have to shed ten thousand for mine own. An escape from suffering would be an escape from the power to sympathise, and that were to be deprecated beyond all things. Luther was right, when he said affliction was the best book in the minister's library. If the man of God who is to minister to others could be always robust, it were perhaps a loss; if he could be always sickly it might be equally so; but for the pastor to be able to range through all the places where the Lord suffers his sheep to go, is doubtless to the advantage of his flock.

Be thankful then, dear brethren, be thankful for trouble; and above all be thankful because it will soon be over, and we shall be in the land where these things will be spoken of with great joy. As soldiers show their scars and talk of battles when they come at last to spend their old age in the country at home, so shall we in the dear land to which we are hastening, speak of the goodness and faithfulness of God which brought us through all the trials of the way. I would not like to stand in that white-robed host and hear it said, "These are they that come out of great tribulation, all except that one." Would you like to be there to see yourself pointed at as the one saint who never knew a sorrow? We will be content to share the battle, for we shall soon wear the crown and wave the palm.

I know while I am preaching some of you have said, "Ah, these people of God have a hard time of it." So have you. The ungodly do not escape from sorrow by their sin. I never heard of a man escaping from poverty through being a spendthrift, I never heard of a man who escaped from headache or heartache by drunkenness; or from bodily pain by licentiousness. I have heard the opposite; and if there be griefs to the holy there are others for you. Only mark this, ungodly ones, mark this. For you these things work no good. You pervert them to mischief; but for the saints they work eternal benefit. For you your sorrows are punishments; they are not so to the child of God. You are punished for your transgressions, and he is not. And let us tell you, too, that if this day you happen to be in peace, and prosperity, and plenty, and happiness—yet there is not one child of God here, in the very deeps of trouble that would change places with you under any consideration whatever. "Let God do as he pleases," we say, "for a while here; we believe our worst state to be better than your best." Do you think we love God for what we get out of him, and for nothing else? Is that your notion of a Christian's love to God? This is how the ungodly talk, and that is what the devil thought was Job's case. Says he: "Does Job fear God for naught? Hast thou not set a hedge about him, and all that he has?" The devil does not understand real love and affection; but the child of God can tell the devil to his face that he loves God if he covers him with sores and sets him on the dunghill, and by God's good help he means to cling to God through troubles tenfold heavier than those he has had to bear, should they come upon him. Is he not a blessed God? Aye, let the beds of our sickness ring with it: he is a blessed God. In the night watches, when we were weary, and our brain is hot and fevered, and our soul is distracted, we yet confess that he is a blessed God. Every ward of the hospital where believers are found, should echo with that note. A blessed God? "Aye, that he is," say the poor and needy here this morning, and so say all God's poor throughout all the land. A blessed God? "Aye," say his dying people, "as he slays us we will bless his name. He loves us, and we love him; and, though all his waves go over us, and his wrath lieth sore upon us, we would not change with kings on their thrones if they are without the love of God."

V

"JESUS WEPT"

"Jesus wept."—John 11: 35.

A GREAT storm was stirring the mind of Jesus. We find, on looking at the original, that he was indignant and troubled. We have a very literal translation in the margin of the Revised Version; and instead of reading, "He groaned in the spirit, and was troubled," we find it, "He was moved with indignation in the spirit, and troubled himself." What was this indignation? We cannot think that it was caused by the unbelief of his friends, or even by the pretended sympathy of those malicious Jews who hastened to accuse him to the Pharisees; but we look further and deeper for the reason of this heat. He now stood face to face with the last enemy, death. He saw what sin had done in destroying life, and even in corrupting the fair handiwork of God in the human body; he marked, also, the share which Satan had in all this, and his indignation was aroused; yea, his whole nature was stirred.

Some read it, "He roused himself," instead of reading, as we have it in our version, "He was troubled." Certainly, there would seem to be an active sense in the expression: it was not so much that he was troubled, as that "He troubled himself." Between indignation at the powers of evil, grief for the family who had been bereaved by death, sorrow over those who stood by in unbelief, and a distressing realization of the effects of sin, the Lord's heart was evidently in a great storm. Instead of the thunder of threatening, and the lightning of a curse, all that was perceptible of the inward tempest was a shower of tears; for "Jesus wept."

"Jesus wept." I have often felt vexed with the man, whoever he was, who chopped up the New Testament into verses. He seems to have let the hatchet drop indiscriminately here and there; but I forgive him a great deal of his blundering for his

wisdom in letting these two words make a verse by themselves:
"Jesus wept." This is a diamond of the first water, and it cannot have another gem set with it, for it is unique. Shortest of
verses in words, but where is there a longer one in sense? Add
a word to the verse, and it would be out of place. No, let it
stand in solitary sublimity and simplicity.

There is infinitely more in these two words than any sermon-
izer, or student of the Word, will ever be able to bring out of
them, even though he should apply the microscope of the most
attentive consideration. "Jesus wept." Instructive fact; simple
but amazing; full of consolation; worthy of our earnest
heed.

Is there a man or woman here who has not wept? Have we
not all, sometimes, felt a sweet relief in tears? Looking round
upon this great assembly, I could point to you, one by one,
and say, "He wept, and he wept; and she wept, and she wept";
and none would wonder that such has been the case. The
marvel is that the sinless Son of God should, in the days of his
flesh, know the meaning of strong crying and tears. The fact
worthy to be noticed and recorded is that "Jesus wept." On
that subject we shall meditate; and may the Lord make our
thoughts profitable!

First, "Jesus wept," for HE IS TRULY MAN. Many facts prove
the completeness of our Lord's taking up of our nature. Not
in phantasm, nor in fiction was Jesus a man; but in reality and
truth he became one of us. He was born of a woman, wrapped
in swaddling bands, fed from the breast. He grew as a child,
was obedient to his parents, and increased in stature and in
wisdom. In manhood he worked, he walked, he wearied. He
ate as we do: we find it mentioned that he fasted, and that
he hungered. After his resurrection, he ate a piece of a broiled
fish, and of a honeycomb, to show that his body was real. His
human nature was sustained, as ours is, by supplying it with
food. Though on one occasion, sustained by divine power,
he fasted forty days and forty nights, yet as man he ordinarily
needed food. He drank also, and gave thanks both for food
and drink. We find him sleeping with his head upon a pillow,
and resting upon the curb of the well of Sychar. He suffered
all the innocent infirmities of our nature. He was an hungered,
and was disappointed when, early in the morning, he came

to a fig-tree seeking fruit, but found none. He was weary: "Jesus, being wearied with his journey, sat thus on the well." That he thirsted we know, for he said to the Samaritan woman, "Give me to drink"; and on the cross he cried in burning fever, "I thirst!" In all things he was made like unto his brethren. "Himself took our infirmities, and bare our sicknesses." His humanity was our humanity to the full, although without sin. Sin is not essential to humanity: it is a disease of nature; it is not a feature found in humanity as it came from the Creator's hand. The Man of men, in whom all true humanity is found in perfection, is Christ Jesus.

The fact that Jesus wept is a clear proof of this. *He wept, for he had human friendships.* Friendship is natural to man. Scarcely is he a man who never had a friend to love. Men in going through the world make many acquaintances, but out of these they have few special objects of esteem, whom they call friends. If they think to have many friends, they are, probably, misusing the name. All wise and good men have about them choice spirits, with whom their intercourse is more free, and in whom their trust is more confident than in all others. Jesus delighted to find retirement in the quiet home at Bethany; and we read that "Jesus loved Martha, and her sister, and Lazarus." Alas, my brethren! every friendship opens a fresh door for grief; for friends are no more immortal than ourselves. "Jesus wept" at the grave of his friend just as you and I have done, and must needs do again. See how human he is in his friendships.

"Jesus wept," for *he was truly human in his sympathies.* He did not merely walk about among us, and look like a man, but at a thousand points he came into contact with us. Jesus was always in touch with sorrow; happy are they that are in touch with *him!* Our Lord saw Mary and Martha weeping, and the Jews weeping that were with her, and he caught the contagion of their grief: "Jesus wept." His sympathies were with sorrowing ones, and for this reason, among others, he was himself "a man of sorrows, and acquainted with grief." He loved first his Father in heaven, whose glory was his main object; but he loved intensely his chosen, and his sympathy with them knew no bounds. "In all their afflictions he was afflicted." Jesus was far more tender towards humanity than any other man has ever been. He was the great Philanthropist. Alas! man is often the cruellest foe of man. None more unkind to man than men. Not the elements in their fury, nor wild beasts in their rage, nor diseases in their terror, have made such havoc among men as men drunk with the war spirit. To this hate our Lord was a perfect stranger. He was love, and only love; and through his love he descended into the depths of grief with the beloved ones whose lot was sorrowful; and he carried out to the full that sacred precept, "Weep with them that weep."

He was a man, for *he was stirred with human emotions.* Every emotion that ever thrilled through your bosom, so far as it is not sinful, has had its like in the bosom of the Lord Jesus Christ. He could be angry: we read in one place that "he looked round about on them with anger." He could be pitiful; when was he not so? He could be moved with compassion for a fainting crowd, or with scorn of a crafty ruler. Did he not speak with great indignation of the scribes and Pharisees? Yet, was he not tender as a nurse with a child, when cheering the penitent? Our Saviour, at the moment described in our text, felt indignation, pity, love, desire, and other emotions. His whole nature shaken with a mighty emotion, as he stood at the grave of Lazarus, confronting death and him that hath the power of it.

Beloved, have a clear faith in the humanity of him whom you rightly worship as your Lord and your God. Holding his divinity without doubt, hold his manhood without mistake. Realize the actual manhood of Jesus in all lights. Three times we read he wept. Doubtless he sorrowed full often when he was not seen; but thrice he was known to weep.

Now, let us change the line of our thought a little, while we say, "Jesus wept," that is, HE WAS NOT ASHAMED OF HIS HUMAN WEAKNESS. He could have repressed his tears—many men do so habitually. I do not doubt that there may be great sorrow, very great sorrow, where there is no open expression of it. In fact, most of you must have felt times when grief has struck you such a stunning blow that you could not weep, you could not recover yourself sufficiently to shed tears: the heart was all on fire with anguish, and the eyes refused the cooling drops. The Saviour could doubtless, if so he wished, have hidden his grief; but he did not choose to do so, for he was never unnatural. As "the holy child Jesus," he was free from pride, and wore his heart where men could see it.

For, first, remember *his talk when he spoke to his disciples.* He never concealed his poverty. There is an idea abroad that respectability is maintained by the pretence of riches, whereby real need is hidden. It is thought disreputable to seem to be poor, even when you are so. There may be something in the affectation, but our Lord did not countenance such a course; for he said, "Foxes have holes, and birds of the air have nests; but the Son of man hath not where to lay his head." Though he was rich, yet for our sakes he became poor, and he was never ashamed to let it be known that he was poor. So, too, he was "despised and rejected of men," and he did not pretend to be unaware of it. He did not try to make out that he was exceedingly popular, and that nobody had a word to say against him; but he owned that they had called the Master of the house Beelzebub. He knew what they had called him, and he was not ashamed of being made the butt of ridicule and the target of reproach. When they ascribed his miracles to the power of Satan he met the charges with an overwhelming reply; but he was not ashamed that slander had befallen him as well as poverty. As for his sufferings and death, how frequently do we find him talking to his disciples about it, till Peter would have stopped him if he could! Our Lord spoke of his being betrayed into the hand of sinners, and despitefully entreated, and spat upon. He spoke openly of his being "lifted up." He even dwelt upon the minute items of his coming passion: he had no wish to deny the fate which he knew awaited him. Why not die, and say nothing about it, if so it must be? Not so the Saviour. He has become a man, and he is not abashed at that which necessarily follows as a part of his humiliation. Being found in fashion as a man he becomes obedient to all that is required of his manhood, and before all observers he takes his place in the ranks. "Jesus wept."

Jesus wept on this occasion, *although it might have been misunderstood and misrepresented.* Do you not think that the Jews who stood there would sneeringly say, "See, he weeps! The miracle-worker weeps! He calls himself the Son of God, and yet he stands weeping there like any ordinary man!" Here was opportunity for scorn at his manifest weakness, and even for blasphemy at the evident token of it; but our Lord did not act upon policy; he allowed his true feeling to be seen. The enemies may say what they please, and even blaspheme both him and his God; but he will not act a part in the hope of silencing them. He acts the truth only, and weeps as his kind heart suggests. He thinks more of Mary and of Martha, and the comfort his sympathy may yield them, than of the cavilling ribaldry of unbelievers, which may forge an excuse for itself out of the loving weakness of his humanity.

"Jesus wept," and thereby *he revealed his love to Lazarus,* so that others saw it and cried, "Behold how he loved him!" This is one proof that our Lord does not hesitate to declare his love to his people. When he sojourned upon earth he was not ashamed to find friends among ordinary mortals. Our glorious Lord, now that he is enthroned, "is not ashamed to call us brethren." He is not ashamed to be written down in the same heavenly register as his poor people. His cheeks were bedewed with tears such as those which drop from our eyes, and by those tears all knew what manner of love he had towards his chosen. Blessed be his name! Many a great man might be willing to befriend a poor man with money, but not with tearful love; but here the blessed Master, in the midst of the assembled multitude, owns dead and rotting Lazarus as his friend, and seals the covenant of his love with tears.

"Jesus wept": *he was not ashamed to own the affliction which sin caused to his holy soul,* nor the gash which the sight of death made in his heart. He could not bear to see the grave and its corruption. May we never think of the sin and misery of our race without sorrow! I confess I can never go through this huge city without feeling unhappy. I never pass from end to end of London without feeling a black and dark cloud, hanging like a pall over my spirit. How my heart breaks for thee, O sinful city of London! Is it not so with you, my brethren? Think of its slums, its sins, its poverty, its ungodliness, its drunkenness, its vice! These may well go through a man's heart like sharp swords. How Jesus would have wept in London! Brethren, holy emotion is not a weakness to be ashamed of. If at any time, in the midst of the world's wickedness and gaiety, you weep, do not hide those tears!

"Jesus wept," *though he was about to work a wonderful miracle.* The glory of his Godhead did not make him ashamed of his manhood. Singular thing, too, that he should weep just before the joy of raising the dead to life. He is God, for he is about to call Lazarus out of the grave; but he is man just as much as ever, and therefore he weeps. Our Lord was as much man when he raised the dead as when he worked in the carpenter's shop at Nazareth. He was not ashamed to own his real manhood while he proved himself the resurrection and the life. This day in the glory of heaven he wears his scars, to show that, though God, he is not ashamed to be recognized as man. He makes this one of his glorious names—"I am he that liveth, and was dead; and, behold, I am alive for evermore"; therein describing his connection with our manhood in life and in death.

Thirdly, OUR LORD JESUS IS OUR INSTRUCTOR IN WEEPING. This is the most practical part of our discourse; be sure that you receive it by the teaching of the Holy Ghost. He wept because *this was his method of prayer on this occasion.* A great miracle was to be wrought, and great power was needed from on high: as man, the Lord Jesus cries to God with intense earnestness, and finds the fittest embodiment for his prayer in weeping. No prayer will ever prevail with God more surely than a liquid petition, which, being distilled from the heart, trickles from the eye, and waters the cheek. Then is God won when he hears the voice of your weeping. The angel at Peniel will slip from your dry hands; but moisten them with tears, and you will hold him fast. Before the Lord Jesus puts forth the power which raises Lazarus from the grave, he appeals to God with strong crying and tears. The Father appears for his weeping Son; and you, if you want to win in prayer, must weep in prayer. Let your soul arouse itself to eager desire, and trouble itself to anguish, and then you will prevail. "Jesus wept" to teach us how to baptize our prayers unto God in a wave of heart-grief.

"Jesus wept" again, because *before he would arouse the dead he would be himself aroused.* A word of his could have wrought the wonder; yea, his mere volition would have been enough. But for our instruction he did not make it so. There was a kind of evil which went not out but with prayer and fasting, and here was a kind of death which would not yield unless the Saviour groaned and wept. Without great exertion of the life of Jesus, the death in Lazarus could not be subdued. Therefore the Lord aroused himself, and stirred up all his strength, troubling all his being for the struggle on which he entered. Learn hence, my brother, that if you think to do any great good in saving sinners, you must not be half-asleep yourself: you must be troubled even to tears. Perhaps the most difficult thing in winning souls is to get ourselves into a fit state. Until a man's whole soul is moved, he will not move his fellow. He might, possibly, succeed with those who are willing to be impressed; but the careless will be unmoved by any man who is unmoved himself. Tears storm a passage for warnings. If Christ's whole self must be stirred before Lazarus is raised, *we* must be thrilled before we can win a soul. We must feel, if others are to feel. Come, you that are going to the Sunday-school class this afternoon, because you must go; you must not go in that spirit. You, who are going to preach or talk to your classes, and have as yet only one eye open; this will never do. Your Lord was all alive, and all sensitive, and you must be the same. You must be quickened into tenderness as he was, or you will not receive his life-giving power.

Jesus wept *in full knowledge of several things which might have prevented his weeping.* You have sometimes thought to yourself when weeping at the grave of a dear child, or wife, or husband, that you have been wrong in so doing; but this may not be the case. Our Saviour wept, though he knew that Lazarus was safe enough. I do not know what had happened to the soul of Lazarus: where Scripture is silent it is not mine to speak; but, wherever he was, he was perfectly safe; and yet "Jesus wept." Moreover, Jesus knew that he was going to raise Lazarus to life; his resurrection was close at hand; and yet "Jesus wept." Sometimes we are told that if we really believed that our friends would rise again, and that they are safe and happy even now, we could not weep. Why not? Jesus did. There cannot be any error in following where Jesus leads the way. Jesus knew, moreover, that the death of Lazarus was for the glory of God: he had said, "This sickness is not unto death, but for the glory of God"; and yet he wept! Have we not thought, "Surely it must be wicked to weep when you know that the bereavement will glorify God?" Not so, or else Jesus would not have wept under similar circumstances. Learn instruction: tears which else we might have regarded as contraband have now free admission into the realm of holiness, since "Jesus wept."

"Jesus wept," but he did not sin. There was not even a particle of evil in any one of the Redeemer's tears. Salt there may have been, but not fault. Beloved, we can weep without sin. I do not suppose we have ever done so; but it is possible. It is not a sin to weep for those whom God has taken away from us, nor for those who are suffering. I will tell you why there was no sin in Christ's weeping: it was because *he wept in his Father's presence.* When he spoke in his sorrow, the first word was, "Father": he said, "Father, I thank thee." If you can weep in such a way that all the while you feel God to be your Father, and can thank him, and know that you are in his presence, your weeping is not blameworthy, but healthful. Let such floods flow on, for Jesus wept, and said, "Father, I thank thee." When you cannot smile nor weep except by forgetting God and his law, then are you offending; but if you can get up to your great Father's bosom, and bury your head there, you may sob away without stint; for that which he permits is evidently no offence.

"Jesus wept": IN THIS HE IS OUR COMFORTER. Let me speak to those who are of heavy heart. "Jesus wept": *herein is our honour.* Thou weepest, my friend, in good company; for Jesus wept. Let no man censure thee lest they not only blame thee, but Jesus also.

"Jesus wept": *herein is our sonship vindicated.* Thou sayest, "Can I be the child of God, and yet go weeping?" Was not Jesus the well-beloved Son? and yet he wept. Ah! the question lies another way: "What son is he whom the father chasteneth not?" What child did God ever have that did not weep? He had one Son without sin; but he never had a son without sorrow. He had a Son that never deserved a stroke of the rod, and yet against that Son the sword was awakened.

See now the real sympathy of Christ with his people, for *herein is comfort.* His sympathy lies not alone in words, not even wholly in deeds—it is more tender than these can be. Only his heart could express his tender sympathy, and then it was by tears—tears which were brought up like gold from the ore-bed of the heart, minted in the eyes, and then put in circulation as current coin of the merchant, each one bearing the King's image and superscription. Jesus is our fellow-sufferer; and this should be our greatest solace. Oh, if we had a High-priest that knew not what it is to suffer as we do, it would be a most unhappy thing for us! If we fled to him for refuge, and found that he had known no grief, and consequently could not understand us, it would be killing to a broken heart. A Jesus who never wept could never wipe away my tears. That were a grief I could not bear, if he could not have fellowship with me, and could not understand my woe.

Beloved, think how bravely our Lord endured: *herein is confidence*. Tears did not drown the Saviour's hope in God. He lived. He triumphed notwithstanding all his sorrow; and because he lives, we shall live also. He says, "Be of good cheer; I have overcome the world." Though our hero had to weep in the fight, yet he was not beaten. He came, he wept, he conquered.

Let this comfort you, too, that, though he wept, he weeps no more: *herein is heaven begun below.* "Death hath no more dominion over him" in any sense or degree. He has done with weeping. So shall it be with us before long. How I love that promise: "Neither shall there be any more pain"! Heaven is without a temple, for it is all devotion; and so is it without a hospital, for it is all health and love. "The inhabitant shall no more say, I am sick." "Oh for the no more weeping!" It will come to us before long, for it has come to Jesus. "The Lord God shall wipe away all tears from their eyes."

Fifthly, and lastly, "Jesus wept": IN THIS HE IS OUR EXAMPLE. We should weep, for Jesus wept. *Jesus wept for others.* I know not that he ever wept for himself. His were sympathetic tears. He embodied that command, "Weep with them that weep." He has a narrow soul who can hold it all within the compass of his ribs. A true soul, a Christly soul, lives in other men's souls and bodies as well as in its own. A perfectly Christly soul finds all the world too narrow for its abode, for it lives and loves; it lives by loving, and loves because it lives. Think of other weepers, and have pity upon the children of grief. To-day I want to touch your heart-strings, and move you to pity the pains, the agonies, of the many now lying within the wards of our hospitals, and the even greater miseries of those who pine for want of medicine and care, because they cannot get into the hospitals, but have to wear themselves out in hopeless disease. How must those suffer who have bad nursing and little food, and in the winter are pinched with cold! You and I may never suffer as they do, but at least let us grieve on their account, and stand ready to succour them to the best of our ability.

In another matter our Lord is our example; learn from him that our indignation against evil will best show itself in *compassion for sinners*. Ah, my dear friend! I heard you declaiming tremendously against drunkenness. I am glad to hear you: you cannot say anything too hard or too heavy about that degrading vice; but, I pray you, wind up your denunciation with weeping over the poor drunkard. I heard you speak, my other friend, on behalf of the League of Purity, and you smote the monsters of lasciviousness with all your force. I wish more strength to your arm! But when you have done, sit down and weep, that such filthiness should defile men and women, who are your fellow-creatures. Appeal to Parliament, if you wish, for the putting down of vice; but Parliament itself first needs correcting and purifying. A flood of tears before the thrice Holy God will do far more than the hugest rolls of petition to our senators. "Jesus wept"; and his tears were mighty weapons against sin and death. You feel indignant at the lazy, idle, loafing vagabonds whose very illness is produced by their own vice: I cannot condemn your virtuous wrath. But if you would in all things imitate Jesus, please note that it is not written that Jesus thundered, but that "Jesus wept." Let indignation have pity mixed with it. You will do more good to offenders, and more good to yourself, and more good to the best of causes, if pity moistens all.

Lastly, when you have wept, *imitate your Saviour—do something!* If the chapter before us had finished with "Jesus wept," it would have been a poor one. Suppose, after they had come to the grave, we had read "Jesus wept, and went about his daily business," I should have felt small comfort in the passage. If nothing had come of it but tears, it would have been a great falling off from the usual ways of our blessed Lord. Tears!

what are they alone? Salt water. A cup of them would be of little worth to anybody. But, beloved, "Jesus wept," and then he commanded, "Roll away the stone." He cried, "Lazarus, come forth!" When Lazarus struggled out of the tomb, Jesus said, "Loose him, and let him go." Some of you are full of pity for the sick; but I hope we shall not end in mere sentiment. Do not let us say, "We were moved to sympathize with the sick, but we gave an awfully bad collection!" I should be ashamed to think of this morning's meditation if it ended so. No, no; if you cannot raise the dead, give something towards rolling away the stone which shuts the poor out of the hospital; if you cannot restore them to health, at least do something towards removing their maladies. Loose them from this crowded city, and send them into the country to a Convalescent Home. Brethren, we can thus practically prove the truth of our sympathy.

VI

"LET NOT YOUR HEART BE TROUBLED"

> "Let not your heart be troubled: ye believe in God, believe
> also in me. In my Father's house are many mansions: if it
> were not so, I would have told you. I go to prepare a place for
> you. And if I go and prepare a place for you, I will come
> again, and receive you unto myself; that where I am, there
> ye may be also. And whither I go ye know, and the way ye
> know."—John 14: 1-4.

WE may well feel glad that God's people, whose lives are
recorded in the Old and New Testaments, were men of
like passions with ourselves. I have known many a poor sinner
pluck up hope as he has observed the sins and struggles of those
who were saved by grace, and I have known many of the heirs
of heaven find consolation as they have observed how imperfect
beings like themselves have prevailed with God in prayer, and
have been delivered in their time of distress. I am very glad
that the Apostles were not perfect men; they would then have
understood all that Jesus said at once, and we should have lost
our Lord's instructive explanations; they would also have
lived above all trouble of mind, and then the Master would not
have said to them these golden words, "Let not your heart be
troubled."

It is, however, most evident from our text that it is not
according to our Lord's mind that any of his servants should
be troubled in heart. He takes no delight in the doubt and disquietude of his people. When he saw that because of what he
had said to them sorrow had filled the hearts of his Apostles,
he pleaded with them in great love, and besought them to be
comforted. Trials depress the hearts of God's children, for
which the most tender ministry fails to afford consolation; and
then it is most sweet for the failing comforter to remember the
unfailing Comforter, and to commit the case of the sorrowful
spirit into the divine hands. Seeing that one Person of the

blessed Trinity has undertaken to be the Comforter, we see how important it is that our hearts should be filled with consolation. Happy religion in which it is our duty to be glad! Blessed gospel by which we are forbidden to be troubled in heart!

Is it not a thing greatly to be admired that the Lord Jesus should think so carefully of his friends at such a time? Great personal sorrows may well be an excuse if the griefs of others are somewhat overlooked. Jesus was going to his last bitter agony, and to death itself, and yet he overflowed with sympathy for his followers. Had it been you or I, we should have asked for sympathy for ourselves. Our cry would have been, "Have pity upon me, O my friends, for the hand of God hath touched me!" But, instead of that, our Lord cast his own crushing sorrows into the background, and bent his mind to the work of sustaining his chosen under their far inferior griefs.

While I admire this condescending tenderness of love, I at the same time cannot help adoring the marvellous confidence of our blessed Lord, who, though he knows that he is to be put to a shameful death, yet feels no fear, but bids his disciples trust implicitly to him. The black darkness of the awful midnight was beginning to surround him, yet how brave his word —"Believe also in me!" He knew in that threatening hour that he had come forth from the Father, and that he was in the Father and the Father in him; and so he says, "Ye believe in God, believe also in me." This association of himself with God as the object of human confidence in the time of trouble, betokens a consciousness of his own divine power and Godhead; and it is a mystery in whose difficulties faith takes pleasure, to see in our Lord Jesus the faith of a man for himself, and the faithfulness of God for others.

First, then, LET US TASTE OF THE BITTER WATERS. "Because I have said these things unto you, sorrow hath filled your heart." I would not confine the comfort to any one form of affliction, for it is a balm for every wound; but still it will be well to enquire what was the particular trouble of the disciples? It may be that some of us are passing through it now, or we may be plunged in it ere long.

It was this—*Jesus was to die:* their Lord, whom they sincerely loved, was about to go from them by a shameful, painful death. What tender heart could bear to think of that? Yet he had told them that it would be so, and they began to remember his former words wherein he had said that the Son of man would be betrayed into the hands of wicked men, and would be scourged and put to death. They were now to pass through all the bitterness of seeing him accused, condemned, and crucified. In a short time he was actually seized, bound, carried to the high priest's house, hurried to Pilate, then to Herod, back again to Pilate, stripped, scourged, mocked, insulted. They saw him conducted through the streets of Jerusalem bearing his cross. They beheld him hanging on the tree between two thieves, and heard him cry, "My God, my God, why hast thou forsaken me?" A bitter draught this! In proportion as they loved their Lord they must have deeply grieved for him: and they needed that he should say, "Let not your heart be troubled."

To-day those who love the Lord Jesus have to behold a spiritual repetition of his shameful treatment at the hands of men; for even now he is crucified afresh by those who account his cross a stumbling-block and the preaching of it foolishness. Ah me! how is Christ still misunderstood, misrepresented, despised, mocked, and rejected of men! They cannot touch him really, for there he sits enthroned in the heaven of heavens; but as far as they can, they slay him over again. A malignant spirit is manifested to the Gospel as once it was to Christ in person. Some with coarse blasphemies, and not a few with cunning assaults upon this part of Scripture, and on that, are doing their best to bruise the heel of the seed of the woman. It is a huge grief to see the mass of mankind pass by the cross with averted eyes as if the Saviour's death was nothing—nothing at least to them. In proportion as you feel a zeal for the Crucified, and for his saving truth, it is wormwood and gall to live in this age of unbelief.

In addition to this, the Apostles had for an outlook the expectation that *their Lord would be away from them.* They did not at first understand his saying, "A little while, and ye shall not see me: and again, a little while, and ye shall see me, because I go to the Father." Now it dawned upon them that they were to be left as sheep without a shepherd; for their Master and head was to be taken from them. This was to them a source of dread and dismay: for they said to themselves,

"What shall we do without him? We are a little flock; how shall we be defended when he is gone, and the wolf is prowling? When the Scribes and Pharisees gather about us, how shall we answer them? As for our Lord's cause and Kingdom, how can it be safe in such trembling hands as ours? Alas for the Gospel of salvation when Jesus is not with us!" This was a bitter sorrow: and something of this kind of feeling often crosses our own hearts as we tremble for the ark of the Lord. My heart is sad when I see the state of religion among us. Oh for an hour of the Son of man in these darkening days! It is written, "There shall come in the last days scoffers"; and they have come, but, oh, that the Lord himself were here in person! Oh, that the Lord would pluck his right hand out of his bosom, and show us once again the wonders of Pentecost, to the confusion of his adversaries, and to the delight of all his friends. He has not come as yet! Well-nigh two thousand years have rolled away since he departed, and the night is dark, and there is no sign of dawn. We know that he is with us in a spiritual sense; but, oh, that we had him in the glory of his power!

But they felt a third grief, and it was this: that *he was to be betrayed by one of themselves*. The twelve were chosen men, but one of them was a devil and sold his Lord. This pierced the hearts of the faithful—"the Son of man is betrayed." He is not taken by open seizure, but he is sold for thirty pieces of silver by one whom he entrusted with his little store. He that dipped with him in the dish had sold him for paltry gain. This cut them to the heart, even as it did the Master himself; for our Lord felt the treachery of his friend. Of this bitter water the faithful at this hour are made to drink: for what see we at this day? What see we in various places but persons that are reputed to be ministers of the Gospel whose main business seems to be to undermine our holy faith, and batter down the truths which are commonly received in the Christian church? Under the banner of "advanced thought," they make war upon those eternal truths for which confessors contended and martyrs bled, and by which the saints of past ages have been sustained in their dying hours. It is not an enemy; then we could have borne and answered it. If the outward and avowed infidel attacks inspiration, let him do so. It is a free country, let him speak; but when a man enters our pulpits, open the sacred volume, and denies that it is inspired, what does he there? How does his conscience allow him to assume an office which he perverts?

Then there came another pang at the back of this; for one of them, though true-hearted and loyal, would that night *deny his Lord*. Peter, in many respects the leader of the little company, had been warned that he would act the craven and vehemently deny his Lord. This is bitterness indeed, of which those that love the Church of God are compelled full often to drink, to see men whom we cannot but believe to be the disciples of Jesus Christ carried away by temptation, by fear of man, or by the fashion of the times, so that Christ and his Gospel are virtually denied by them. The fear of being thought dogmatic or Puritanic closes many a mouth which ought to be declaring him to be the Son of God with power, and extolling his glorious majesty in defiance of all that dare oppose him. The hearts of some who best love Jesus grow heavy at the sight of the worldliness and lukewarmness of many of his professed followers.

Under our second head LET US DRINK OF THE SWEET WATERS and refresh our souls.

First, in this wonderful text our Master indicates to us the true means of comfort under every sort of disquietude. How puts he it? "Let not your heart be troubled"—*believe*. Kindly look down your Bibles, and you will see that this direction is repeated. He says in the opening of the eleventh verse, "Believe me"; and then, again, in the second clause, "Believe me." I thought as I tried to enter into the meaning of this sacred utterance that I heard Jesus at my side saying thrice to me, "Believe me! believe me! believe me!" Could any one of the eleven that were with him have disbelieved their present Lord? He says, "Believe me! believe me! believe me!"—as if there was great need to urge them to faith in him. Is there no other cure, then, for a troubled heart? No other is required. This is all-sufficient through God. If believing in Jesus you still are troubled, believe in him again yet more thoroughly and heartily. If even that should not take away the perturbation of your mind, believe in him to a third degree, and continue to do so with increasing simplicity and force. Regard this as the one and only physic for the disease of fear and trouble. Jesus prescribes, "Believe, believe, believe in *me*!"

Believe not only in certain doctrines, but in Jesus himself— in him as able to carry out every promise that he has made. Believe in him as you believe in God. One has been at times apt to think it easier to believe in Jesus than in God, but this is a thought of spiritual infancy; more advanced believers find it not so. To a Jew this was certainly the right way of putting it, and I think to us Gentiles it is so also, when we have been long in the faith; for we get to believe in God as a matter of course, and faith in Jesus requires a further confidence. I believe in God's power in creation: he can make what he wills, and shape what he has made. I believe in his power in providence, that he can bring to pass his eternal purposes, and do as he wills among the armies in heaven and among the inhabitants of this lower world. I believe concerning God that all things are possible unto him. Just in that way I am called upon to believe in Jesus that he is as omnipotent in power and as sure in his working as the Lord from whom come all the forces of nature; and just as certain to accomplish his purposes as God is to achieve his design in the works of providence. Relying upon the Saviour with the implicit faith which every right-minded man renders towards God, we shall only give our Lord the faith which he justly claims. He is faithful and true, and his power can effect his promise: let us depend trustfully upon him, and perfect peace shall come into our hearts. Believe him, and sorrow and sighing will flee away.

Believe in him as ever living, even as you believe in the eternity of God. You believe in the eternal existence of the Most High whom you have not seen, even so believe in the everlasting life of the Son of God. Aye, though you see him die, though you see him laid in the grave, yet believe in him that he has not ceased to be. Look for his reappearance, even as ye believe in God. Yea, and when he is gone from you, and a cloud has received him out of your sight, believe that he liveth, even as God liveth; and because he lives, you shall live also. "Even as ye believe in God," saith Jesus, "believe also in me." Faith in Jesus Christ himself as an ever-living and divine Person, is the best quietus for every kind of fear.

But now our Lord proceeded to say that though he was

going from them *he was only going to his Father's house.* "In my Father's house are many mansions." Aye, but this was sweet comfort. "I am going," said he, "and on my way you will see me scourged, bleeding, mocked, and buffeted; but I shall pass through all this to the joy and rest, and honour of my Father's house." God is everywhere present, and yet as on earth he had a tabernacle wherein he specially manifested himself, so there is a place where he in a peculiar manner is revealed. The temple was a type of that matchless abode of God which eye hath not seen; we call it heaven, the pavilion of God, the home of holy angels and of those pure spirits who dwell in his immediate presence. In heaven God may be said in special to have his habitation, and Jesus was going there to be received on his return to all the honour which awaited his finished service. He was, in fact, going home, as a son who is returning to his father's house, from which he had gone upon his father's business. He was going where he would be with the Father, where he would be perfectly at rest, where he would be above the assaults of the wicked; where he would never suffer or die again; he was going to reassume the glory which he had with the Father or ever the world was. Oh, if they had perfectly understood this, they would have understood the Saviour's words, "If ye loved me, ye would rejoice, because I said, I go unto the Father." Imagination fails to picture the glory of our Lord's return, the honourable escort which heralded his approach to the Eternal City, the heartiness of the welcome of the Conqueror to the skies.

"He was seen of angels." They beheld that "joyous re-entry," the opening of the eternal doors to the King of Glory, and the triumph through the celestial streets of him who led captivity captive and scattered gifts among men. They saw the enthronement of Jesus who was made a little lower than the angels for the suffering of death, but was then and there crowned with glory and honour. These are not things of which these stammering lips of mine can speak, but they are things for you to consider when the Spirit of the Lord is upon you. Muse upon them for your delectation.

Jesus has gone by the way of Calvary up to his Father's house: all his work and warfare done, he is rewarded for his sojourn among men as man. All the shame which his work necessitated is now lost in the splendour of his mediatorial reign. Ye people of God, be no more troubled, for your Lord is King, your Saviour reigns! Men may still scoff at him, but they cannot rob him of a ray of glory! They may reject him, but the Lord God omnipotent has crowned him! They may deny his existence, but he lives! They may rebelliously cry, "Let us break his bands asunder, and cast his cords from us," but the Lord hath set his King upon his holy hill of Zion, and none can thrust him from his throne. Hallelujah! "God hath highly exalted him, and given him a name which is above every name: that at the name of Jesus every knee should bow." Wherefore let not your hearts be troubled by the noise of controversy, and the blasphemy and rebuke of an evil age. Again let us say, "Hallelujah!" The Prince hath come unto his own again; he hath entered into his Father's palace; the heavens have received him. Why should we be troubled?

Thirdly, our Lord gave his servants comfort in another way: *he gave them to understand by implication that a great many would follow him to the Father's house.* He did not only assure them that he was going to his Father's house, but he said, "In my Father's house are many mansions." These mansions are not built to stand empty. God doeth nothing in vain; therefore it is natural to conclude that a multitude of spirits, innumerable beyond all count, will rise in due time to occupy those many mansions in the Father's house. Now I see in this great comfort to them, because they doubtless feared that if their Lord was absent his Kingdom might fail. How would there be converts if he were crucified? How could they expect, poor creatures as they were, to set up a kingdom of righteousness on the earth? How could they turn the world upside down and bring multitudes to his feet whom he had purchased with his blood, if his conquering right arm was not seen at their head? The Lord Jesus in effect said, "I am going, but I shall lead the way for a vast host who will come to the prepared abodes. Like the corn of wheat which is cast into the ground to die, I shall bring forth much fruit, which shall be housed in the abiding resting-places."

This is one part of our comfort at this hour. Little boots it how men fight against the Gospel for the Lord knoweth them that are his, and he will ransom by power those redeemed by blood. He has a multitude according to the election of grace whom he will bring in. Though they seem to-day to be a small remnant, yet he will fill the many mansions. This stands fast as a rock—"All that the Father giveth me shall come to me; and him that cometh to me I will in no wise cast out." They boast that "they will not come unto Christ"; but the Spirit of God foresaw that they would reject the salvation of the Lord. What said Jesus to those like them? "Ye believe not, because ye are not of my sheep, as I said unto you. My sheep hear my voice, and I know them, and they follow me: and I give unto them eternal life." The wicked unbelief of men is their own condemnation; but Jesus loses not the reward of his passion. We fling back into the faces of the despisers of Christ the scorn which they pour upon him, and remind them that those who despise him shall be lightly esteemed, their names shall be written in the earth. What if *they* come not to him? it is their own loss, and well did he say of them, "No man can come to me except the Father which hath sent me draw him." Their wickedness is their inability and their destruction. But "the redeemed of the Lord shall come to Zion with songs and ever-lasting joy upon their heads." "He shall see of the travail of his soul, and shall be satisfied." There shall be no failure as to the Lord's redeeming work, even though the froward reject the counsel of God against themselves. What Jesus has bought with blood he will not lose; what he died to accomplish shall surely be performed; and what he rose again to carry out shall be effected though all the devils in hell and unbelievers upon earth should join in league against him.

But our Lord went much further, for he said, *"I go to prepare a place for you."* I think he did not only refer to the many mansions for our spirits, but to the ultimate *place* of our risen bodies, of which I will speak before long. In our Lord's going away, as well as in his continuance in his Father's presence he would be engaged in preparing a place for his own. He was going that he might clear all impediment out of the way. Their sins blocked the road; like mountains their iniquities opposed all passage; but he hath broken down every wall of partition, and every iron gate he hath opened. The way into the kingdom is opened for all believers. He passed through death to resur-rection and ascension to remove every obstacle from our path.

He went from us also to fulfil every condition: for it was absolutely needful that all who entered heaven should wear a perfect righteousness, and should be made perfect in character, seeing no sin can enter the holy city. Now the saints could not be perfected without being washed in his precious blood, and renewed by the Holy Spirit; and so the Saviour endured the death of the cross; and when he arose he sent us the sanctifying Spirit, that we might be fitted for his rest.

He went away also that he might be in a position to secure that place for all his people. He entered the glory-land as our Forerunner, to occupy the place in our name, to take possession of heaven as the representative of all his people. He was going that he might in heaven itself act as Intercessor, pleading before the throne, and therefore be able to save to the uttermost all that come to God by him. By being in heaven our Lord occupies a vantage-ground for the sure accomplishing of his purposes of love. As Joseph went down into Egypt to store the granaries, to prepare for Israel a home in Goshen, and to sit upon the throne for their protection, so hath our Lord gone away into the glory for our good, and he is doing for us upon his throne what could not so advantageously have been done for us here.

At the same time, I am inclined to think that there is a special sense in these words over and above the preparing of heaven for us. I think our Lord Jesus meant to say, "I go to prepare a place for you" in this sense—that there would in the end be a place found for their entire manhood. Mark that word, *"a place."* We are too apt to entertain cloudy ideas of the ultimate inheritance of those who attain unto the resurrection of the dead. "Heaven is a state," says somebody. Yes, certainly, it is a state; but it is *a place* too, and in the future it will be more distinctly a place. Observe that our blessed Lord went away in body; not as a disembodied spirit, but as one who had eaten with his disciples, and whose body had been handled by them. His body needed a *"place,"* and he is gone to prepare a place for us, not only as we shall be for a while, pure spirits, but as we are to be ultimately—body, and soul, and spirit. When a child of God dies, where does his spirit go? There is no question about that matter: we are informed by the inspired Apostle— "absent from the body, present with the Lord." But that is a spiritual matter, and something yet remains. My spirit is not the whole of myself, for I am taught so to respect my body as to regard it as a precious portion of my complete self—the temple of God. The Lord Jesus Christ did not redeem my spirit alone, but my body too, and consequently he means to have a "place" where I, this person who is here, in the wholeness of my individuality, may rest for ever. Jesus means to have a place made for the entire manhood of his chosen, that they may be where he is and as he is. Our ultimate abode will be a state of blessedness, but it must also be *a place* suited for our risen bodies. It is not, therefore, a cloud-land, an airy something, impalpable and dreamy. Oh, no, it will be as really a place as this earth is a place. Come, you that think you will never rise again, you who imagine that the scattering of our dust forbids all hope of the restoration of our bodies; we shall go where Christ has gone, and as he has gone. He leads the way in his body, and we shall follow in ours. Ultimately there shall be the complete redemption of the purchased possession, and not a bone shall be left in the regions of death, not a relic for the devil to glory over.

The next consolation was *the promise of his sure return*: "If I go away to prepare a place for you, I will come again." Listen, then! Jesus is coming again. In the same manner as he ascended he will return—that is, really, literally, and in bodily form. He meant no play upon words when he so plainly said, without proverb, "I will come again," or more sweetly still, "I go away and come again *unto you*." This is our loudest joy-note, "Behold, he cometh!" This is our never-failing comfort. Observe that the Saviour, in this place, says nothing about the peace and rest of believers till he is come; for he looks on to the end. It is not necessary to put every truth into one sentence; and so our Lord is content to mention the brightest of our hopes, and leave other blessings for mention at other times. Here the consolation is that he will come, come personally to gather us in. He will not send an angel, nor even a host of cherubim to fetch us up into our eternal state; but the Lord himself will descend from heaven. It is to be our marriage-day, and the glorious Bridegroom will come in person. When the Bride is prepared for her Husband, will he not come to fetch her to his home? O beloved, do you not see where our Lord's thoughts were? He was dwelling upon the happy day of his ultimate victory, when he shall come to be admired in all them that believe. That is where he would have his people's thoughts to be; but alas! they forget his advent. The Lord shall come; let your hearts anticipate that day of days. His enemies cannot stop his coming! "Let not your heart be troubled." They may hate him, but they cannot hinder him; they cannot impede his glorious return, not by the twinkling of an eye. What an answer will his coming be to every adversary! How will they weep and wail because of him! As surely as he lives he will come; and what confusion this will bring upon the wise men who at this hour are reasoning against his Deity and ridiculing his atonement! Again I say, "Let not your heart be troubled" as to the present state of religion; it will not last long.

For that is the next comfort—*he will receive us.* When he comes he will receive his followers with a courtly reception. It will be their marriage reception; it shall be the marriage supper of the Son of God. Then shall descend out of heaven the new Jerusalem prepared as a bride for her husband. Then shall come the day of the resurrection, and the dead in Christ shall rise. Then all his people who are alive at the time of his coming shall be suddenly transformed, so as to be delivered from all the frailties and imperfections of their mortal bodies: "The dead shall be raised incorruptible, and we shall be changed." Then we shall be presented spirit, soul, and body "without spot, or wrinkle, or any such thing"; in the clear and absolute perfection of our sanctified manhood, presented unto Christ himself. This is the sweetest idea of heaven that can be, that we shall be with Christ, that we shall see him, that we shall speak to him, that we shall commune with him most intimately, that we shall glorify him, that he will glorify us, and that we shall never be divided from him for ever and ever. "Let not your heart be troubled," all this is near at hand, and our Lord's going away has secured it to us.

For this was the last point of the consolation, that when he came and received his people to himself *he would place them eternally where he is, that they may be with him.* Oh, joy! joy! joy! unutterable joy! Can we not now, once for all, dismiss every fear in the prospect of the endless bliss reserved for us?

The Lord talks to us as if we now knew all about his goings and doings; and so we do as far as all practical purposes are concerned. He says, "Whither I go ye know." He is not gone to a place unknown, remote, dangerous. He has only gone home. "Whither I go ye know." When a mother sends her boy to Australia she is usually troubled because she may never see him again; but he replies, "Dear mother, the distance is nothing now, we cross the ocean in a very few weeks, and I shall speedily come back again." Then the mother is cheered; she thinks of the ocean as a little bit of blue between her and her son, and looks for him to return, if need be. So the Saviour says, "Whither I go ye know." He could not reach his crown except by the cross, nor his mediatorial glory except by death: but that way once made in his own person is open for all who believe in him. Thus you know where the Lord has gone, and you know the road; therefore, be encouraged, for he is not far away; he is not inaccessible; you shall be with him soon. "Let not your heart be troubled."

VII

"OUR LIGHT AFFLICTION"

"Our light affliction."—2 Cor. 4: 17.

PERHAPS someone here thoughtlessly says, "Well, whoever calls affliction 'light' must have been a person who knew very little about what affliction really is. If he had suffered as I have done, he would not have written about 'our light affliction.' He must have been in robust health, and known nothing of sickness and pain." "Just so," says another, "and if he had been as poor as I am, and had to work as hard as I do to maintain a sickly wife, and a large family, he would not have written about 'our light affliction.' I expect the gentleman who used that expression lived very much at his ease, and had all that his heart could wish." "Aye," says another, "and if he had stood by an open grave, and had to lament the loss of loved ones, as I have done, and if he had known what it was to be desolate and forsaken, as I have known it, he would not have written about 'our light affliction.'"

Now, if you do talk like that, you are all of you mistaken, for the man who wrote these words was probably afflicted more than any of us have ever been. The list of his afflictions that he gives us is perfectly appalling: "in stripes above measure, in prisons more frequent, in deaths oft. Thrice was I beaten with rods, once was I stoned, thrice I suffered shipwreck, a night and a day I have been in the deep; in journeyings often, in perils of waters, in perils of robbers, in perils by mine own countrymen, in perils by the heathen, in perils in the city, in perils in the wilderness, in perils in the sea, in perils among false brethren; in weariness and painfulness, in watchings often, in hunger and thirst, in fastings often, in cold and nakedness." Is there anyone who could truthfully make out such a catalogue of personal afflictions as the apostle Paul endured?

"Well then," says one, "he must have been so hardened that he took no notice of it, like the Red Indian who will endure terrible torture without a groan, or like the Stoic philosopher who concealed his inward feelings beneath an unmoved countenance." No; you also are mistaken. If you read Paul's letters to his private friends and to the churches, you will see that they bear abundant evidences that he was a man of great tenderness of spirit and of intense emotion, one who could suffer and who did suffer most acutely.

"Well then," says another, "he must have been one of those careless, light-hearted people who never trouble about anything that happens, and whose motto is, 'Let us eat and drink, for to-morrow we die.'" Oh, no! the Apostle Paul was not at all that kind of man; he was the most thoughtful, logical, careful, considerate man of whom I have ever read. He knew what it was to be joyful, yet there was never any sign of levity about him. He had a grandly buoyant spirit which lifted him above waves of sorrow in which most men would have sunk, yet he was never frivolous. He wrote of "our light affliction" even when he was heavily afflicted, and while he acutely felt that affliction.

We must not forget that Paul had afflictions which were peculiarly his own. There are afflictions which Christians have because they are Christians, and which those who are not Christians do not have; and Paul, as an Apostle of Jesus Christ, had sufferings which were peculiarly his because he was an apostle. Because he was specially called to be the Apostle of the Gentiles, because he was chosen to carry the Gospel to many nations, because he was called to stand even before the cruel Emperor Nero,—for that very reason, he who was peculiarly gifted and specially chosen above all others to do most arduous and onerous work was also called to endure unusual trial. He had spelt out the word "AFFLICTION" as perhaps no other mere man had done, he had seen it written in capital letters across his whole life; so he could speak, not as a novice, but as one who had graduated in the school of affliction, and yet he wrote concerning "our light affliction."

I am going to speak, first, specially TO CHRISTIAN WORKERS; and to them I would say: Dear brethren and sisters in Christ, *our affliction is light compared with the objects we have in view.*

Much of the affliction that the Apostle had to endure came upon him because he was seeking the conversion of the heathen and the ingathering of the elect into the Kingdom of Christ. If this is the object you also have in view, and you are made to suffer through your sedulous and faithful pursuit of it, I think you may truly call anything you have to endure a light affliction. If you have ever seen a mother sit up night after night with her sick child, you must have sometimes wondered that her eyes did not close in slumber. You were amazed that she did not permit someone else to share her task, but she seemed to think nothing of the cost to herself if she might only be the means of saving her little one's life. 'Twas love that made her labour light, and he who truly loves the souls of sinners will willingly bear any affliction for their sakes if he may but bring them to the Saviour. Yes, and he will also patiently endure affliction from them as he remembers how, in his own wilfulness and waywardness, he caused his Saviour to suffer on his behalf. If a man could know that, all through his life, he would have to wear a threadbare garment and exist upon very scanty fare; if he were sure that, throughout his life, he would meet with but little kindness from Christians, and with nothing but persecution from worldlings; and if, at the close of his career, he could only expect to be devoured by dogs or his body to be cast to the carrion crows, yet might he think all this to be but a light affliction if he might but win one soul from the unquenchable flame.

Still speaking to Christian workers, I have next to say that *our affliction is light compared with our great motive.* What should be the great motive of all who seek to spread the Gospel, and to win sinners for Christ? Surely there is no motive comparable to that of seeking to bring glory to God by gathering into the Kingdom of Christ those for whom he shed his precious blood. Ever keep in memory, beloved, what Jesus has done for us. He left his radiant throne in glory, and condescended to take upon himself our nature, and also our sin.

Saved by his almighty grace, cleansed by his ever-precious blood, living because we have been made partakers of his life, how can we help loving him who has made us what we are? When that sacred passion burns vehemently within our hearts, we feel that any affliction that we have to endure in order to

glorify Christ is too light to be even worth mentioning. O ye
devoted lovers of the Saviour, have ye not known hours when
ye have envied the martyrs, and wished that ye too might be
allowed to wear the ruby crown? When you have read about
how they had to lie for years in cold, damp dungeons, and
then at last were dragged forth to die at the block, the stake,
or the scaffold, have you not felt that your lives were poor and
mean compared with theirs, and that you would gladly sacrifice
all the comforts you now enjoy if you might be permitted to
die for Christ as they did?

Now, secondly, I am going to speak TO THOSE WHO COM-
PLAIN OF THE WEIGHT OF THEIR AFFLICTION. Let me remind
you that *your affliction is light compared with that of many
others*. Think of the horrors of a battlefield, and of the agonies
of the poor wounded men who have to lie there so long un-
tended. Living in peace in our happy island home, it is difficult for us to realize the misery and wretchedness that are
being endured by those besieged in Paris even while I am
preaching to you [during the Franco-Prussian war]. Some of
you complain of shortness of bread, but you have not to suffer
the pangs of hunger as so many of the inhabitants of the
French capital are at this moment suffering. There are some
who are miserable as soon as any little ache or pain seizes
them, yet their affliction is very light compared with that of
many who never know what it is to be well and strong. Even
if we are called to suffer pain, let us thank God that we have
not been deprived of our reason. If we could go through the
wards of Bethlehem Hospital, not far away from us, and see
the many forms of madness represented, I think each one of
us would be moved to say, "My God, I thank thee that, however poor or sick I am, thou hast preserved me from such
mental affliction as many have to bear." How thankful we
all ought to be that we are not in prison! Does it seem im-
probable that such good people as we are could ever be
numbered amongst the law-breakers of the land? You know
how Hazael said to Elisha, "Is thy servant a dog, that he
should do this great thing?" yet he did all that the prophet
foretold; and but for the restraining grace of God, you and
I, dear friends, might have been suffering the agony and
remorse that many are to-night enduring in the prisons of

this and other lands. I need not go on multiplying instances of those who are suffering in various ways in mind or body or estate; but I think I have said sufficient to convince you that our affliction, whatever form it may assume, is light compared with that of many others.

Next, *our affliction is light compared with our deserts.* We can truly say, with the psalmist, "He hath not dealt with us after our sins; nor rewarded us according to our iniquities." If the Lord had not dealt with us in mercy and in grace, we might have been at this moment beyond the reach of hope, like that rich man who in vain begged "Father Abraham" to send Lazarus to dip his finger in water to cool his parched tongue. Yes, ungodly one, you might have been in hell tonight, in that outer darkness where there is weeping and wailing and gnashing of teeth. Let the goodness of God in preserving you alive until now lead you to repent of your sin, and to trust in the Saviour. Thank God, you are still out of the pit; the iron gate has not yet been opened to admit you, and then been closed upon you for ever. Yet remember that you are, as it were, standing upon a narrow neck of land between two unbounded seas, and that the waves are every moment washing away the sand from beneath your feet, and rest no longer upon such an unsafe footing, lest it should give way altogether, and you should sink down into the fathomless abyss. As for any affliction that you ever can have to endure on earth, it is not merely light, it is absolutely unworthy of mention in comparison with the eternal woe that is the portion of the lost. Be thankful that, up to the present moment, this has not been your portion; and lest it should be, flee at once for refuge to lay hold upon the hope set before you in the gospel.

Then next, *our affliction is very light compared with that of our Lord.* Do you murmur at the bitterness of the draught in the cup which is put into your hand? But what heart can conceive of the bitterness of that cup of which Jesus drank? Yet he said, "The cup which my Father hath given me, shall I not drink it?" Is the disciple to be above his Master, and the servant above his Lord? Did Christ have to swim through stormy seas, and—

"Must I be carried to the skies
On flowery beds of ease?"

I think there is no consolation for an afflicted child of God so rich as that which arises from the contemplation of the sufferings of Jesus. The remembrance of the agony and bloody sweat of Gethsemane has often dried up the sweat of terror upon the anguished brow of the believer. The stripes of Jesus have often brought healing to his wounded followers. The thirst, the desertion, and the death on Golgotha—all the incidents of our Saviour's suffering, and the terrible climax of it all,—have been most helpful in assuaging the sorrows of stricken saints. Brethren and sisters in Christ, your sufferings are not worth a moment's thought when compared with the immeasurable agonies of Jesus your Redeemer. My soul would prostrate herself at his dear pierced feet, and say, "I have never seen any other affliction like thine affliction. I have beheld and seen, but I have never seen any sorrow like unto thy sorrow. Thou art indeed the incomparable Monarch of misery, the unapproachable King of the whole realm of grief. Of old, thou wert the 'Man of sorrows, and acquainted with grief,' and no man has ever been able to rob thee of thy peculiar title." I think that such reflections as these will help us to realize that, however heavy our affliction appears to us to be, it is very light compared with that of our dear Lord and Master.

And further, beloved, *our affliction is very light compared with the blessing which we enjoy*. Many of us have had our sins forgiven for Christ's sake, and the blessing of full and free forgiveness must far outweigh any affliction that we ever have to endure. When we were lying in the gloomy dungeon of conviction, and had not a single ray of hope to lighten the darkness, we thought that, even though we had to be kept in prison all our days, and to be fed only upon bread and water, we could be quite joyous if we could but be assured that God's righteous anger was turned away from us, and that our sins and iniquities he would remember against us no more for ever. Well, that is just what many of us have experienced; our transgressions have been forgiven, and our sin has been covered by the great atoning sacrifice of Jesus Christ our Lord and Saviour. Then let us rejoice and be glad all our days. But this is not all the blessing that we have received, for we have been clothed in the righteousness of Christ, and adopted into the family of God. Now we are heirs of God, and joint-heirs with Jesus

Christ. We share even now in all the privileges of the children of God, and there are still greater favours and honours reserved for us in the future, as the apostle John saith, "Beloved, now are we the sons of God, and it doth not yet appear what we shall be; but we know that, when he shall appear, we shall be like him; for we shall see him as he is." We already have a foretaste of the bliss that is laid up in store for us, for—

> *"The men of grace have found*
> *Glory begun below;*
> *Celestial fruits on earthly ground*
> *From faith and hope do grow."*

So it is quite true that, in comparison with our blessings and privileges, our affliction is indeed light.

And we specially realize that *our affliction is light as we prove the power of the Lord's sustaining grace.* Some of you have never personally proved its power, but many of you do know by practical experience what I mean. There are times when, through acute physical pain or great mental anguish, the soul is at first utterly prostrate; but at last it falls back, in sheer helplessness, upon the bosom of Jesus, gives up struggling, and resigns itself absolutely to his will; and then—I speak what I do know, and testify what I have felt—there comes into the soul a great calm, a quiet joy so deep and so pure as never is experienced at any other time. I have sometimes looked back upon nights of pain—pain so excruciating that it has forced the tears from my eyes—and I have almost asked to have such suffering repeated if I might but have a repetition of the seraphic bliss that I have often enjoyed under such circumstances. I made a mistake when I said "seraphic" bliss, for seraphs have not the capacity for suffering that we have, and therefore they can never experience that deep, intense, indescribable bliss that is our portion when, by grace, we are enabled to glorify God even in the furnace of affliction.

We may well say that no affliction weighs more than a gnat resting upon an elephant when the Lord's upholding grace is sweetly manifested to our soul in times of perplexity, anxiety, and pain. It is just then that Jesus often so graciously reveals himself to us that we even come to love the cross that brings him specially near to us. I can understand that strange speech of Samuel Rutherford, as some have regarded it, when he said that he sometimes feared lest he should make his cross into an idol by loving affliction too much because of the blessed results that flowed from it. The bark of the tree of affliction may be bitter as gall; but if you get to the pith of it, you will find that it is as sweet as honey.

Once more, affliction—*sanctified affliction becomes very light when we see to what it leads.* Sin is our great curse, and anything that can help to deliver us from the dominion of sin is a blessing to us. It seems that, in the constitution of our nature, and in the divine discipline under which we are being trained, our growth in grace is greatly assisted by affliction and trial. There are certain propensities to evil that can only be removed in the furnace, as the dross is burnt away from the pure metal; and surely, brethren, you who know the exceeding sinfulness of sin would not think any affliction too severe that should humble your pride, or subdue your passions, or slay your sloth, or overcome any other sin that so easily besets you. You will not merely acquiesce in the Lord's dealings with you, but you will devoutly thank him for using the sharp knife of affliction to separate you from your sin. A wise patient will gratefully thank the surgeon who cuts his flesh, and makes it bleed, and who will not allow it to heal up too quickly; and when God, by his gracious Spirit's operation, uses the stern surgery of trial to eradicate the propensity to sin, we do well to kiss the hand that holds the knife, and to say with cheerfulness as well as with resignation, "The will of the Lord be done."

Now, lastly, *our affliction is light compared with the glory which is so soon to be revealed to us and in us.* Some of us are much nearer to our heavenly home than we have ever imagined. Possibly, we are reckoning upon another twenty or even forty years of service, yet the shadows of our life's day are already lengthening although we are unaware that it is so. Perhaps we are anticipating long periods of fightings without and fears within, but those anticipations will never be realized, for the day of our final victory is close at hand, and then doubts and fears shall never again be able to assail our spirits. In this house to-night there may be some who are sitting on the very banks of the Jordan, and just across the river lies the land that floweth with milk and honey, the land which is reserved as the inheritance of the true children of God. Their eyes are so dimmed with tears that they cannot see—"Canaan's fair and happy land, Where their possessions lie." They even imagine that they are captives by the waters of Babylon, and they hang their harps upon the willows, for they fear there are many years of banishment still before them. Yet the King's messenger is already on the way with the summons to bid them to appear before him very soon. Even if the call does not come to some of us at once, if the Master has need of us in this world a little longer, how soon our mortal life must end! What is our life? "It is even a vapour, that appeareth for a little time, and then vanisheth away." "As for man, his days are as grass; as a flower of the field, so he flourisheth. For the wind passeth over it, and it is gone; and the place thereof shall know it no more." But does the brevity of life cause us any anxiety? Oh, no! "For we know that if our earthly house of this tabernacle were dissolved, we have a building of God, a house not made with hands, eternal in the heavens"; and when once we reach that blest abode of all the saints, and look back upon our earthly experiences, we shall feel that any affliction we had to endure was light indeed compared with the unutterable bliss that shall then be our eternal portion. We are pilgrims to Zion's city bound, and we necessarily have certain privations and difficulties; but when our journey is at an end, "One hour with our God will make up for it all."

If we have not this good hope through grace, we may well say that our affliction is *not* light. I cannot imagine how any of you, my hearers, can go on living without a Saviour—you poor people, you hard-working people, you sickly, consumptive people, how can you live without a Saviour? I wonder how those who are rich, and who have an abundance of earthly comforts, can live on year after year without any hope (except a false one) of comfort and blessing in the life that is to come. But as for you who have so few earthly comforts, you whose life is one long struggle for bare existence, you who scarcely know what it is to have a day without pain, how can *you* live without a Saviour? Remember that "godliness is profitable unto all things, having promise of the life that now is, and of that which is to come." So, "seek ye the Lord while he may be found, call ye upon him while he is near: let the wicked forsake his way, and the unrighteous man his thoughts: and let him return unto the Lord, and he will have mercy upon him; and to our God, for he will abundantly pardon."

VIII

GOOD NEWS FOR OUTCASTS

"He gathereth together the outcasts of Israel."—Ps. 147 : 2.

DOES not this show us the great gentleness and infinite mercy of God? And as we know most of God in the person of our Lord Jesus Christ, should it not charm us to remember that when he came on earth he did not visit kings and princes, but he came unto the humble and simple folk. He did not seek out Pharisees, wrapped up in their own supposed righteousness, but he sought out the guilty, for he said, "They that are whole have no need of the physician, but they that are sick." The Son of man has come to seek and to save that which was lost.

When I read that the Lord gathers together the outcasts of Israel, and when I see the text is truly applicable to the Lord Jesus Christ, because this is just what he did, I see an illustration of the gentleness of his heart, who said, "Take my yoke upon you, for I am meek and lowly of heart, and ye shall find rest unto your souls." Be glad that we gather around such a Saviour as this, from whom all pride and self-seeking are absent, and who, coming down among us in gentleness and meekness, comes to gather those whom no man cares for—those who are judged to be worthless and irreclaimable.

Applying this text to our Lord Jesus Christ we not only see his gentleness, but we also clearly see an illustration of his love to men, as men. If you seek only after rich men the suspicion arises, and it is more than a suspicion, that you rather seek their wealth than them. If you aim only at the benefit of wise men, it is probably true that it is their wisdom which attracts you, and not their manhood: but the Lord Jesus Christ did not love men because of any advantageous circumstances, or any commendable incidents of their condition: his love was to

manhood. He loved his own chosen people as men, not as this
or that among men. He had no respect for rank, nor care for
wealth. Where Jesus Christ sees a man, though he be an outcast, an outlaw, one condemned by the law of his own country,
he sees a human being there—a creature capable of awful sin
and terrible misery, but yet, renewed by grace, capable of
bringing wondrous glory to the Most High. Our Lord Jesus
Christ, by gathering together the outcasts, proves to demonstra-
tion that it is not the things which surround men, but the
men themselves that he cares for. He considers not so much
where a man is, but *what* he is; not what he has learned,
or what he is thought of, or what he has done; but what he
is.

Another thing is also clear. If Jesus gathers together the
outcasts of Israel, it proves his power over the hearts of men.
There is a certain class of men who follow that which is morally
good because the Lord has given them a noble disposition.
Thank God, he has in mercy been pleased to give some men a
desire after that which is beautiful and true. They, too, are
merchantmen seeking goodly pearls, and it is not difficult,
when the heart is brought into such a desirable state, for the
excellence and beauty of Jesus Christ to attract it. But here
is the tug of war: there are men still left in the guilt and filthiness of human nature who have no desire after that which is
good, but whose entire longings are after evil, only evil, and
that continually. These have no more eye to anything that is
high and noble than the swine hath for the stars. The minister
of Christ may appeal to them, but he will appeal in vain; and
providence may warn them by the deaths of others, and by
personal sickness, but they are not to be separated from the
earth to which they are glued. Yet our Lord Jesus can gather
together even these, the outcasts of Israel. Such is his power
that he does not stay till he sees good desires in men, but he
imparts those desires to those who have them not. No ground-
work of goodness is asked or expected from any man that Christ
may come and act upon it; but he takes man in his ruin, and
in the extremity of his depravity, and begins with him there
and then. When the good Samaritan came to the wounded
man, he did not wait for him to make the first advance, or
come a little towards him, but he came unto him where he

was, and poured into his wounds the oil and the wine: so the
Lord comes where human nature is, and, bad as its condition
is, he stoops to it, and he gathers together the outcasts of
Israel.

Oh, it is a wonderful thing this, that there should be attrac-
tions about the Lord Jesus Christ which can draw to him those
whom nothing else that is good can possibly stir! You may
preach virtue to the sinner; but he does not practically yield
to its charms; you may preach to the drunkard, to the un-
chaste, to the immoral, the beauties and excellencies of honesty
and of all the virtues and the graces, but little good will come
of it; the result is infinitesimal. You may charm very wisely
upon these subjects, but these deaf adders do not care for
charming. We have heard of a divine who said that he had
preached honesty till he had not an honest person left in the
parish, and preached virtue till he did not know where Diogenes
with his lantern could find it. Nothing worth having comes of
preaching when Christ is not its theme. You may preach the
law, and men will be frightened by it, but they will forget their
fears; yet if Jesus Christ be preached he draws all men unto
him. The most wicked will listen to the news of him who is able
to save unto the uttermost them that come unto God by him.
The most obdurate have been known to weep when they have
heard the story of his grief and of his love, the proudest have
found themselves suddenly humbled at his feet, whereof some
of us are witnesses, for we marvelled to find the hardness and
loftiness of our hearts suddenly removed by a sense of his
goodness.

First, then, TO WHOM MAY THIS TEXT APPLY—"He gathereth
together *the outcasts of Israel*"? It refers to several classes in
different ways. First, it is a fact that our Lord Jesus did gather
together some of the very *poorest and most despised among
men,* who might under some respects be regarded as outcasts;
and it is certain that, to this day, the Gospel comes in the largest
measure of power to the poor of this world. Often, too, it comes
with amazing power to those who are despised by others, or
are regarded as being of inferior degree. You know that at this
time it is boastfully said by the enemies of the Gospel, that the
culture, the brain, the intellect, the education of England is
all on the side of scepticism. I am not sure about it. When

people say that they possess a deal of brain, I am not certain that their claim is correct, unless it be that as sheep have a good deal of brain, and yet are not the wisest animals in the world, so these gentlemen also are no wiser than they should be. As to those gentlemen who so evidently claim to be the cultured people, who monopolize all the sweetness and the light, I am not clear that they have all the modesty. It does seem to me that if they talked in a lower key it would be as well; and if they thought a little less of their own culture, and allowed a little more to other people, we might have more faith in this wonderful "culture" of theirs. Some of us have failed to see the deep thought and the profound learning we were told to look for in the books of the sceptical cultured mind, and therefore we are the less patient when we hear the perpetual bragging of our foes. Still, let it stand so. We will not quarrel with it. Suppose it to be so—that none but foolish people embrace the old-fashioned faith—the Puritanism, which they say is nearly dead—the old evangelism which they ridicule as being exploded: be it so, that we are an inferior order of people, with very little brain, and all that. Well, we are not out of heart on that account, because we find that is so happened in our Saviour's day, and has happened all days since, that the wisdom of the world has been at enmity with God; and it has also turned out that the foolishness of God has been wiser than men, and God has mastered human wisdom by the foolishness of preaching. By that Gospel which wise men laughed at as being folly God has brought carnal wisdom to naught. The Lord Jesus Christ looks with love on those whom others look down upon with scorn.

I am thankful when I meet with poor saints, and see what a grip humble men and women get of the promises of God. Labouring men, humble shepherds, and the like, have often been more distinguished for deep insight into the mysteries of grace than learned doctors of divinity. Where there has been little in the cupboard, and the provision on the table has been but slender, there has been more enjoyment of the favour of God than amongst the great ones of the earth. They may regard those who still stand by the old-fashioned truth as being outcasts from the commonwealth of letters, and not worthy to be named amongst the cultured intellects of the age, but if the

Lord will but gather us continually to his bosom and refresh us with himself, we shall be well content. The text should be a source of joy to us if any of us happen to be extremely poor —so poor that even Christian men are so ungenerous as to give us the cold shoulder, or if we happen to be the despised ones of our family. Here and there, sad to say it, there will be in families a better one than the rest, less thought of than the others—a Joseph whom his brothers hate, because he loves his God. Well, you may become as a stranger to your mother's children, and you may have no one to give you a good word, yet may you put this verse under your tongue as a sweet morsel—"He gathereth together the outcasts of Israel."

The text may be applied very well to those *who have made themselves outcasts by their wickedness and are deservedly cast out of society*. May God grant that none of us may be or may have been amongst that number; but if I should be addressing any such at this time, I have a word for them. If there should be some such here who do not often attend places of worship, but have dropped in from curiosity I may suppose your case to be that of one who has broken a mother's heart and brought a father's grey hairs to the grave with grief. You have lived such a life that your own brothers could scarcely be expected to acknowledge you. You have sinned, and sinned terribly. Man or woman—for woman also becomes an outcast, she is too severely treated, as a general rule, and oftener becomes an outcast than the man who deserves it more—if I address such, it is a great joy to me to know that our Lord Jesus Christ can save the most wicked of the wicked, the most fallen of the fallen, the most depraved of the depraved. If you have sunk so low that there is not much to choose between you and a devil, and some men and women do get as low as that, yet Jesus Christ can lift you up. If your life-story is such that it would be a pity it should ever be told, and most grievous that it should ever have been enacted, yet Jesus can wash all the stains of your life away, and save you, even you. "Though your sins be as scarlet they shall be as snow: though they be red like crimson they shall be as wool." Jesus is able to wash away every transgression from those who are steeped in guilt. Countless iniquities dissolve and disappear before the presence of his mighty love, for he, even Jesus, gathereth together the outcasts of Israel.

A third class of persons consists of *those who judge themselves to be outcasts,* though as to outward actions they certainly do not deserve the character. Many who have written about John Bunyan have been surprised at the description which he gives of his own life, for it does not appear that, with the sole exception of the use of blasphemous language, John Bunyan was one of the very worst of mankind; but he thought himself to be so. Now it often happens—I do not say always, but I think it is generally so—that when the Spirit of God comes with power to the conscience and awakens it, the man judges himself to be the very chief of sinners. For see, it may be that you have never gone into actual vice; you have never been a blasphemer or dishonest, you have, on the contrary, from the instructions of your childhood, been led into the path of right; and yet when you are awakened you may feel yourself to be the vilest of the vile. Everything that is lovely and of good report has been found in you, you do not know the time in which you would not have been shocked to hear a blasphemous word, and yet when the Holy Spirit arouses you, you will plead guilty among the very worst.

I know that, in my own case, I had a horror of ungodliness, and yet when the Spirit of God came to me I felt myself to be far worse than the swearer or the drunkard, for this reason— that I knew that many who indulged in those open sins did so ignorantly, did so from the imitation of those in whose society they had been brought up; but as for me, with a godly parentage, with a mother's prayers and tears, with light and knowledge, understanding the letter of the Gospel, having read the Bible from my youth up, I felt that my sins were blacker than those of others, because I had sinned against light and knowledge. And you must have felt the same, I am persuaded; perhaps you are even now feeling it. You recollect that night when you stifled conviction, when conscience had an earnest battle with you, and it seemed that you must yield to God and to his Christ; but you deliberately did violence to the inward principle, and resolved to go on in sin. Do you remember that? If you do, it will sting you as doth a serpent now that you are under conviction of sin, and you will feel yourself to be the very chief of sinners on account of it, though no public sin may ever have stained your life.

Well, I should not wonder, if such be your condition, that you also judge that there is no salvation for you—that God might save your mother, your brother, or your friend, but not you. You believe the blood of Jesus to be very precious, but you think it never will be applied to you. You heard the other day of the conversion of a friend, and you felt glad, but at the same time you thought, "Grace will never come to me." When the preacher has exhorted his hearers to believe in Jesus Christ you have said, "Ah, but I—I cannot. I am in a condition in which that Gospel does not avail me." You think yourself an outcast. You feel that you deserve to be. You are not content to be so, but, at the same time, you could not blame the Lord if he left you to perish. Now, listen, thou who hast condemned thyself. The Lord absolves thee. Thou who has shut thyself out as an outcast, thou shalt be gathered; for whereas they call thee an outcast, whom no man seeketh after, thou shalt be called Hephzibah, for the Lord's delight is in thee. Only believe thou in Jesus Christ, and cast thyself upon him. Outcasts of this sort are the people who most gladly welcome Christ. People who have nowhere else to go but to him—people so cast down, so full of sin, so everything but what they ought to be —these are the people to whom Christ is very precious. "Oh," says one, "but I do not feel like that. I cannot feel my guilt as I should." Very well, then, you are one of the outcasts among the outcasts: you do not think yourself to be so good even as they are. You are in your own esteem one of the veriest outcasts of them all, because you lack even the feeling of your needs. You say, "I have a hard heart. I cannot see sin as others have seen it who have found Christ: I wish I could. I smite my breast and mourn that I cannot mourn, for if aught is felt it is only pain to find that I cannot feel. I seem made of hell-hardened steel which will not melt or break." Well, I see what you are, but "such were some of us," we also knew our insensibility, and lamented that we could not lament. But he gathered us, and there stands the text, "He gathereth together the outcasts of Israel." If you have not a broken heart, only Christ can give it you. If you cannot come to him *with* it, come to him *for* it. If you cannot come to him wounded, come to him that he may wound you and make you whole. You need bring nothing to Jesus.

There is another sort of people who are even more truly the outcasts of Israel, whom Jesus gathers. I mean *the backsliders from the Church*—the outcasts of Israel who have been put out, and properly put out, for their unholy lives and inconsistent actions: those whom the Church is obliged, alas, to look upon as diseased members that must be removed; sickly sheep that infect the flock, and that must be put away; lepers that must be set aside from the camp. O wanderer, banished from a church, there is a word in the Gospel to thee also, even the backslider! The Lord calls back his wandering children. Though his Church does right to put out those who do dishonour to his holy name, yet she would do wrong if she did not follow her Lord in saying, "Return, ye backsliding children." It is not easy to persuade one who has been a backslider to come back to his first love. The return journey is uphill, and flesh and blood do not assist us in it. Many new converts come, but the old wanderers remain outside, and sometimes they do this because they fancy they will not be welcome. But if you are sincerely repenting of the sin which has put you away from the Church, the Church of Christ will be glad to receive you; and if you be indeed the Lord's believing one, though you have defiled yourself yet he does not forget you. He does earnestly remember you still, and he bids you come in all your defilement and wash in his atoning blood.

The expression of the text may certainly be applied to *those who have loved the Lord for years, but who have fallen into great depression of spirit.* We happen, every now and then, to meet with some of the best of God's people who get into the Slough of Despond, and stick there by the month together— aye, by the year together. There are believers who take periodically to despondency, as birds do to moulting, and when the fit is on them you cannot cheer or comfort them. Then they write bitter things against themselves, and call themselves all the ugly names in the dictionary, until they make us smile to hear them because we know how mistaken they are. What a mercy it is that, when you who love the Lord thus sit down and commune with your despondencies—I mean you, Miss Much-afraid, you, Mr. Ready-to-halt, and you, Mr. Feeble-mind—my Lord does not leave you, nor judge you as you judge yourselves, but he is pleased to gather together in mercy those who think themselves outcasts in Israel.

Lastly, upon this point, there are some who become outcasts through their love to Christ, and of these the text is peculiarly true. I mean *those who suffer for righteousness' sake, till they are regarded as the offscouring of all things.* Who that serves God faithfully has escaped the trial of cruel mockings? The world is not worthy of them, and yet their enemies think they are hardly worthy to live in the world. We do not hear much about persecution now-a-days, but in private life there is a world of it; the cold shoulder is given where once friendship was sought; hard, cruel, cutting things are said where once admiration was expressed; and separations take place between very friends because of Christ. It is still true in the Christian's case that a man's foes are they of his own household. Blessed are those who are outcasts for Christ! Rich are those who are so honoured as to be permitted to become poor for him! Happy they who have had this grace given them to be permitted to lay life itself down for Jesus Christ's sake!

Now a few words upon the second point—IN WHAT SENSE THE LORD JESUS GATHERS TOGETHER THESE OUTCASTS OF DIFFERENT CLASSES. Of course I should have to vary the explanation to suit each case, but as that would take a long time, let me say that the Lord Jesus has several ways of gathering together the outcasts.

He gathers them *to hear the Gospel.* Preach Jesus Christ and they will come. Both outcast saints and outcast sinners will come to hear the charming sound of his blessed name. They cannot help it. Nothing draws like Jesus Christ. Jesus Christ next gathers them *to himself.* The parable of the wedding feast is repeated over again, "Go out into the highways and hedges, and compel them to come in, that my house may be filled." "Bring in hither the poor, and the maimed, and the halt, and the blind." In this sort the Lord Jesus Christ gathers multitudes where he is faithfully preached. He gathers all sorts of characters, and especially the odds and ends of society—the despised of men and the despised of themselves. He gathers them to himself. And oh, what a blessed gathering-place that is where there is cleansing for their filthiness, health for their disease, clothing for their nakedness, and all sufficient supplies for their abundant necessities.

When he has done that, he gathers them *into the divine family*. He takes the outcasts and makes them children of God —heirs with himself. From the dunghill he lifts them, and sets them among princes. He takes them from the swine-trough, and puts the ring on their fingers and the shoes on their feet, and they sit down at the Father's table to feast and to be glad. Jesus Christ, as the good Shepherd, gathers the lost sheep, the lame, the halt, the diseased, and feeds them, and makes them to lie down, and restores their souls, and finally leads them to the rich pastures of the glory-land.

In due time the Lord gathers together the outcasts *into his visible Church*. As David enrolled a company of men that were in debt, and discontented, so does Jesus Christ still gather the indebted ones and the malcontents and makes them his soldiers; and these are known as the Church militant. Surely as David did great exploits by those Pelethites and Cherethites, and Gittites, and strange men of foreign extraction whom he gathered to himself, so does Jesus of Nazareth do great things by those great sinners whom he greatly forgives—those hard-hearted ones whom he so strangely changes and makes to be the Old Guard of his army.

And when he has done that, he gathers them *into heaven*. What a surprise it must be for any man to find himself in heaven, when he remembers where he once was; but for the outcast to remember the ale-bench on which he sat and soaked himself in liquor till he degraded himself below the brute beast, and now to be cleansed in the Redeemer's blood, and to sit among the angels—this will be surprising grace indeed. "Oh, to think," one might well say, "that I who was once in lewd company, polluted and defiled, am now made to wear a crown, and sit at the Redeemer's feet!" When we reach heaven, brethren, I do not suppose that we shall forget all the past; and sometimes it must burst in upon us as a strangely divine instance of love that Christ should have brought *us* there, and set *us* among the peers of his realm. And yet he means to do it; and you, Mrs. Much-afraid—you will be there; and you who think "surely Satan will have me!" you will be there.

Well, now, WHAT IS THE LESSON OF THIS? I think there are three lessons, and I will just hint at them.

One is this—*encouragement to those who are unworthy, or who think themselves so, to go to Jesus Christ to-night.* I have been trying to think of all I know, and I have lifted up my heart to the Holy Spirit to guide me that I may cheer some discouraged one. I believe there are some here whom God has sent me after who really believe themselves to be out of the region of hope. If God gathers together the outcasts, why should he not gather you? And if it be true that Jesus Christ does not look for goodness, but that he only considers our sin and misery, why should he not look upon you? May I urge you to go and try my Master; and if you go to him, confessing your unworthiness and trusting yourself with him, if he does not save you I would like to know it, because you will be the first person I have ever heard of that did trust himself with Jesus and was rejected. It shall not be the case, whatever your condition may be, however desperate your state. You think your condition to be worse than I have pictured it to be, and you fancy that I cannot know anything about how bad you are. Well, I do not know your special form of rebellion, but you are the very person I mean for all that. I say, if thou be as black as hell, if thou be as foul as the Stygian bog, if thou have sinned till thy sins cannot be counted, and if thy crimes be so heinous that infinite wrath is their just desert, yet come and look to those five wounds and to that sacred head once wounded, and to that heart pierced with the spear. There is life in a look at Jesus crucified. Wilt thou try it? Like "as Moses lifted up the serpent in the wilderness, even so must the Son of man be lifted up: that whosoever believeth in him should not perish, but have eternal life." O that thou wouldst believe on Jesus now.

The second reflection is this. *If Jesus Christ received some of us when we felt ourselves to be outcasts, how we ought to love him!* It does us good to look back to the hole of the pit whence we were digged. We get to be very top-lofty at times, my brethren. If we recollected our lost and ruined state by nature, I am sure that we should not lift our heads so very loftily, and want to have respect paid to us in the church, or think that God ought not to deal so very hardly with us, as if we had cause for complaint. Let us remember what we used to be, and that will keep us low in our own esteem. But, oh, how it will fire us with zeal to remember from what a depth he has lifted us up. Did Jesus save such a wretch as I was? Then for him would I live and for him would I die. This ought to be the utterance of us all.

Then, again, let us always feel that *if the Lord Jesus Christ took us up when we were not worth having, we will never be ashamed to try and pick up others who are in a like condition.* We will not count it any lowering of our dignity to go after the most fallen of all. We will reckon that they are no worse than we were if we were viewed from a certain point, and we will therefore aim at their conversion, hope for it, and expect it. If you really feel yourselves to have been outcasts, and yet have been received into the divine family, and are now on the road to heaven, I ask you to pay every attention to any whom you meet with who are now what you were once. If you meet with any in great despair of soul, say, "Ah, I must be a comforter here, for I have gone through this; and I will never let this poor soul go till by God's help I have cheered him." If you meet with one who is an open sinner, perhaps you will have to say to yourself, "I was an open sinner too"; but if not, say, "My sins were more secret, but still they were as bad as his; and therefore I have hope of this poor soul, and will try whether he cannot be loved to Christ by me." Mark my expression— "loved to Christ," for this is the power we must use—sinners are to be loved to Christ. The Holy Spirit uses the love of saints to bring poor sinners to know the love of Christ. Search after them, and do not let them perish.

The outcast, when converted, should seek after his brother outcasts. Young man, did you ever swear? seek the conversion of swearers. Young man, have you been fond of the card-table? Have you been a frequenter of low resorts of pleasure? Then addict yourself to looking after persons of the same sort. George Whitefield says that after his own conversion his first concern was the conversion of those with whom he had taken pleasure in sin; and he had the privilege of seeing many of them brought to Christ. Have you been a man of business, and have you been associated in wrongdoing with others? Seek the salvation of those who were associated with you. It is a natural obligation which Christ imposes upon all of any special sort, that they should seek those of their own sort, and labour to bring them to repentance.

IX

THE JOY OF REDEMPTION

"Sing, O ye heavens; for the LORD hath done it: shout, ye
lower parts of the earth: break forth into singing, ye mountains, O forest, and every tree therein: for the LORD hath
redeemed Jacob, and glorified himself in Israel."—Isaiah 44 : 23.

WHEN the human mind is on the stretch of emotion,
whether it be under the influence of grief or joy, it often
thinks that the whole world is in sympathy with itself. It seems
to wrap the mantle of the universe round about its spiritual
nature as a garment. If it be joyous, it puts on nature as a
spangled robe; and if it be wretched, it finds its sackcloth
and ashes in the world round about it. You know how the
prophet—poet as well as prophet—says of us in our joyous
moments, "Ye shall go out with joy, and be led forth with
peace: the mountains and the hills shall break forth before
you into singing, and all the trees of the field shall clap their
hands." When the heart is happy, nature seems to ring marriage peals in unison with the music within the heart. Let the
eye be clear, and all nature will be bright. The earth seems
glad when we are so. On the other hand, it is a part of the
nature of grief to be able to transpose itself into the world
around. Does not old Master Herbert cry,—

"O who will give me tears? Come, all ye springs,
Dwell in my head and eyes; come, clouds and rain:
My grief hath need of all the watery things
That nature hath produced. Let every vein
Suck up a river to supply mine eyes,
My weary, weeping eyes, too dry for me,
Unless they get new conduits, new supplies,
To bear them out, and with my state agree"?

Fain would he make the world weep with him when he wept,
as others have made the world sorrow when they grieved, and

rejoice when they were full of joy. The fact is, the world is one great organ, and it is man that plays it, and when he is full of joy and gladness, he puts his tiny fingers upon the keys, and wakes the world to a majesty of joy; or if his soul be gloomy, then he plays some pensive, dolorous dirge, and thus the world without keeps pace with the other little world within.

The prophet, in this chapter, had been studying the great redemption which God had wrought for his people, and he was so happy and delighted with it, so overjoyed, so charmed, so enraptured, that he could not help saying, "*Sing, O ye heavens.*" There were the angels looking down on man with eyes of sympathy. "Sing," said he, "ye angels, that sinners can be saved, yea, that sinners have been saved! Rejoice to think that repenting sinners can have their sins forgiven them! Sing, ye stars, that all night long, like the bright eyes of God, look down on this poor world, so dark but for you! Sing, for God hath blessed your sister star, unwrapt her from her gloom, and made her shine more radiant in mercy than any one of you! Sing, O blue sky of heights profound! O thou unnavigated ether, be thou stirred with song, and let space become one mighty mouth for melody! Sing, O ye heavens!" Then, when he must come down from those lofty heights, he looks upon *the earth,* and he says, "O earth, echo, echo with song, and ye lower parts of the earth, ye valleys and plains, the sea with its million hands, the deep places of the earth, and the hollow caverns thereof—let them all sound with joy, because Jehovah hath redeemed man, and in mercy has come down to his poor erring creatures." And then, as if he heard all earth getting vocal with the voices of happy ones, and felt it would not do for the praise to be limited even to the tongues of men, he thinks of those mountains where man cannot climb, those virgin snows, undefiled by human feet, and he says, "*Sing, ye mountains!*" Then he thinks of the shaggy woods upon their brows, and he bids them sing in admiration—"*Sing, ye forests!*" Let every tree break forth in melody!

Do you catch his thought? Do you not see how the great poet-prophet, in a mighty fervency of delight, wakes the whole earth, and even heaven itself, to one mighty burst of song? And what is the subject of it? "The Lord hath redeemed his people, and glorified himself in Israel." Oh, that I could stir in your hearts songs of joy for the redemption which God has wrought for his people, and for the glory which God has gotten to himself by this wonderful act of grace!

There are three redemptions which may well make all hearts rejoice: the first is, *redemption by blood*; the second is, *redemption by power*; and the third is the completion of the two, *redemption in perfection*.

The first is, REDEMPTION BY BLOOD.

You know the story. Man had sinned against his God, and God, the Just One, must punish sin. But it was agreed that, if a plan could be devised by which justice should be satisfied, mercy should have full play for all her kind designs. What a day was that when the eternal wisdom revealed to man the plan by which the Son of God should suffer instead of us, that so justice might have its claims discharged in full, and yet mercy enjoy its boundless, unlimited sway! Sing, ye heavens, because of the wisdom which devised so benevolent a scheme! Rejoice, O earth, because of the marvellous, matchless understanding which framed so wise a plan!

The terms or preamble thus agreed upon, it was necessary that someone should suffer instead of man, in order that man might escape. *Will the Eternal Son undertake to do this?* He is God; his glory is excessive; angels veil their faces as they adore him. Is it possible that he will ever become a man, to bleed, to be spit upon, to be scourged, to be crucified? Will he undertake to do it? He said unto his Father, "Lo, I come: in the volume of the book it is written of me, I delight to do thy will, O my God!" Sing again, ye heavens! Let your hallelujahs rise aloft, ye angels! The Son of God has undertaken the redemption of men! That which was once only a scheme, has now become a covenant. That which was but a plan in the divine mind is now a compact between the Father and the Son.

But though Christ has undertaken it, *will he perform it?* The years roll on, the world gets grey, and yet he does not come. But on a sudden, when the shepherds were keeping their flocks by night, there was heard a sound up yonder, and straightway a multitude of the heavenly host appeared, singing, "Glory to God in the highest, and on earth peace, goodwill toward men!" What means this? It is Jesus, the Son of God, come to do what he undertook to do; and there he is, lying in a manger, wrapped in swaddling bands, and God is born into the world. God has become flesh. He, without whom was not anything made that was made, has come down to tabernacle among us, that we may behold his glory, the glory as of the only begotten of the Father, and yet a man of the substance of his mother, like ourselves. Sing, ye angels! Let the carols of that first Christmas night never cease, for that which was once a scheme, and then a covenant, has now commenced to be a work in real earnest.

He has come to do it, *but will he ever fulfil it?* Will he ever accomplish the stupendous obligation? Two and thirty years roll over him, during which he is despised and rejected of men, the Man of sorrows and acquainted with grief. But will he ever achieve that last, that dreadful task? Will he ever be able to perform it? Will he give his back to the smiters, and his cheeks to them that pluck off the hair? Will he verily be led like a sheep to the slaughter? Can it ever be that the Lord of life and immortality will actually die the death of a criminal, and be buried in a borrowed tomb?

My brethren, not only will it be, but it has been. Recall to memory that eventful night when Judas betrayed him with a perfidious kiss, when, in Gethsemane, he was covered with a bloody sweat, a sweat caused by your sins and mine. Do you not see him led away by those who have arrested him? Do you not see the Lord of glory mocked and set at nought, made an object of ridicule, the jeer of sarcasm, and the butt of scorn? *"Ecce Homo!"* Behold the man covered with an old robe, the cloak of some common soldier, and his back laid bare to show you that it is covered with another crimson, the crimson of his own most precious blood, fetched by the accursed scourge from those blessed shoulders? Do you see him staggering along beneath the weight of that heavy cross, hurried and hounded through the streets of Jerusalem? Do you mark him as he bids the daughters of Jerusalem stay their tears, and weep not for him, but for themselves and their children? Can you not see him as they fling him on his back, stretch out his hands and feet to the wood, and then drive the cruel nails through their tenderest parts? Can you not see him as they lift him high between earth and heaven, and then dash the cross into its place, dislocating all his bones, till he cries out, "I am poured out like water, and all my bones are out of joint. Thou hast brought me into the dust of death"? Yes, he is accomplishing it all. Jehovah's wrath is pouring over him, wave after wave, and he is meekly bowing his head to it all! Jehovah's sword is being driven into his heart, and he is baring his breast to receive it, for your sakes and for mine! Sinner, he does it altogether. He can do it. He is doing it, he has done it, for he bowed his head, saying, "It is finished!" and gave up the ghost. That which was first a purpose, then a covenant, and then a work initiated, is now a work achieved. Jesus Christ has redeemed his people with his most precious blood.

But they took his mangled corpse down from the cross. They put it in the tomb. It remained a question whether he really had accomplished the work, for if he had, God would set two seals to it: first, by his rising from the tomb, and secondly, by his ascending into heaven. See then, believer. On the third day, the mighty Sleeper unwound his grave-clothes; an angel came from heaven, and rolled away the stone, and in the glory of a life unshackled by the trammels of vanity to which our poor creatureship is made subject, he rose from the dead. And when he had shown himself to his disciples, and to others, for forty days, he took them out to Olivet, and as he communed with them and blessed them, he went up into heaven, and a cloud received him out of their sight. Can you not, in the devout exercise of imagination, track him past those clouds? Do you not see heaven's heroes as they meet him and welcome him? See you not his chariot waiting for him? Do you not behold him as he mounts it, and they sing in advance of him till they come to the crystal gates, and then, from over the gates, the watchers cry, "Who is this King of glory?" while others shout, "Lift up your heads, O ye gates; and be ye lift up, ye everlasting doors; and the King of glory shall come in!" Yes, in he rides, up to his Father's throne, and there he sits in state, God over all, blessed for ever; the Lamb once slain, no more to die. Sing, ye heavens, and be glad, O earth! The work which was accomplished is accepted. The deed which was finished is stamped and recognized by heaven, and now there is peace "through the blood of the everlasting covenant."

Ah! I know what would make some of you very happy. Should you come to-night to the cross, look up and trust Christ to save you, your joy would then be unspeakable. Never did a soul trust Christ in vain. You would receive pardon, you would get peace, you would feel as if heaven did sing, and as if earth did rejoice. You would say, "Here am I, a poor, guilty sinner, having nothing to trust to of my own, but I know my sins were laid on Christ, and if they were laid on Christ, they cannot be in two places at one time; consequently, they cannot be put on me when I trust in Jesus; they were put on his bleeding back, and they are gone, and there is not one left in the Book of God against me." O, if thou believest in Christ, thou art perfectly absolved. Thou needest not a priest to say, "*Absolvo te,*" "I absolve thee." There is no condemnation to them that are in Christ Jesus. Who can lay anything to the charge of God's elect, since Jesus died? If you rest in Jesus Christ, he has paid all your debts; you are out of debt; Christ has discharged all your liabilities, and you are free. Let your soul, then, be happy. Let your soul be so happy that it transfers its joy to all nature, and makes heaven and earth glad with its own gladness.

Let us strike another key, and celebrate the second theme that redemption unfolds—REDEMPTION BY POWER.

Those for whom the Saviour shed his blood, and so redeemed them by price, are by-and-by redeemed by power. The Spirit of God finds them, like other men, fond of sin; like other men, blind to the beauties of the Saviour, deaf to the commands of Christ; but if Christ has bought them with his blood, he never paid for what he will not have. The price was too precious to be paid for those who are not saved. If Christ has paid his blood for a soul, he will have that soul. Neither will God's honour rob him of his purchase, nor will Christ be content to lose what he so dearly bought.

This second redemption, which is conversion and regeneration, is equally a subject of holy joy; very briefly I will set it forth. What sort of people are those whom Christ saves? Why, *some of them were the very worst of the worst.* Some of them were the companions of the lost; nay, they were lost themselves. But when the grace of God met with them, it washed them, and made new men of them. There is many a man who has been a captain in the devil's service, but whom the Lord has taken, and made a valiant man for the truth. Oh, what a great sinner John Newton was before his conversion! You who have read his life know that he went about as far as a man could go. What an offender was John Bunyan before the Lord met with him! What a blood-thirsty wretch was Saul of Tarsus! What a horrible life had the thief led with whom Christ met at the last! Now, when I think of these being saved, I feel as if I could say, "Sing, ye heavens, and be joyful, O earth!"

Sometimes, at our church-meetings, when some brethren have told the story of their past lives, we have felt inclined to stop and sing. Some have said, "I never entered a place of worship for years; I cursed at the very thought of it; the Sabbath I never regarded; yea, the very name of God himself I despised; but eternal mercy met with me." Aye, and the greatest wonder to every one of you will be that ever God's mercy saved you! I can understand very well his saving any of you; but I often cannot comprehend why he should save me. Oh! this will be the wonder of heaven to each one of us, to find ourselves there; and how will we say, "Sing, O heaven, and be joyful, O earth!" if once our poor guilty feet tread that golden pavement; and if, once being washed in the precious blood of Jesus, we shall be permitted to sit down with Abraham, and Isaac, and Jacob, in the kingdom of heaven!

Does it not enhance the joy that *they were in such a miserable plight before they were saved?* They were prejudiced against the Gospel, but God knew how to knock their prejudices over. They were blind, and would not see the beauties of it; but the Lord has a blessed way of opening blind eyes. Their hearts were as hard as granite, but God knew how to use the hammer, and shiver the rock in pieces. Very likely they derided the very idea of being converted, and yet they were made partakers of the saving change. Aye, and I have noticed that some of the most hardened are the very first who are met with; some of those who seemed the most unlikely subjects of divine grace have been chosen by divine sovereignty, and have been made wonders of divine power.

And still further, think of *what these souls are saved from.* But for grace, the hottest hell would have been our portion;

but we are saved from it. We should have been made to drink of the bitter cup of wrath for ever; but we shall never drink a drop of it now. And then consider *what the man of God is saved to.* He is saved for heaven. He is made meet to be a partaker of the inheritance of the saints in light. His head shall wear the crown. His hands shall sweep the strings of harps of gold. Sing, O heavens, and be joyful, O earth!

Mighty as is the power, are we not often constrained to marvel at the weakness of the instruments which the Lord employs? Sometimes a soul is saved by Christ's grace through a poor preacher, who is despised by many, and who in himself is humble, and weak, and feeble. By means of a tract, or a quotation from the Bible, or something of that sort, the heart is turned. Any instrument in the hand of God, though it seem most unlikely, is capable of bringing a soul to Christ.

And now, lastly, what a song will that be as heaven and earth, mountains and forests, rejoice WHEN THE BELIEVER IS PERFECTLY REDEEMED! On earth he was still the subject of temptation, and he wrestled hard with inbred sins; but when death comes, he shall be perfect. There shall not be a rag of corruption, nor a relic of the old man. Brethren, will you not make the heavens and the earth ring when you find yourselves made like unto Christ; when you shall find that nothing that old Adam gave you is left, but that all sin is gone, and that you are like the angels of God? Surely there shall be no voice in heaven more exulting, more joyous, than that of men delivered from strong passions and deep depravity, and made perfectly like the Lord Jesus.

And there we shall be perfectly free from all the cares and troubles of this mortal life. No sweat to wipe from aching brows! No tossing upon beds of weariness! No nights of languishing! No question of "What shall I eat, and what shall I drink, and wherewithal shall I be clothed?" "The Lord God shall wipe away all tears from their eyes." There shall be no more spiritual battles and conflicts. Death and hell shall no more annoy us, nor sinners vex the righteous with their ungodly conversation.

Oh, blissful hour! Oh, happy moment! when "We shall be near and like our God!" Brethren, does it not make you long to be gone, when you think of the perfection of redemption? The body will be redeemed. It will rise from the dead. This poor dishonoured body will be made like unto Christ's glorious body; and then body and soul together shall, like twin angels, glorify God throughout eternity.

Alas! I fear there are some of you who will have no part or lot in this matter! If you would have this last redemption, begin with the first. Faith first! Look to the price—to the blood—and then the Holy Spirit will graciously give you the redemption which is by power. Your faith will be the first proof that you are so redeemed, and will lead you on until you attain that perfection for which we groan, that adoption for which we wait, to wit, the redemption of the body. Bought with the blood of Jesus, quickened into newness of life by the power of his resurrection, and at length gathered unto Jesus, to be with him where he is, the joy of his salvation shall swell into a mighty chorus, in which heaven and earth shall ring out their loud-sounding music, while our tongues shall sing Immanuel's praise for ever and ever.

X

HOPE FOR THE WORST BACKSLIDERS

"Return, ye backsliding children, and I will heal your back-slidings. Behold, we come unto thee; for thou art the Lord our God. Truly in vain is salvation hoped for from the hills, and from the multitude of mountains: truly in the LORD our God is the salvation of Israel."—Jer. 3 : 22, 23.

SIN is quite sure to cause sorrow; and the longer the sorrow is delayed, the heavier it will be when it comes. This ship may be long at sea, but it will come home at last with a terrible cargo. There was never a man who broke the law of God who had not in the end to rue it. "He that diggeth a pit shall fall into it; and whoso breaketh a hedge, a serpent shall bite him," is one of Solomon's sayings, and it is most certainly true. How many there are in this world who have now upon them a load of sorrow which is plainly and evidently the result of their own folly and iniquity. Their sin procured it for themselves.

The other day, I read in the paper a story, which certainly did surprise me; and undoubtedly it is an instance of wonderful patience and forbearance on the part of a loving woman. I do not think that I have heard or read the like of it in all my days, and I should think that such action as hers never was excelled. The wretch of whom I speak must have been the meanest man who ever lived, and died without being hanged, and the woman must have been one of the most wonderful of women ever seen upon the face of the earth. According to the account I read, the man had not been long married, but he did not prosper in his profession, and feeling that he had talent and ability, he came to London by his wife's permission, and with her consent, that he might make his way in the world. He did make his way, and became afterwards a portrait painter of considerable eminence, so that he obtained admission into fashionable society, and lived upon the fat of the land. He had told his wife, when he wrote to her once, that if she came she might be a burden to him, so he never fetched her up to London; indeed, he never but on that one occasion communicated with her, and never sent her even a solitary sixpence.

That state of things lasted for forty years, and the wife remained true and faithful to him notwithstanding all the heartbreak caused by his cruel conduct. In process of time, he spent all his money, and reduced himself to beggary; beside that, he was full of disease, yet he was mean enough to crawl to the door of the woman he had neglected all those years, and, strange as it may seem, she opened it with delight, and welcomed him back to her heart. She put him in her bedroom, she carefully nursed and cared for him, and she wore her own life away by sitting at his bedside till he died. Was it not splendid on her part? What monument ought not to be raised to such a loving woman as that?

But I merely tell you this story in order to say that this woman's forgiveness of her unworthy husband is but a faint picture of the great love of God towards ungodly men. He feeds them, and supplies their every need; they are always dependent upon him, they could not live an instant without his permission; yet some whom I know have never communicated with their God for forty years. Forty years, did I say? Fifty, sixty, or perhaps even more years than that they have lived as if there were no God; and worse still, they have perhaps only used his name for the purposes of blasphemy. They have made a mock of holy things, they have provoked the Lord to jealousy; and yet even now, though they are decrepit and old, if they are not only sick but sorry, if they are broken down and despairing, if they will but come creeping to God's door, he will say, "Come in, and welcome." He never yet refused to receive a soul that came to him by Jesus Christ his Son; and Jesus Christ himself has said, "Him that cometh to me I will in no wise cast out." Oh! how many old sinners have come to Christ even at eighty years of age, and he has never uttered a word about those eighty wicked years; but he has said to each one of them, "Come in; I died for thee; come in, and welcome." There have been many, many sins of the most aggravated kind committed, yet those who committed them have been freely forgiven. What did the Lord Jesus say to Saul of Tarsus? "I am Jesus whom thou persecutest: it is hard for thee to kick against the pricks." Yet, having asked, "Why persecutest thou me?" he had nothing more to say to him by way of reproof or rebuke, but he blotted out his sin, and more than that, he counted him worthy, putting him into the ministry, so that this very man could afterwards say, "To me, who am less than the least of all saints, is this grace given, that I should preach among the Gentiles the unsearchable riches of Christ."

To begin, then, here is THE CALL FROM GOD: "Return, ye backsliding children, and I will heal your backslidings."

You observe that it is a call to come back to God; and that means, first, *remember him*; begin to think of him; let him be a living God to you. Come back to him in your thoughts. The Lord Jehovah is the greatest factor in the universe; he works all things. He is the great unit without which all the rest of the figures would be but ciphers. He made you; you are dependent upon him from day to day; before long, your spirit must return to God who gave it; and you will have to stand before his judgment-seat. Why, of all the persons in the world, must God be forgotten? Why, of all the things that are, should you forget this chief of all things, the great I AM?

Do you say that there is no God? Ah! then, I have nothing to do with you; your conduct in forgetting him may be quite consistent with that declaration, though I am sure that you know better. But if there be a God, and you believe that he is, begin to think of him in due proportion. I mean that, as he is the greatest of all beings, give to him your greatest and highest thoughts; and as he is most to be reverenced, give him your most reverent and careful consideration. I think that I am not asking too much of you. Certainly, if you are sorry for your sin, and wish the Lord to forgive you, the very first thing for you to do is to obey that ancient command, "Acquaint now thyself with him, and be at peace: thereby good shall come unto thee." I know that the thought of your sin sometimes troubles you; so it ought, and it will do you good to be troubled if it leads you back to the Lord against whom you have sinned. If you have offended anyone, go and confess your offence, and make matters right. Perhaps you say that you do not like the person, and you are not willing to go to the person. Of course, you are not; but that only proves how very right it would be for you to do so. That dislike of yours has sprung out of two things—first, your having been the offender, and secondly, your not being acquainted with the offended one. Now, if those two things are owned, and confessed, and remedied, you will soon find it to be the most joyful thing in all the world to think of God. It will be your delight above all things to rejoice in him, and in all that he does. Begin, then, to think of God, for this is what he means when he says to you, "Return, ye backsliding children."

The next thing is, really *turn to him*. I know that you must have been shocked with the figure used in this chapter; that sense of shame I cannot help. As God used this symbol, it is good enough for me, and I am sure that there is an instructive meaning in it. I must turn again to that figure. We will suppose —and, alas! bad as the case is, we need not go very far to find the like of it—that a woman has grievously offended against the honour of her husband, she has gone away and left him, and plunged into all sorts of sin and vice. Well now, suppose that there should come to her the word, "Return. He knows it all; he realizes all that it means; he has grieved over it all, yet he says to you, Return." She says, "I have spent all. I am in rags. I have but a miserable lodging. Those who once flattered me, and lived with me in sin, have forsaken me. I am a poor cast-off wretch, whom even a reformatory refuses." Then the husband writes to her, and says, "Return. Return to me, and all shall be forgiven you, whatever it may be." Do you not fancy that you can see her starting to go back to him? If there is anything left in her that is worth saving, she makes haste to accept the invitation; yet she is very timid, and very much afraid. Oh, how her sad face is covered with the blushes of shame! How the tears fall down her furrowed cheeks! Sometimes, she can hardly believe that such wonderful love can be exhibited to so undeserving a woman as she is. Perhaps she is troubled, and rightly troubled, by the thought that no man would do such a thing as her husband appeared to have done, and that it would not be right that he should do so. She therefore stops a while, and considers the matter; yet it is all true. Her husband is one of a million, perhaps there is no other quite as loving and forgiving as he is. "Come back," he says; "only confess your transgression, and come back to me just as you are." Methinks, she must be a wretch indeed if she does not feel that she will lay all the rest of her life out in service and love to such a forgiving husband as she has.

Now, this is just how the Lord offers to deal with you. He says, "Come back. I will say nothing about the past. 'I have blotted out, as a thick cloud, thy transgressions, and, as a cloud, thy sins: return unto me; for I have redeemed thee.' I have forgiven thine iniquities, I laid them all on my dear Son. He died for thee, his precious blood has washed all thy guilt away. Come back to me. Come back to me. 'I have loved thee with an everlasting love: therefore with loving-kindness have I drawn thee.' Come back to me. 'The Lord, the God of Israel, saith that he hateth putting away.' I have not put you away, notwithstanding all your sin and all your iniquity. Here is the message of my love and mercy, 'Return, ye backsliding children,' for I am married unto you, saith the Lord your God."

Well now, in some such way as that striking figure would import, come back to your God at once, poor wandering sinner, confessing all your wrong, wondering that there should be mercy for you, trusting that what the Lord says is indeed true because he says it, and resolve henceforth to live and to die at his dear feet, his servant as well as his beloved. This is the way to come back to God, so I would entreat you thus to return unto him.

There is one word in this call from God which proves that *you are invited to come back just as you are.* He says, "Return, ye *backsliding* children." I notice that he does not say, "Return, ye penitent children." He pictures you in your worst colours, yet he says, "Return, ye backsliding children." I notice also that he does not say, "Heal your wounds first, and then come back to me"; but he says, "Return, ye backsliding children," with all your backslidings unhealed—"and I will heal your backslidings." Many sinners seem to suppose that they must make themselves better, and then come to Christ— a most unworthy supposition, and an utterly unfounded one. Come just as you are, with no goodness, or virtue, or hope of any; come to Christ for it all. "But all who would be saved must believe in Jesus, and repent of their sins," says one. Exactly so, but Christ does not want you to begin the work of salvation, and then to let him finish it. He never came to be a make-weight to add the last half-ounce to all that you had gathered. Come to him with nothing, and he will fill the scale. Come empty, ragged, filthy, just as you are, and believe in God that justifieth the ungodly. Cast yourselves on him who came to call, not the righteous, but sinners to repentance. Bow in humility and penitence before him who flashes the lightnings of Sinai in the face of every self-righteous sinner, but who kindles the milder, genial rays of Calvary to guide every truly humble and repentant sinner into the port of peace and everlasting love.

Thus have I put before you the call from God: "Return, ye backsliding children, and I will heal your backslidings."

Now, in the second place, I want to show you THE METHOD OF OBEYING THIS CALL.

There are two things in the text that are specially noteworthy. First, he who would return to God, and find salvation, must distinctly *renounce all other trust except that which God himself gives him,* and sets before him in the gospel. Listen: "Truly in vain is salvation hoped for from the hills, and from the multitude of mountains." Judæa was a hilly country, and wherever there was the peak of a mountain, or the summit of a hill, there was an idol temple; and wherever there was a grove of oaks, there would be an idolatrous shrine; whenever the people travelled through the valleys, they kept looking up to these shrines, so their trust was in the hills, and in the multitudes of mountains. They had gods everywhere, blocks of wood and stone; so the Lord said to them, "If I am to receive you back, you must renounce all this idolatry." The spiritual meaning of this passage is this—if you are to be saved by the grace of God, you must solemnly, formally, and heartily renounce all confidence in any but the living God and his Son, Jesus Christ.

First, there must be a distinct renunciation of all righteousness of your own. You are a very excellent person in your own estimation, you think yourself well up to the mark; what have you ever done that is wrong? Ah! friend, there is no salvation for you on that ground. Your righteousness must in your own esteem become as filthy rags; you must own yourself to be defiled and undone, or there is no hope for you. The man who clings to his own righteousness is like a man who grasps a millstone to prevent himself from sinking in the flood. Your righteousness will damn you if you trust in it, as surely as will your sins, for it is a false proud lie, there is no truth in it, and no dependence must be placed upon it. There is not a man living who, by nature, doeth good and sinneth not, and the soul that sins must die. We have not any one of us a righteousness that will stand the test of the all-searching eye of God, and in our heart of hearts we know it is so. Therefore, away with that lie, once for all.

When I came to Christ, this matter did not trouble me, for I had not any righteousness of my own to which I could trust; and there are many poor souls who are in much the same condition in which I was. They do not want to keep the counterfeit money which they once reckoned to be great riches; they are anxious to be rid of it! Yes, brethren, and even at this present moment, I do not know of anything that I have ever been, or done, or thought, or said, that I could patch up into a righteousness upon which I could place the slightest reliance. I have not anything to trust to, except the blood and righteousness of Jesus Christ, my Lord and Saviour; and, what is more, I never wish to have, and never shall have any other ground of confidence; and I am sure, beloved, that you must build on the same foundation, or else Christ will never save you. You must altogether renounce any trust in your own righteousness.

The next thing that you must renounce is, your own strength. There is many a young man whom I have known, who has been going into impurity and into drunkenness, and he has been warned by kind friends to see the wrong in his course of action, and he has said, "Yes, I see it, but I shall make everything right; I shall become a total abstainer, I shall forsake evil companions, I shall keep out of harm's way, I shall be as right as a trivet, I know that I shall. I have great strength of mind, and I always could command myself." Excuse me, dear friend, but I should like very politely and very kindly to tell you that you are a fool. You have not any strength; and, what is more, if you have, you will certainly be lost, for I read concerning those who are saved, "When we were yet *without strength*, in due time Christ died for the ungodly"; so that those for whom he died had not any strength. Believe me, you have not any strength. Oh! I have seen many a young man, with splendid moral principle, trusting in himself; but where has his moral principle been when a woman's pretty lips and smiling face have enticed him to wantonness, or when in gay company he has been chaffed into that other glass of wine that has upset his balance of mind, and has led him to say things which he never thought could have come out of his mouth?

Poor Hazael was told by the prophet Elisha of the enormities he would commit, and he said, "Is thy servant a dog, that he should do this great thing?" No, he was not a dog; but he was much worse than a dog, for he was a devil, yet he did not know it; and there is many a man who is fair to look upon, who is like John Bunyan's tree, which was green on the outside, but inwardly it was as rotten as to be only fit to be tinder for the devil's tinder-box. You must give up your own strength; there is not much of it to give up, but whatever there is, give it all up, renounce all trust in your own strength as well as in your own righteousness.

With that must also go all trust in your own knowledge and abilities, and even in your own understanding. Yet this is the bane and ruin of many men, they know so much that, like Solomon's sluggard, they are wiser in their own conceit than seven men who can render a reason. See how they treat the Bible itself; when they open it, it is not that they may hear what God says in it, but that they may tell God what he ought to have said. When they condescend to listen to the Gospel, it is not that they may hear what the Gospel is, but that they may note how the man preaches it. Is he an eloquent orator? Does he use fine words? That is all that many care to hear. Sirs! if I could use grand words, I would loathe to use them lest I should ruin your souls. As the Apostle Paul said, so say I, "Not with wisdom of words, lest the cross of Christ should be made of none effect." If I could get you to heaven by using the plainest words that can be uttered, I would sooner do it than I would leave any to perish in their sins, because I was anxious to display the niceties of language and the beauties of style. There are some men who are so wonderfully wise that they would quarrel with the angel Gabriel, or with the archangel Michael himself. Solomon—well, Solomon did not know everything; but these men do; according to their own ideas, they not only know everything, but they know a little more besides! If ever we want anybody to rule the nation, I would undertake to find fifty prime ministers, so wise in their own esteem are many men, who are, I must add, so little and so foolish when they come to be weighed in the balance of the sanctuary, and the unerring scales that God holds in his hand. Hear ye this, ye great ones of the earth, "Except ye be converted, and become as little children, ye shall not enter into the kingdom of heaven." He must become as a little child who would become a child of God. To be saved, we must not only—

> *"Cast our deadly 'doing' down,*
> *Down at Jesus' feet,"*

but we must also—

> *"Lay our boasted reason down,*
> *Down at Jesus' feet,"*

and ask that he may be made of God unto us "wisdom, and righteousness, and sanctification, and redemption."

Now, what say you to this? Are you willing to give up your own mind to God, and simply to believe what he tells you in his Word? Are you willing also to give up self-rule? "We are our own," says one; "we may do as we like. Our tongues are our own, we may say what we like. We are free thinkers and free livers." Let me tell you that, if you are saved by Christ, you shall find the only true freedom you can ever enjoy; but there must first be a complete surrender of yourself to your God. Come now, who is to rule? Shall it be his will, or your will? Shall it be his way, or your way? If it is to be your way, it will be your ruin; but if it is to be God's way, it shall be your salvation. When the Romans attacked a city, and the people yielded to them, they usually drew up a declaration which ran something like this: —"We, craving mercy at the hands of the powers of Rome, surrender up ourselves, our houses, our goods, our bodies, our souls, all that we have, and all that we are, to be dealt with by the Roman power exactly according to its will." It was so worded that there could be no escape from it, and it contained no stipulations and no conditions; and then, as soon as it was signed, the Roman conqueror, in the generosity of his power, said, "You have yielded to me, now you are free." God demands just that kind of submission. If thou art to be forgiven, thou must yield thyself up body, soul, and spirit, purse, heart, brain, everything, to belong wholly to Christ henceforth and for ever. I wish that yielding were over with all of you. If you would be saved, that submission must be yours; oh, then, let it be so at once! Will you keep your sins and go to hell, or leave your sins and go to heaven? Will you have sin or the Saviour? Which shall it be? Oh, that the blessed Spirit may lead you to the right decision, and lead you to that decision at once!

Finally, it is clear from the text that there must also be a *hearty, true-minded acceptance of God alone as our one hope.* Read the passage again: "Behold, we come unto thee; for thou art the Lord our God. . . . Truly in the Lord our God is the salvation of Israel."

There is but one living and true God. Men have made almost as many gods as there are sands on the sea-shore. There is, however, but one God, whose name is Jehovah, the Creator of all things, in whom we live, and move, and have our being. Will you have this God to be your God? Will you say, "This God is our God for ever and ever: he will be our guide even unto death"? Will you take him to be yours, not regarding him merely as another man's God, but henceforth as your God, whom you love, whom you embrace, not comprehending him by thought, but apprehending him by love?

Will you take God to be your God, and shall he be truly yours? Notice how the text says, *"Truly* in the Lord our God is the salvation of Israel." There must be no playing at this acceptance of God as our one hope, there must be no mocking of God by a pretended yielding up of ourselves to him. It must be a true acceptance of God, to be our God henceforth and for ever.

To help you do this, let me remind you that there is a blessed Trinity in Unity. There is, first, the ever-blessed Father. What sayest thou? Wilt thou have this Father to be thy Father? Thou hast sinned against him, wilt thou crave his forgiveness for Christ's sake? Wilt thou ask to be admitted into his house by the blood-stained door of his Son's atoning sacrifice? Wilt thou honour him as thy Father? Will not each of you young people from this time cry unto him, "My Father, thou art the Guide of my youth"?

The next blessed and adorable Person of the United Trinity is the Son of God. Wilt thou have this Son of God as thy Saviour? He died that sinners might live; wilt thou have his death to be thy life? He poured out his blood to cleanse the guilty from every stain of sin; wilt thou be washed in the crimson stream? Shall Christ be Prophet unto thee? Wilt thou sit at his feet, and learn of him? Shall Christ be Priest for thee? Wilt thou trust him to present his sacrifice for thee, and to intercede for thee? Christ is a King; wilt thou have him as King to reign over thee? In fine, wilt thou have him in all his offices and in all his relationships, in the majesty of his glorious Godhead, and in the humiliation of his perfect manhood? Wilt thou have this Man as thine? I put the question to you as one of old put it to the damsel he met at the well, "Wilt thou go with this man?" Wilt thou have Christ, to have and to hold, for better, for worse, for richer, for poorer, so that death itself shall not part thee from him? If so, have him and welcome, for he is prepared to give himself to every soul that is willing to accept him.

There is a third Person of this blessed Unity, and that is, the Holy Ghost. Art thou willing to let the Holy Ghost come and dwell in thee? It is he who must regenerate thee if thou art to be born again. It is he who must teach thee; it is he who must sanctify thee; it is he who must illuminate thee; it is he who must comfort and guide thee. Without him, thou canst do nothing. The Holy Ghost is the very life of the Christian. What the Father decreed, what the Son purchased, that the Holy Ghost applies; and without that Holy Ghost, there is nothing for thee. Wilt thou obey his monitions? Wilt thou put thyself under his superintendence? Wilt thou resign thy body to be his temple?

If thou wilt do all this, God helping thee, then believe on the Lord Jesus Christ, and thou shalt be saved. His own word is, "He that believeth and is baptized shall be saved." With the heart, believe on him; then let the body be washed with pure water in baptism. These two things the Lord Jesus Christ asks of thee; again I remind you that it is he who says, "He that believeth and is baptized shall be saved." Demur not to either of these Gospel words. Come at once, and do what he bids thee, and enter into life, for he that believeth in him hath everlasting life; and then at once make the Scriptural confession of your faith, as they did who heard the apostle Peter on the day of Pentecost: "Then they that gladly received his word were baptized: and the same day there were added unto them about three thousand souls."

XI

BEAUTY FOR ASHES

"To appoint unto them that mourn in Zion, to give unto
them beauty for ashes, the oil of joy for mourning, the garment of praise for the spirit of heaviness; that they might be
called trees of righteousness, the planting of the Lord, that he
might be glorified."—Isaiah 61 : 3.

WHEN soldiers are on the march, or advancing to the
battle, military men think it wise to let the trumpet
sound, that the warriors may be stimulated by the thrilling
music. Many a weary soldier has tramped on with new vigour
when the band has struck up a lively march, or a soul-moving
tune. In the midst of our present Christian service, my brethren,
when I trust all of you have resolved to come to the help of
the Lord—to the help of the Lord against the mighty—we would
bid the silver trumpets of Gospel promise sound aloud, that
the hosts of God as they march on in battle array may feel
their pulses quickened and their souls cheered. May times of
Revival be also seasons of refreshing. In times of great toil and
eminent service much extra refreshment may with wisdom be
dealt out. Harvest men require substantial meals amid their
exhausting toil; and, as I feel that the Lord of the harvest
would not have his labourers treated niggardly, I have to
regale each of you with a portion of bread, a good piece of
flesh, and a flagon of wine. Melchisedek met Abraham with
bread and wine—not on some fine holiday when he had been
musing in the plains of Mamre, but when he returned from
the slaughter of the kings. After hard fighting comes sweet
refreshment, and any here who have striven diligently to
serve the Master, and have been pursuing their sacred calling
even unto faintness, will be entitled to come and sit down,
and partake of the nourishing bread and wine, which such
a text as this prepares for all the sons of the Father of the
faithful.

First then, WHO GIVES THIS WORD? It is a word to mourners in Zion, meant for their consolation. But who gives it? The answer is not far to seek. It comes from him who said, "The Spirit of the Lord God is upon me"; "he hath sent me to bind up the broken-hearted." Now, in a very inferior and subordinate sense, Christian ministers have the Spirit of God resting upon them, and they are sent to bind up the broken-hearted; but they can only do so in the name of Jesus, and in strength given from him. This word is not spoken by them, nor by prophets or apostles either, but by the great Lord and Master of apostles and prophets, and ministers, even by Jesus Christ himself. If he declares that he will comfort us, then we may rest assured we shall be comforted! The stars in his right hand may fail to penetrate the darkness, but the rising of the Sun of Righteousness effectually scatters the gloom. If the consolation of Israel himself comes forth for the uplifting of his downcast people, then their doubts and fears may well fly apace, since his presence is light and peace.

But, who is this anointed one who comes to comfort mourners? He is described in the preface to the text as a *preacher*. "The Spirit of the Lord God is upon me; because the Lord hath appointed me to *preach* good tidings unto the meek." Remember what kind of preacher Jesus was. "Never man spake like this man." He was a son of consolation indeed. It was said of him, "A bruised reed shall he not break, and the smoking flax shall he not quench." He was gentleness itself: his speech did not fall like a hail shower, it dropped like the rain, and distilled as the dew, as the small rain upon the tender herb. He came down like the soft vernal shower upon the new-mown grass, scattering refreshment and revival wherever his words were heard. The widow at the gates of Nain dried her eyes when he spake, and Jairus no longer mourned for his child. Magdalene gave over weeping, and Thomas ceased from doubting, when Jesus showed himself. Heavy hearts leaped for joy, and dim eyes sparkled with delight at his bidding. Now, if such be the person who declares he will comfort the broken-hearted, if he be such a preacher, we may rest assured he will accomplish his work.

In addition to his being a preacher, he is described as a *physician*. "He hath sent me to bind up the broken-hearted."

Some hearts want more than words. The choicest consolations that can be conveyed in human speech will not reach their case; the wounds of their hearts are deep, they are not flesh cuts, but horrible gashes which lay bare the bone, and threaten ere long to kill unless they be skilfully closed. It is, therefore, a great joy to know that the generous friend who, in the text, promises to deal with the sorrowing, is fully competent to meet the most frightful cases. Jehovah Rophi is the name of Jesus of Nazareth; he is in his own person the Lord that healeth us. He is the beloved physician of men's souls. "By his stripes we are healed." Himself took our infirmities, and bare our sickness, and he is able now with a word to heal all our diseases, whatever they may be. Joy to you, ye sons of mourning; congratulation to you, ye daughters of despondency: he who comes to comfort you can not only preach with his tongue, but he can bind up with his hand. "He healeth the broken in heart, and bindeth up their wounds. He telleth the number of the stars; he called them all by their names."

As if this were not enough, our gracious helper is next described as a *liberator*. "He hath sent me to proclaim liberty to the captives, and the opening of the prison to them that are bound." There were many downcast persons in Israel in the olden times—persons who had become bankrupt, and, therefore, had lost their estates, and had even sunk yet further into debt, till they were obliged to sell their children into slavery, and to become themselves bondsmen. Their yoke was very heavy, and their trouble was very sore. But the fiftieth year came round, and never was there heard music so sweet in all Judæa's land, as when the silver trumpet was taken down on the jubilee morn, and a loud shrill blast was blown in every city, and hamlet, and village, in all Israel, from Dan even to Beer-sheba. What meant that clarion sound? It meant this: "Israelite, thou art free. If thou hast sold thyself, go forth without money, for the year of jubilee has come." Go back, go back, ye who have lost your lands; seek out the old homestead, and the acres from whence ye have been driven: they are yours again. Go back, and plough, and sow, and reap once more, and sit each man under his vine and his fig-tree, for all your heritages are restored. This made great joy among all the tribes, but Jesus has come with a similiar message. He, too, publishes a jubilee for bankrupt and enslaved sinners. He breaks the fetters of sin, and gives believers the freedom of the truth. None can hold in captivity the souls whom Jesus declares to be the Lord's free men.

Surely, if the Saviour has power, as the text declares, to proclaim liberty to the captive, and if he can break open prison doors, and set free those convicted and condemned, he is just the one who can comfort your soul and mine, though we be mourning in Zion. Let us rejoice at his coming, and cry Hosanna, blessed is he that cometh in the name of the Lord. Happy are we that we live in an age when Jesus breaks the gates of brass and cuts the bars of iron in sunder.

As if this were not all and not enough, one other matter is mentioned concerning our Lord, and he is pictured as being sent as *the herald of good tidings* of all sorts to us the sons of men. Read the second verse: "To proclaim the acceptable year of the Lord." God has taken upon himself human flesh. The infinite Jehovah came down from heaven and became an infant; lived among us, and then died for us. Behold in the person of the incarnate God the sure pledge of divine benevolence. "He that spared not his own Son, but freely delivered him up for us all, how shall he not with him also freely give us all things?"

Beloved, the very fact that a Saviour came to the world should be a source of hope to us, and when we think what a Saviour he was, how he suffered, how he finished the work that was given him to do, and what a salvation it is which he has wrought out for us, we may well feel that the comfort of mourners is work for which he is well suited, and which he can execute most effectually. How beautiful upon Olivet and Calvary are the feet of him that bringeth, in his person and his work, "good tidings, that publisheth peace, that bringeth good tidings of good, that publisheth salvation."

Secondly, TO WHOM IS THIS WORD SPOKEN? It is spoken to those who mourn in Zion. They are in Zion. They are the Lord's people, but they mourn. To mourn is not always a mark of grace. Nature mourns. Fallen human nature will have to mourn for ever, except grace change it. But the mourning here meant is a mourning in Zion—a mourning of gracious souls. Let me try and describe what kind of mourning it is. It assumes various shapes. It begins in most hearts with *lamentation over past sin.* I have broken God's just commandments, I have done evil against my God, I have destroyed my soul; my heart feels this, and bitterly mourns. It is one thing to say formally, "I am a miserable sinner"; it is a very different thing to be one. To say it may be gross hypocrisy, to feel it is a mark of grace. Oh that every one of us, if we have never felt mourning for sin, may feel it at this hour. May we mourn to think that we have pierced the Saviour, that we have transgressed against a God so good, and a Redeemer so generous. Those who mourn for the guilt of past sin, before long, reach a higher point. Mourners are not suffered long to tarry; grace takes their load of guilt away. Their transgressions are covered. Do they leave off mourning then? Oh, no, they mourn in another way. There is a sweet mourning concerning my past sin which I would never wish to lose. It is forgiven, every sin of mine is blotted out, and my soul, therefore, with a sweet bitterness, would mourn over it more and more.

True hearts, however, mourn not only for their past transgressions, but they also *sorrow over their present imperfections.* If you are what you should be, I am quite certain you see a great deal in yourself to grieve over. You cannot live as you would live. Whenever I meet with a person who feels that he is perfect, I conceive at once that he has not yet attained even a remote conception of what true perfection must be. The savage of Australia is satisfied with his weapons of war so long as he has never seen a rifle or heard of a cannon: to him his hovel is a model of architecture, for he has never heard of a cathedral or a palace. I have no doubt that a barn-door fowl would be quite surprised at the complaint which an eagle might make about its inability to mount as high as it desires to do. The fowl is perfect—perfect up to the condition of its barn-door, barley-scratching life, it knows nothing higher than its roosting place, and so it concludes itself absolutely perfect and fit for all that is desirable in flight. But oh, could it know where the thunders dwell, and sail above the clouds where the callow lightnings wait the bidding of the Lord, then would the creature feel something of the aspirations and the griefs which torment the heart of the royal bird.

Men know not what God is, nor the infinity of his perfections, nor the majesty of his purity, else, when highest would they cry, "Higher, higher, higher," and mourn because they have not yet attained, and need still to mount as on eagle's wings. Brethren, I speak for you all when I say, there is not a day in which our service satisfies us, not a deed we have ever performed that contents us. We see our spots, and would fain wash them out with tears if we could, though we bless God they are removed by the precious blood of Jesus. Those are among the blessed who mourn because they cannot live a perfect life as they desire. To mourn after more holiness is a sign of holiness; to mourn after greater conformity to the image of Christ proves that we are already in a measure conformed thereunto; to sigh after more complete subordination of our entire life to the will of God is a mourning for which Jesus Christ will bring rich comfort.

The Christian mourner *laments, also, because he cannot be more continually in communion with God.* He knows the sweetness of fellowship with the Father and with the Son. He cannot bear to have it broken. If but the thinnest cloud pass between him and the sun of God's love, he is distressed directly, for he is sensitive lest he should lose the delights of communion. A native of sunny Italy deplores the absence of heaven's bright blue, when made to dwell in this land of the fleecy clouds; and he who has dwelt in unclouded fellowship with the Lord bemoans his hard lot, if even for a while he beholds not that face which is as the sun shining in its strength. Love cannot endure absence, much less, coldness. True grace finds its life in fellowship, and pines if it be denied it.

The real Christian mourns, again, *because he cannot be more useful.* He wishes he were like a pillar of fire and light, so that he might evermore by day and by night enlighten the ignorant, and inspire the dull and laggard. He wishes not so much for more talent as for more grace to make use of the talent which he has. He would fain bring in a great rental to the owner of the vineyard who has placed him as a husbandman among the vines. He longs to bring up priceless pearls from the deep seas of sin, wherewith to adorn the diadem of his Lord and King.

He sighs because thorns and thistles will spring up where he looked for a hundred-fold harvest: this makes him groan out, "Who hath believed our report, and to whom is the arm of the Lord revealed?"

Moreover, like his Lord, *he mourns for others*. He mourns in Zion because of the deadness of the Christian church, its divisions, its errors, its carelessness towards the souls of sinners. He cries with Jeremiah, "How is the gold become dim! How is the much fine gold changed!" But, he mourns most of all for the unconverted. He sees their state of alienation from God, and knowing the danger of it, his heart shrinks within him, as with prophetic glance he sees what their end will be: when "there shall be wailing and gnashing of teeth." His heart breaks for the sins and sorrows of others, and, like his Saviour, he could weep over the cities that reject divine love; he could say like Moses that he was almost willing to have his name blotted out of the Book of Life if others might be saved: he feels such sorrow and heaviness of heart for his kinsmen according to the flesh who are strangers to Christ, that he has no rest in his flesh concerning them.

What is that, then, in the third place, WHICH IS SPOKEN in the text to those that mourn? I would draw particular attention to the words here, "To appoint unto them that mourn in Zion, to give unto them beauty for ashes." Come, mourning souls, who mourn in the way described, come ye gladly hither: there is comfort *appointed* for you, and there is also comfort *given* to you. It is the prerogative of King Jesus both to appoint and to give. How cheering is the thought that as our griefs are appointed, so also are our consolations. God has allotted a portion to every one of his mourners, even as Joseph allotted a mess to each of his brethren at the feast. You shall have your due share at the table of grace, and if you are a little one, and have double sorrows, you shall have a double portion of comfort. "To *appoint* unto them." This is a word full of strong consolation; for if God appoints me a portion, who can deprive me of it? If he appoints my comfort, who dare stand in the way? If he appoints it, it is mine by right. But then, to make the appointment secure, he adds the word "To *give*." The Holy One of Israel in the midst of Zion gives as well as appoints. The rich comforts of the Gospel are conferred by the Holy

Spirit, at the command of Jesus Christ, upon every true mourner in the time when he needs them; they are given to each spiritual mourner in the time when he would faint for lack of them. He can effectually give the comfort appointed for each particular case. This is the happy experience of all the saints.

> *"Sometimes a light surprises*
> *The Christian while he sings:*
> *It is the Lord who rises*
> *With healing in his wings.*
> *When comforts are declining,*
> *He grants the soul again,*
> *A season of clear shining,*
> *To cheer it, after rain."*

Our ever gracious and almighty Lord knows how to comfort his children, and be assured he will not leave them comfortless. He who bids his ministers again and again attend to this duty, and says, "Comfort ye, comfort ye my people," will not himself neglect to give them consolation. If you are very heavy, there is the more room for the display of his grace in you, by making you very joyful in his ways. Do not despair; do not say, "I have fallen too low, my harp has been so long upon the willows that it has forgotten Zion's joyful tunes." Oh, no, you shall lay your fingers amongst the old accustomed strings, and the art of making melody shall come back to you, and your heart shall once more be glad. He appoints and he gives —the two words put together afford double hope to us—he appoints and he gives comfort to his mourners.

Observe, in the text, the change Christ promises to work for his mourners. First, here is *beauty* given *for ashes*. In the Hebrew there is a ring in the words which cannot be conveyed in the English. The ashes that men put upon their head in the East in the time of sorrow made a grim tiara for the brow of the mourner; the Lord promises to put all these ashes away, and to substitute for them a glorious head dress—a diadem of beauty. Or, if we run away from the words, and take the inner sense, we may look at it thus: —mourning makes the face wan and emaciated, and so takes away the beauty; but Jesus promises that he will so come and reveal joy to the sorrowing

soul, that the face shall fill up again: the eyes that were dull
and cloudy shall sparkle again, and the countenance, yea, and
the whole person shall be once more radiant with the beauty
which sorrow had so grievously marred.

I thank God I have sometimes seen this change take place in
precious saints who have been cast down in soul. There has
even seemed to be a visible beauty put upon them when they
have found peace in Jesus Christ, and this beauty is far more
lovely and striking, because it is evidently a beauty of the
mind, a spiritual lustre, far superior to the surface comeliness
of the flesh. When the Lord shines full upon his servants' faces,
he makes them fair as the moon, when at her full she reflects
the light of the sun. A gracious and unchanging God sheds on
his people a gracious and unfading loveliness. O mourning
soul, thou hast made thine eyes red with weeping, and thy
cheeks are marred with furrows, down which the scalding tears
have burned their way; but the Lord that healeth thee, the
Lord Almighty who wipeth all tears from human eyes, shall visit
thee yet; and, if thou now believest in Jesus, he shall visit thee
now, and chase these cloudy griefs away, and thy face shall be
bright and clear again, fair as the morning, and sparkling as
the dew. Thou shalt rejoice in the God of thy salvation, even
in God, thy exceeding joy.

Then, it is added, "He will give the *oil of joy for mourning.*"
Here we have first beauty, and then unction. The Orientals
used rich perfumed oils on their persons—used them largely
and lavishly in times of great joy. Now, the Holy Spirit comes
upon those who believe in Jesus, and gives them an anointing
of perfume, most precious, more sweet and costly than the nard
of Araby. An unction, such as royalty has never received,
sheds its costly moisture over all the redeemed when the Spirit
of the Lord rests upon them. "We have an unction from the
Holy One," said the Apostle. "Thou anointest my head with
oil, my cup runneth over." Oh, how favoured are those who
have the Spirit of God upon them! You remember that the
oil which was poured on Aaron's head went down to the skirts
of his garment, so that the same oil was on his skirts that had
been on his head. It is the same Spirit that rests on the believer
as that which rests on Jesus Christ, and he that is joined unto
Christ is one Spirit. What favour is here! Instead of mourning,

the Christian shall receive the Holy Spirit, the Comforter, who shall take of the things of Christ, and reveal them unto him, and make him not merely glad, but honoured and esteemed.

Then, it is added, to give still greater fulness to the cheering promise, that the Lord will give *"the garment of praise for the spirit of heaviness."* The man is first made beautiful, next he has the anointing, then afterwards he is arrayed in robes of splendour. What garments these are! Surely Solomon in all his glory wore not such right royal apparel. "The garment of praise," what a dress is this! Speak of wrought gold, or fine linen, or needlework of divers colours, or taffeta, or damasks, or gorgeous silks most rich and rare which come from far off lands—where is anything compared with "the garment of praise?" When a man wraps himself about, as it were, with psalmody, and lives for ever a chorister, singing not with equal voice, but with the same earnest heart as they do who day and night keep up the never ending hymn before the throne of the infinite I AM, what a life is his, what a man is he! O mourner, this is to be your portion; take it now; Jesus Christ will cover you, even at this hour, with the garment of praise; so grateful shall you be for sins forgiven, for infirmity overcome, for watchfulness bestowed, for the church revived, for sinners saved, that you shall undergo the greatest conceivable change, and the sordid garments of your woe shall be put aside for the brilliant array of delight. It shall not be the *spirit* of praise for the *spirit* of heaviness, though that were a fair exchange, but as your heaviness you tried to keep to yourself, so your praise you shall not keep to yourself, it shall be a *garment* to you, external and visible, as well as inward and profound. Wherever you are it shall be displayed to others, and they shall see and take knowledge of you that God has done great things for you whereof you are glad.

We close by noticing what will be the result of this appointment, and the text concludes, by saying, *"That they might be called trees of righteousness, the planting of the Lord, that he might be glorified."* We learn, here, that those mourning souls who are cast down, and have put ashes on their heads, shall, when Jesus Christ in infinite mercy comes to them, be made

like trees—like "oaks"; the original is, like "oaks of righteousness," that is, they shall become strong, firmly rooted, covered
with verdure; they shall be like a well-watered tree for pleasantness and delight. Thou sayest, "I am a dry tree, a sere branch,
I am a cast off, fruitless bough; Oh that I were visited of God
and saved! I mourn because I cannot be what I would."
Mourner, thou shalt be all thou wouldst be, and much more
if Jesus visit thee. Breath the prayer to him now; look to
him, trust him. He can change thee from a withered tree that
seems twice dead into a tree standing by the rivers of water,
whose leaf is unwithering, and whose fruit ripens in its
season.

But, the very pith of the text lies in a little word to which
you must look. "Ye shall be *called* trees of righteousness."
Now, there are many mourning saints who are trees of
righteousness, but nobody calls them so, they are so despond-
ing that they give a doubtful idea to others. Observers ask,
"Is this a Christian?" And those who watch and observe them
are not at all struck with their Christian character. Indeed, I
may be speaking to some here who are true believers in Jesus,
but they are all their lifetime subject to bondage; they hardly
know themselves whether they are saved, and therefore, they
cannot expect that others should be very much impressed by
their godly character and fruitful conversation. But, O
mourners! if Jesus visits you, and gives you the oil of joy,
men shall call you "trees of righteousness," they shall see grace
in you, they shall not be able to help owning it, it shall be so
distinct in the happiness of your life, that they shall be compelled to see it. I know some Christian people who, wherever
they go, are attractive advertisements of the Gospel. Nobody
could be with them for a half-an-hour without saying, "Whence
do they gain this calm, this peace, this tranquillity, this holy
delight and joy?" Many have been attracted to the cross of
Christ by the holy pleasantness and cheerful conversation of
those whom Christ has visited with the abundance of his love.
I wish we were all such. When a man is contented—more than
that, when he is happy under all circumstances, when "his
spirit doth rejoice in God his Saviour" in deep distress, when
he can sing in the fires of affliction, when he can rejoice on the
bed of sickness, when his shout of triumph grows louder as his

conflict waxes more and more severe, and when he can utter the sweetest song of victory in his departing moments, then all who see such people call them trees of righteousness, they confess that they are the people of God.

Note, still, the result of all this goes further, "They shall be called trees of righteousness, *the planting of the Lord*," that is to say, where there is joy imparted, and unction given from the Holy Spirit, instead of despondency, men will say, "It is God's work, it is a tree that God has planted, it could not grow like that if anybody else had planted it; this man is a man of God's making, his joy is a joy of God's giving." I feel sure that in the case of some of us we were under such sadness of heart before conversion, through a sense of sin, that when we did find peace, everybody noticed the change there was in us, and they said one to another, "Who has made this man so happy, for he was just now most heavy and depressed?" And, when we told them where we lost our burden, they said, "Ah, there is something in religion after all." "Then said they among the heathen the Lord hath done great things for them." Remember poor Christian in Pilgrim's Progress. Mark what heavy sighs he heaved, what tears fell from his eyes, what a wretched man he was when he wrung his hands, and said, "The city wherein I dwell is to be burned up with fire from heaven, and I shall be consumed in it, and, besides, I am myself undone by reason of a burden that lieth hard upon me. Oh that I could get rid of it!" Do you remember John Bunyan's description of how he got rid of the burden? He stood at the foot of the cross, and there was a sepulchre hard by, and as he stood and looked, and saw one hanging on the tree, suddenly the bands that bound his burden cracked, and the load rolled right away into the sepulchre, and when he looked for it, it could not be found. And what did he do? Why, he gave three great leaps for joy, and sang,

> *"Bless'd cross! bless'd sepulchre! bless'd rather be*
> *The man that there was put to shame for me."*

If those who knew the pilgrim in his wretchedness had met him on the other side of that never-to-be-forgotten sepulchre, they would have said, "Are you the same man?" If Christiana had met him that day, she would have said, "My husband, are you the same? What a change has come over you"; and, when she and the children marked the father's cheerful conversation, they would have been compelled to say, "It is the Lord's doing, and it is wondrous in our eyes." Oh live such a happy life that you may compel the most wicked man to ask where you learned the art of living.

Another word remains. That other word is this, *"The planting of the Lord, that he might be glorified."* That is the end of it all, that is the great result we drive at, and that is the object even of God himself, "that he might be glorified." For when men see the cheerful Christian, and perceive that this is God's work, then they own the power of God: not always, perhaps, with their hearts as they should, but still they are obliged to confess "this is the finger of God." Meanwhile, the saints, comforted by your example, praise and bless God, and all the church lifts up a song to the Most High. Whatever your circumstances are, "Rejoice in the Lord always, and again I say rejoice." Think what Jesus has given you, your sins are pardoned for his name sake, your heaven is made secure to you, and all that is wanted to bring you there; you have grace in your hearts, and glory awaits you; you have already grace within you, and greater grace shall be granted you; you are renewed by the Spirit of Christ in your inner man, the good work is begun, and God will never leave it till he has finished it; your names are in his book, nay, graven on the palms of his hands; his love never changes, his power never diminishes, his grace never fails, his truth is firm as the hills, and his faithfulness is like the great mountains. Lean on the love of his heart, on the might of his arm, on the merit of his blood, on the power of his plea, and the indwelling of his Spirit.

Peradventure, I speak to some for whom the promises of God have no charm; let me, then, remind them that his threatenings are as sure as his promises. He can bless, but he can also curse. He appoints mourning for those who laugh now with sinful merriment; he will give to his enemies vengeance for all their rebellions. He has himself said, "And it shall come to pass, that instead of sweet smell there shall be stink; and instead of a girdle a rent; and instead of well set hair baldness;

and instead of a stomacher a girdling of sackcloth ; and burning instead of beauty." Beware, then, ye that forget God, lest
he overthrow you in his hot displeasure. Seek ye the Saviour
now, lest the acceptable year of the Lord be closed with a long
winter of utter despair.

XII

AN ENCOURAGING WORD IN
TROUBLOUS TIMES

"Wherefore, sirs, be of good cheer: for I believe God, that it
shall be even as it was told me."—Acts 27: 25.

THE presence of a brave man in the hour of danger is a very
great comfort to his companions. It is a grand thing to
observe Paul so bold, so calm, in the midst of all the hurly-
burly of the storm, and talking so cheerfully, and so encourag-
ingly, to the crew and to the soldiery and to the prisoners. You
must have seen in many events in history that it is the one man,
after all, that wins the battle: all the rest play their parts well
when the one heroic spirit lifts the standard. Every now and
then we hear some simpleton or other talking against a "one-
man ministry," when it has been a one-man ministry from the
commencement of the world to the present day; and whenever
you try to have any other form of ministry, except that of each
individual saint discharging his own ministry, and doing it
thoroughly and heartily and independently and bravely in the
sight of God, you very soon run upon quicksands. Recollect,
Christian man, that wherever you are placed you are to be *the*
one man, and you are to have courage and independence of
spirit and strength of mind received from God, that with it you
may comfort those around you who are of the weaker sort. So
act that your confidence in God shall strengthen the weak hands
and confirm the feeble knees, and your calm quiet look shall
say to them that are of a faint heart, "Be strong; fear not."

If you are to do this, and I trust you will do it, in the sick
chamber, in the midst of the troubles of life, in the church, and
everywhere else, *you must be strong yourself*. Take it as a good
rule that nothing can come out of you that is not in you. You
cannot render real encouragement to others unless you have
courage within yourself. Now, the reason why Paul was able

to embolden his companions was that he had encouraged himself in his God; he was calm, or else he could not have calmed those around him. Imagine him excited and all in a tremble, and yet saying, "Sirs, be of good cheer." Why they would have thought that he mocked them, and they would have replied, "Be of good cheer yourself, sir, before you encourage us." So you must trust God and be calm and strong, or else you will not be of such service in the world and in the church as you ought to be. Get full, and then you will run over, but you can never fill others till you become full yourselves. Be yourselves "strong in the Lord, and in the power of his might," and then you will be as a standard lifted up to which the timid will rally.

First, then, PAUL WAS STRONG BECAUSE HE BELIEVED. Faith makes men strong—not in the head, but in the heart. Doubting people are generally headstrong—the Thomas-sort of people who obstinately declare that they will not believe unless they can have proofs of their own choosing. If you read certain newspapers, journals, quarterly reviews, and so on, you will see that the doubting people who are always extolling scepticism and making out that there is more faith in their doubt than in half the creeds, and so on, are particularly strong in the upper region, namely, in the head, only it is that sort of head-strength which implies real weakness, for obstinacy seldom goes with wisdom. They are always sneering at believers as a feeble folk, which is a clear sign that they are not very strong themselves; for evermore is this a rule without exception, that when a man despises his opponent he is himself the party who ought to be despised.

When certain writers rave about "evangelical platitudes," as they commonly do, they only see in others a fault with which they are largely chargeable themselves. Anybody who glances at the sceptical literature of the present day will bear me out that the platitudes have gone over to the doubting side of the house. No people can write such fluent nonsense, and talk such absurdity, as the school of modern doubt and "culture": they think themselves the wisest of the wise, but, professing to be wise, they have become fools. When a man leaves faith he leaves strength; when he takes up with "liberal" views in religion, and does not believe anything in particular, he has lost the bone and sinew of his soul. It is true all round, in all things, that he who firmly believes has an element of power which the doubter knows nothing of. Paul was a believer in God, and so became strong in heart, and was on board the foundering vessel the centre of hope, the mainstay of courage.

But notice that *Paul's faith was faith in God.* "I believe God," said he. Nobody else in the ship could see any hope in God. With the exception of one or two like-minded with Paul they thought that God had forsaken them, if indeed they thought of God at all. But there had that night stood by Paul's side an angel fresh from heaven, bright with the divine presence, and, strengthened by his message, Paul said, "I believe God." That was something more than saying "I believe *in* God": this many do and derive but slender comfort from the belief. But "I believe *God*, believe *him*, believe his truthfulness, believe the word that he has spoken, believe his mercy and his power. I believe God." This made Paul calm, peaceful, strong. Would to God that all professing Christians did really believe God.

Believing God, *he believed the message that God had sent him,* drank in every word and was revived by it. God had said "Fear not, Paul, I have given thee all them that sail with thee." He believed it. He felt certain that God, having promised it, was able to perform it; and amidst the howling of the winds Paul clung to that promise. He was sure that no hair of any man's head would be harmed. The Lord had said the preserving word and it was enough for his servant. Has he said it, and shall he not do it? Has he spoken it, and shall it not come to pass?

And he did that—mark you—*when there was nothing else to believe in.* "I believe God," said he The ship was breaking up. They had put ropes all round her, undergirding her; but he could clearly perceive that all this would not avail. The fierce Euroclydon was sweeping the vessel hither and thither, and driving her towards the shore: but he calmly said, "I believe God." Ah, that is a grand thing—to believe God when the winds are out—to believe God when the waves howl like so many wild beasts, and follow one upon another like a pack of wolves all seeking to devour you. "I believe God." This is the genuine breed of faith—this which can brave a tempest.

The common run of men's faith is fair-weather faith, faith which loves to see its beautiful image mirrored in the glassy wave, but is far away when the storm clouds are marshalling the battle. The faith of God's elect is the faith that can see in the dark, the faith that is calm in the tumult, the faith that can sing in the midst of sorrow, the faith that is brightest when everything around her is black as midnight. "I believe God," said he, when he had nothing else to believe in. "My soul, wait thou only upon God, for my expectation is from him."

Since the Apostle Paul believed God thus truly and really, *he was not ashamed to say so.* He said openly to all those around him, "There shall not a hair of your heads perish, for I believe God." Now, it is not so easy to thrust out your faith and expose it to rough weathers, and to the hearing of rough men. Many a man has believed the promise but has not quite liked to say so, for there has been the whisper in his soul, "Suppose it should not come true, then how the enemy will rejoice! How those that listened to me will be saddened when they find that I was mistaken." Thus does the devil cause faith to be dumb, and God is robbed of his honour. Under the name of prudence there lurks an unbelieving selfishness. Brother, lend me your ear that I may whisper in it—"You do not believe at all." That is not the legitimate sort of believing. Genuine faith in God speaks out and says, "God is true, and I will stake everything on his word." It is not ashamed to say, "The Lord Jesus, whose I am and whom I serve, stood by me this night, and spoke with me, and I avow it." I would to God all Christians were prepared to throw down the gauntlet, and to come out straight; for if God be not true let us not pretend to trust him, and if the Gospel be a lie let us be honest enough to confess it. But if it be true, wherefore should we doubt it and speak with bated breath? If God's promise be true why should we distrust it? What excuse is there for this hesitancy? "Oh," says one, "but that might be running great risks." Risks with God, sir? Risks about God's keeping his word? It cannot be. "Let God be true and every man a liar."

Now, if we have any measure of the faith of Paul, let us try whether we cannot CHEER OTHERS AS PAUL DID. Let the language of the text be on our tongues, "Wherefore, sirs, be of good cheer: for I believe God, that it shall be even as it was told me."

First, you will meet with *seeking souls*. They have not found Christ yet, but they are hungering and thirsting after him. They are saying, "Oh that I knew where I might find him!" You that believe God are bound to speak comfortably to them, and say, "Sirs, be of good cheer: for I believe God, that it shall be even as it was told me." There is one that is sorrowing for sin. Go and tell him that sorrow for sin is sweet sorrow, and that no man should ever regret that he mourns his faults, but should be glad that God has enabled him to feel a holy grief, a penitential pain.

Gotthold tells us that he was called one day to see a man who, when he entered his chamber, burst into many tears; and it was a long time before the good divine could discover what made him so unhappy. At last the man broke out, saying, "Oh, my sin, how I hate it! My sin, how I sorrow over it!" Whereupon Gotthold, who had been sad at the sight of his sadness, smiled and said, "Friend, thy sadness is my gladness. I never behold a happier sight than when I see a man sorrowing for his sin." "Oh," said the other, "say you so?" "Yes, indeed," said he; "there are many mourners who mourn for others, but blessed are they that mourn for themselves. There are many who are sorry because they cannot have their own will; but," said he, "there are few enough that sorrow because they have had their own will, and have disregarded the will of the Lord. I rejoice," said he, "for such as you are those for whom Jesus died. Come and trust him, for when there is sorrow for sin there will soon be joy for pardon."

Perhaps you will meet with another whose condition is that he is *pleading daily for mercy*. "Oh," saith he, "I have been praying, and praying, and praying. I cannot let a day pass without asking for forgiveness; but somehow my prayers seem to come back to me. I get no favourable replies." Brother, to a man in this plight you should speak up, and say, "Be of good cheer, friend, for I believe God, that it shall be even as he told me, and he told me this—'Ask, and it shall be given you: seek, and ye shall find: knock, and it shall be opened.'" Tell the praying soul that praying breath was never spent in vain, and that in due time "he that asketh receiveth." To withhold your testimony will be cruelty to the seeking one, and a robbery of God, to whose honour you are bound to speak.

Possibly you will meet with another who is saying, "I am beginning now to *venture myself upon Christ.* I am desiring to believe; but oh! mine is such a feeble confidence. I think I trust him, but I am afraid I do not. I know there is no other Saviour, and I do give myself to him; but still I am jealous of my heart, lest mine be not true faith." Tell that soul that Jesus has plainly said, "Him that cometh to me I will in nowise cast out," and then say, "Be of good cheer: for I believe God, that it shall be even as he hath told me." Tell the trembling heart that Jesus never did yet respect one believer, however trembling might be his trust. Whosoever believeth in him is not condemned.

Perhaps you will find one who says, "*I desire the renewal of my nature.* I am so sinful. I can believe in Christ for pardon, but my heart is terribly deceitful, and I feel such strong passions and evil habits binding me that I am sore afraid." Go and say to that soul, "His name is called Jesus, for he shall save his people from their sins." Tell that anxious one that the Lord can take away a heart of stone and give a heart of flesh. Say that Christ has come to bring liberty to the captives, and to set men free from the bonds of sin; and tell them that you believe God, that it will be even as he has told you; and he has told you, and you know it is true, that he will purge you from sin and sanctify you wholly.

Now, there is another set of people who are saved, but they are *Little-faiths,* and I want you strong-faith people to encourage them, by telling them that you believe God that it shall be even as it was told you. Some of these Little-faiths are conscious of very great inward sin. They thought when they believed in Christ that they would never feel any more conflicts: their notion was that they should be saved from the assaults of sin the moment they were born unto God. But now they discover that the old viper within is not dead. He has had a blow on the head, but he is not dead; they see lusts and corruptions moving within their hearts, and they cannot make it out. Go and tell them that you feel the same, but that, thanks be to God, he giveth you the victory through our Lord Jesus Christ. The poor young soul that is just struggling out of darkness into light, and beginning to contend with inward corruption, will be greatly comforted if you thus state your experience, and declare your faith in the ultimate issue.

In the case of some others of these Feeble-faiths, the trouble is that they are *vexed with outward temptation.* Many a young man says, "It is hard to be a Christian where I work." Many a young woman has to say, "Father and mother are against me." Others have to complain that all their associations in business tempt them to that which is evil, and that they have few to help them. Go and tell them of the Lord all-sufficient. Remind them that "He keepeth the feet of his saints." Tell them to pray day by day, "Lead us not into temptation, but deliver us from evil." Tell them that there is strength enough in Christ to preserve his own.

You will find others whose lamentation is, *"I am so weak. If I am a Christian yet I am good for nothing. I have little liberty in prayer, or power to edify anybody. I think I am the most useless of all the family."* Tell them that "He giveth power to the weak, and to him that hath no strength he increaseth might." Tell them that the Lord does not cast away the little ones, but he "carrieth the lambs in his bosom, and doth gently lead those that are with young." Tell them of the faithfulness and tenderness of the Good Shepherd, and say, "Sirs, be of good cheer: weak as you are, the Lord's strength will sustain you; and as he has promised to preserve his own, and has evermore preserved me, do not doubt, for it shall be to you even as the Lord has told me."

Perhaps they will say, "Ah, but *I am beset by Satan.* Blasphemous thoughts are injected into my soul. I am driven to my wits' end." Then tell them that the Lord enables his people to cry, "Rejoice not over me, O mine enemy, for though I fall yet shall I rise again." Tell them that when the enemy cometh in like a flood, the Spirit of the Lord will lift up a standard against him. As they feel their danger, point them to their great protector, the Lord Jesus, who has come to destroy the works of the devil, and say, "You will conquer him, you will conquer him yet. The Lord will bruise Satan under our feet shortly. Sirs, be of good cheer: for I believe God, that it shall be even as he has told me."

Now, if you have performed these tasks, I commend to your

attention a third class of persons, namely, *those who are greatly tried*. God has a very tried people abroad in the world. I learned a lesson the other day which, I think, I never can forget. I was asked after preaching a sermon to go and see a lady who suffered from rheumatism. Now, I know by bitter experience what rheumatism is, but when I saw one whose fingers and hands had all lost their form through pain, so that she was incapable of any motion beyond the mere lifting up of her hand, and the letting it fall again—when I saw the pain marked on her countenance, and knew that for two-and-twenty years she had suffered an agony, then I said, "You have preached me a sermon upon patience, and I hope I shall profit by it. How dare I be impatient if you have to suffer so?" Now, if you go and see sick folk—and I suppose you do, and if not sickness comes to your own house—say to them, "Sirs, be of good cheer, for it shall be even as God has told me"; and what has he told me? Why, that he will support his people in the severest afflictions. "In six troubles I will be with thee, and in seven there shall no evil touch thee!" Tell them that the Lord will bless his people's troubles, for "all things work together for good to them that love God." Tell them that God will bring his people out of the trouble some way or other, for he has said, "Many are the afflictions of the righteous, but the Lord delivereth him out of them all." And if you will tell them these precious things, believing them yourself—for that is the main point—having experienced the truth of them yourself, your testimony will comfort them.

You will meet with some that have been bereaved, who have lost the light of their house, and have seen the desire of their eyes taken away with a stroke. Cheer them, and tell them of the sweet things that God has said concerning the bereaved. He is "the Judge of the widow, and the Father of the fatherless," and do you make a point of declaring your belief that he is so.

You will meet with godly folks who are under testing trials. Many young people have to go through severe tests. I mean trials like this: —"Will you take this situation, young man? The wages are sufficient, are they not?" "Yes, sir, I should be well content, I do not think I shall get a better situation as far as money goes." "You understand that you will not have the

Sabbath day to yourself and that we want no religion here."
Now, young man, what do you say to that? Do not think twice
about it, my friend, but say, "No; 'what shall it profit a man
if he gain the whole world, and lose his own soul?'" Speak
right straight out, and do not be afraid to throw up the tempt-
ing offer. Many Christians can tell you, "to be of good cheer,"
for if you do this God will bless you. You shall have even in
this life your recompense, as well as in the life to come, if you
can be decided and steadfast to stand for God and keep his
way. I could mention many Christians who would tell you that
when they were tested the Lord helped them to stand fast, and
that they have to bless him for it every day of their lives;
whereas certain others have temporized and given way a little,
and they have got out of God's ways, and have had to run
from pillar to post all their lives long, and though they are
still Christians yet they never enter into the joy of their
Lord.

I have yet another set of good folks to speak to. We have
some Christian people about who tremble greatly for the ark
of the Lord. I occasionally meet with good brethren, very good
brethren, who are tempted to commit the sin of Uzzah—to put
forth their hand to steady the ark because the oxen shake it; as
if God could not protect his own cause. Some say that the good
men are all dying: I have even heard that they are all dead,
but I am not quite sure of it! and they ask as the fathers fall
asleep, and one after another of the pillars of the house of God
are taken away, what will become of the Church? What will
become of the Church? What will become of the truth, the
cause, and the Church? You know the good Methodist woman's
outcry at the funeral sermon when the minister said, "Now
that this eminent servant of the Lord is departed we know of
no one to fill his place. The standard-bearers are removed and
we have none left at all to be compared with them. It seems as
if the glory were departing and the faithful failing from among
men." The worthy mother in Israel called out from the aisle.
"Glory be to God, that's a lie!" Well, I have often felt inclined
to say the same when I have heard a wailing over the absence
of good and great men, and melancholy prophecies of the awful
times to come, "Glory be to God, he will never let his Church
die out for want of leaders; he has a grand reserve somewhere."

If all the men who preach the gospel to-day were struck down in the pulpit with apoplectic fits to-morrow, the Holy Spirit would still qualify men to preach the Gospel of Jesus Christ. We are none of us necessary to him, nor is any mere man necessary to God. Do not get into that state of mind which makes you attach undue value to men or means. The salvation of souls is God's work, and if it be God's work it will go on.

Many minds are in a state of great distress about the spread of error. I do not know what is going to happen to England according to the weeping prophets. The signs of the times are very bad, and the would-be prophets say that a dreadful storm is coming on. My barometer does not indicate anything of the kind, but theirs stands at "much rain," or "stormy." Not long ago I walked with a very excellent man, whose name I will not mention, because I think he must have been ill that morning. He told me that he believed that he should live to see the streets of London run with blood, on account of the unbridled democracy, the atheism, and the radicalism of the times. In fact, he thought that everything was out of joint, and we were going—I do not know where. It is not long ago, and I remember that I pulled him by the sleeve, and said, "But, my dear friend, God is not dead." Now, that is my comfort. God is not dead, and he will beat the devil yet. As surely as Jesus Christ won the victory on the cross, he will win the victory over the world's sin.

It is true it is a hard time for Christianity, and infidels are fighting us with new arguments; but when I think of them I feel inclined to say what the Duke of Wellington said at Waterloo to the generals "Hard pounding, gentlemen! hard pounding! but we will see which will pound the longest." And so we say. It may be "hard pounding" for the Christian church, but we shall see who can pound the longest. Hitherto—these eighteen hundred years or more—the Gospel gun has gone on pounding, and has neither been spiked nor worn out. As for our opponents, they have changed their guns a good many times. Our Gospel cannon has blown their guns and gun carriages and gunners all to pieces; and they have had to set up new batteries every year or two. They change their modes, their arguments, their tactics, but we glory in the same cross as Paul did, and preach the same gospel as Augustine, and Calvin, and Whitefield, and the like. All along the testimony of Jesus Christ has still been the same. The precious blood has been exalted, and men have been bidden to believe in Jesus. Pound away, gentlemen! We shall pound the longest, and we shall win the day. If we believe God in that fashion, let us turn round to our discomfited brethren, and say to them, "Sirs, be of good cheer: for I believe God, that it shall be even as it was told me."

The last class that I shall notice will be our brethren and sisters who are labouring for Christ. Sometimes workers for the Lord get cast down. "I have taught a class for years," says one, "and seen no fruit." "I have been preaching at the corner of the street for months but have never heard of a conversion," says another. "I have been visiting the lodging-houses, but I have never met with a convert." Well, dear brother, do you think that you have preached Jesus Christ, and nothing has come of it? If you do, you must be a very unbelieving brother. I do not believe it for a moment. I believe God, that it shall be even as he has told me, and he has said, "My word shall not return unto me void, but it shall prosper in the thing whereto I sent it." Perhaps you preach unbelievingly. Now, an unbelieving word is not God's word. If you preach confidently, and teach trustfully, believing in the power of the Spirit of God, and so exhibiting Jesus Christ to your children and to your hearers, there are sure to be results. The raindrops return not to heaven, and the snow flakes climb not back to the treasure-house, but water the earth, and make it bring forth and bud: and even so shall God's word be. It must prosper in the thing whereto he has sent it. Beloved brother, do not give up. Dear sister, do not be discouraged. Go on! Go on! If you do not see results to-day you must wait and work on, for the harvest will come. "He that goeth forth and weepeth, bearing precious seed, shall doubtless come again rejoicing, bringing his sheaves with him." Be not so cowardly as to say, "I will leave the work." You are not to win a battle in a moment, or reap a harvest as soon as you sow the seed. Keep on! "Be steadfast, unmovable, always abounding in the work of the Lord, forasmuch as ye know that your labour is not vain in the Lord." We say this to you because we are confident ourselves, and would have you confident also. Sirs, be of good cheer. God has been true to us, and given us success; and we believe that it shall be to you even as he has told us.

Now, to give ONE OR TWO WORDS OF PERSONAL TESTIMONY TO THE FAITHFULNESS OF GOD by declaring that the Lord has always acted to me as he has promised me. I will give one or two. When I was converted to God, as I read the Scriptures I found that believers ought to be baptized. Now, nobody around me saw things in that light: but it did not matter to me what they thought, for I looked at it carefully for myself. Parents, friends, all differed, but believers' baptism seemed to me to be Scriptural, and, though I was a lad, God gave me grace to be honest to my conscience, and to follow the Lord in that respect as fully as I could. Have I had any cause to regret it? It seemed then that I might soon have grave cause for doing so, but I have had none: it has, on the other hand, often been a great comfort to my soul to feel that I did not trifle with my convictions. And I should like to urge you, young people, whether on that matter or any other, if you have received light from God, never to trifle with it. Follow the Lord fully, and I can say, as the result of actual experience, "Sirs, be of good cheer. No harm will come to you if you are faithful to God and to your consciences."

Again, when I came to London as a young minister, I knew very well that the doctrines which I preached were by no means popular, but I for that very reason brought them out with all the more emphasis. What a storm was raised! I was reading the other day a tirade of abuse which was poured upon me about twenty years ago. I must have been a horridly bad fellow, according to that description, but I was pleased to observe that it was not *I* that was bad, but the doctrines which I preached. I teach the same truths now; and after having preached them these four-and-twenty years or so, what can I say of the results? Why, that no man loses anything by bringing the truth right straight out. If he believes a doctrine, let him speak it boldly.

Now, how has it turned out with me? I wish to bear this witness, not about myself, mark, but about the truth which I have preached. Nothing has succeeded better than preaching out boldly what I have believed, and standing to it in defiance of all opposition, and never caring a snap of the fingers whether it offended or whether it pleased. Young man, if you are beginning life now, I charge you begin so that you can keep on, with a straightforward, honest reliance in God, for be sure of this, the truth will reward those who love it, and all who lose for its sake are great gainers. Be steadfast in following your convictions. I cannot help saying it, because some of you, perhaps, are beginning to temporize a little. I would say to you, "Stand up straight, and tell out the truth, and then be of good cheer, for I believe God, that it shall be even as he has told me."

Believe God. Take every letter of his Book and hang to it as for dear life, and in little as well as in great things keep to the statutes and precepts and ordinances and doctrines of the Lord, as they are committed to you. As surely as you do this the Lord of Hosts will bless you. First rest in Jesus by a simple faith in him, and then treasure up his every word, and keep his every command. So shall the blessing of God be with you henceforth and for ever.

XIII

THE DRAWINGS OF LOVE

"The Lord hath appeared of old unto me, saying, Yea, I have loved thee with an everlasting love; therefore, with loving-kindness have I drawn thee."—Jer. 31 : 3.

FROM the connection it is clear that this passage primarily refers to God's ancient people, the natural descendants of Abraham. He chose them from of old, and separated them from the nations of the world. Their election fills a large chapter in history, and it shines with resplendent lustre in prophecy. There is an interval during which they have experienced strange vicissitudes, been visited with heavy chastisements, and acquired an ill-reputation for the perverseness of their mind and the obstinacy of their heart. Yet a future glory awaits them when they shall turn unto the Lord their God again, be restored to their land, and acknowledge Jesus of Nazareth as the King of the Jews, their own anointed King. Without abating, however, a jot or tittle from the literal significance of these words as they were addressed by the Hebrew prophet to the Hebrew race, we may accept them as an oracle of God referring to the entire Church of his redeemed family, and pertaining to every distinct member of that sacred community. Every Christian, therefore, whose faith can grasp the testimony may appropriate it to himself. As many a believer has heard, so every believer may hear the voice of the Holy Spirit sounding in his ear these words, "Yea, I have loved thee with an everlasting love; therefore, with loving-kindness have I drawn thee."

There are two things of which we propose to speak—*the unspeakable boon*, "I have loved thee with an everlasting love"; and *the unmistakable evidence*, "therefore, with loving-kindness have I drawn *thee*."

How exceedingly great and precious this assurance, how priceless this blessing, to be embraced with the love, the everlasting love of God? Our God is a God of infinite benevolence. Towards all his creatures he shows his goodwill. His tender mercies are over all his works. He wisheth well to all mankind. With what force and with what feeling he asserts it! "As I live, saith the Lord God, I have no pleasure in the death of the wicked, but that the wicked turn from his way and live" (Ezekiel 33: 11). And whosoever of the whole human race, penitent for past sins, will turn to Jesus, the Saviour of sinners, he shall find in him pardon for the past and grace for the future. This general truth, which we have always steadfastly maintained, which we never saw any reason to doubt, and which we have proclaimed as widely as our ministry could reach, is not at all inconsistent with the fact that God hath a chosen people amongst the children of men who were beloved of him, foreknown to him, and ordained by him to inherit all spiritual blessings before the foundation of the world. As an elect people, they are the special objects of his love. On their behalf the covenant of grace was made; for them the blood of Christ was shed on Calvary; in them the Spirit of God worketh effectually to their salvation. Of them and to them it is that such words as these are spoken, "I have loved thee with an everlasting love"; a love far superior to mere benevolence—towering above it as the mountain above the sea; love kindlier, deeper, sweeter far than that bounty of providence which gilds the earth with sunshine, or scatters the drops of morning dew; a love that reveals its preciousness in the drops of blood distilled from the Saviour's heart, and manifests its personal, immutable favour to souls beloved in the gift of the Holy Spirit, which is the seal of their redemption and the sign of their adoption. So the Spirit itself beareth witness with our spirit that we are the children of God.

Now think for a little while of THIS INESTIMABLE BOON.

Let us consider the text word by word. "I have loved thee." *Who is the speaker?* "I"; the great "I am," Jehovah the Lord. There is but one God, and that God filleth all things. "By him all things were made, and through him all things consist." He is not far away, to be spoken of as though he were at an infinite distance from us, though heaven is his throne; for he is here with us. We live in him, move in him, and have our being in him. Imagination's utmost stretch fails to grasp any true con-

ception of what God is. The strong wing of reason, though it
were stronger than that of the far-famed albatross, would
utterly fail if it should attempt to find out God. Incomprehen-
sible art thou, O Jehovah! thy Being is too great for mortal
mind to compass! Yet this we understand—thy voice hath
reached us; from the excellent glory it has broken in tones
distinctly on our ears: "Yea, I have loved thee." Believer in
Christ, hast thou heard it? The love of any creature is precious.
We prize the love of the beggar in the street. We are flattered
by it. We cannot estimate it by silver or gold. Most men
court the acquaintance or esteem the friendship of those among
their fellow-creatures who are in anywise distinguished for
rank, for learning, or for wealth. There is a charm in living
in the esteem of those who themselves are estimable; but no
passion of our nature will supply me with an adequate comparison when I ask, what must it be to be loved with the love
of God; to be loved by him whose dignity is beyond degree,
whose power to bless is infinite, whose faithfulness never varies,
whose immutability standeth fast like great mountains—to be
loved by him who dieth not, and who will be with us when we
die; to be caressed by him who changeth not in all our cares,
to be shielded by his love when we stand at the judgment-seat
and pass the last dread ordeal that responsible creatures have
to undergo!

Oh! to be beloved of God! Had ye the hatred of all mankind, this honey would turn their gall into sweetness. It were
enough to make you start up from the dungeon of wretchedness,
from the chamber of poverty; aye, or from the bed of death.
How like an angel you might feel; and know that such thou art,
a prince of the blood Imperial. If this be true of thee, my
friend, in joy unspeakable thou mayest emulate the bliss of
spirits blest, who see Jehovah and adore him before his throne.
Who is loved? "*I have loved thee.*" Drink that in if thou canst,
Christian. Repeat the words to yourself with fitting emphasis,
"Yea, I have loved thee." Is it not a wonder that the Mighty
God should love any of the race of Adam—so insignificant,
so ephemeral, so soon to pass away? For the eternal God to
love a finite man is a marvel of marvels! And yet had he loved
all men everywhere, save and except myself, it had not so
amazed me as when I grasp the truth in relation to myself that

he has loved me. Let me hear his voice, saying, "Yea, I have loved thee," and forthwith I sit down abashed with humility and overwhelmed with gratitude, to exclaim with David, "What am I, and what is my father's house, that thou hast brought me hither? Why hast thou loved me?" Surely there was nothing in my natural constitution, nothing in my circumstances, nothing in my transient career, that could merit thy esteem or regard, O my God! Wherefore, then, hast thou spoken thus unto thy servant, saying, "I have loved thee!"

Thou wast, perhaps, once a drunkard, yet he loved thee; a swearer, yet he loved thee; thou hadst a furious temper, yet he loved thee; and thou hast, even now, infirmities and imperfections that make thee sometimes loathe thyself and lie down in shame, weary of life, chafed with the conflict in which you have to fight with such besetting sins day by day—evil thoughts and evil desires, so degrading to thy nature, so disgusting to thyself, so dishonouring to thy God. Still, he saith, "Yea, I have loved thee." Come, brothers and sisters, hear the word, and heed it; do not fritter away the sweetness of the text with vexatious questions. Here it is. In large and legible letters it is written. Take your fill and slake your thirst with this love divine. If you believe in Jesus, what though you be poor, obscure, illiterate, and compassed with infirmities, which make you despise yourself, yet he who cannot lie saith, "I have loved thee." These words have been said to Magdalen; they have been spoken to one possessed with seven devils; they were whispered in the heart of the dying thief. Within the tenfold darkness of despair itself they have sounded their note of cheer. Blessed be the name of the Lord, you and I can hear the voice of his Spirit, as he bears witness with our spirit, "Yea, I have loved thee." What a disparity by nature, what a conjunction by grace between these two, the "I" and the "thee"—the infinite "I" and the insignificant "thee"—the first person so grand, the second so paltry!

Whenever I attempt to speak about God's love, I feel that I would rather hold my tongue, sit down to muse, and ask believers to be kind enough to join me in meditation, rather than wait upon my feeble expressions. If the love of God utterly surpasseth human knowledge, how much more a mortal's speech? *What is it he bestows?* That God should be merciful to us is a theme for praise; that he should pity us is a cause for gratitude; but that he should love us is a subject for constant wonder, as well as praise and gratitude. Love us! Why, the beggars in the street may excite our pity, and towards the criminals in our jails we may be moved with compassion; but we feel we could not love many whom we would cheerfully help. Yet God loves those whom he has saved from their sins, and delivered from the wrath to come. Between that great heart in heaven and this poor throbbing, aching heart on earth there is love established—love of the dearest, truest, sweetest and most faithful kind. In fact, the love of woman, the mother's love, the love of the spouse, these are but the water; but the love of God is the wine; these are but the things of the earth, but the love of God is the celestial. The mother's love mirrors the love of God, as the dewdrop mirrors the sun; but as the dewdrop compasseth not that mighty orb, so no love that beats in human bosom can ever compass, as no words can express the height, depth, length, and breadth of the love of God, which is in Christ Jesus our Lord. "Yea, I have loved thee." Oh! come thou near then, Christian. Thy Father, he that chastened thee yesterday, loves thee; he whom thou forgettest so often, and against whom thou hast offended so constantly, yet loves thee. Thou knowest what it is to love. Translate the love thou bearest to thy dearest friend, and look at it and say, "God loves me better than this." Think you there are some thou couldst die for cheerfully, whose pain thou wouldst freely take if thou couldst ease them of it for a while, upon whose weary bed thou wouldst cheerfully lie down if a night of suffering could be spared him; but thy Father loves thee better than that, and Jesus proves it to thee. He took thy sins, thy sorrows, thy death, thy grave, that thou mightest be pardoned, accepted, and received into divine favour, and so mightest live and be blessed for evermore.

Passing on with our meditation, let us observe that *there is incomparable strength,* as well as inexhaustible sweetness in this assurance, "I have loved thee with an everlasting love." That word "everlasting" is the very marrow of the Gospel. Take it away, and you have robbed the sacred oracle of its divinest part. The love of God is "everlasting." The word bears three ideas within it. *It has never had a beginning.* God never began to love his people. Or ever Adam fell; ere man was made, ere the mountains were brought forth, before the blue heavens were stretched abroad, there were thoughts of love in his heart towards us. He began to create, he began actually to redeem, but he never began to love. It is eternal love which glows in the bosom of God towards every one of his chosen people.

Some of our hearers, strange to say, take no delight in this doctrine; but if you know that everlasting love is yours, you will rejoice to hear it proclaimed again and again. You will welcome the joyful sound. Ah! God's love is no mushroom growth. It sprung not up yesterday, nor will it perish to-morrow; but, like the eternal hills, it standeth fast.

The second idea is that *he loves his people without cessation.* It would not be everlasting if it came now and then to a halt; if it were like the Australian rivers, which flow on, become dry, and flow on again. The love of God is not so. It swells and flows on like some mighty river of Europe or America, ever expanding—a mighty, joyous river; returning again into the eternal ocean from whence it came. It never pauses. Christian, thy God loves thee always the same. He cannot love thee more; he will not love thee less. Never, when afflictions multiply, when terrors affright thee, or when thy distresses abound, does God's love falter or flag. Let the rod fall never so heavily upon thee, the hand that moves, like the heart that prompts the stroke, is full of love. Judge not the Lord by feeble sense, but trust him for his grace. Whether he brings thee down into the depths of misery, or lifts thee up into the seventh heaven of delight, his faithful love never varies or fluctuates; it is everlasting in its continuity.

And, being everlasting, the third thought is, *it never ends.* You will grow grey soon, but the love of God shall still have its locks bushy and black as a raven, with the verdure of youth. You will die soon, but the love of God will not expire. Your spirit will mount and traverse tracts unknown, but that love shall encompass you there ; and at the bar of judgment, amidst the splendours of the resurrection morning in the millennial glory, and in the eternity that shall follow, the love of God shall be your unfailing portion. Never shall that love desert thee. A destiny how splendid! For thy soul an heritage, how boundless! Thou art his, and thou shalt be his when worlds shall pass away and time shall cease to be. There is infinitely more solace and satisfaction here than I can bring out. Sure I am there is no more delightful manna for the pilgrims in the wilderness to feed upon than this doctrine applied to the heart. The love of God towards us personally in Jesus Christ is an everlasting love.

Now we come to the second point, which is, THE UNMISTAKABLE MANIFESTATION, the manifestation by which this love is made known. Good people often get puzzled with the doctrine of election. In their simplicity they sometimes ask, "How can we know whether we are the Lord's chosen, or ascertain if our names are written in the Lamb's book of Life?" You cannot scan that mystic roll, or pry between those folded leaves. Had you an angel's wing and a seraph's eye, you could not read what God has written in his book. The Lord knoweth them that are his. No man shall know by any revelation, save that which the Holy Spirit gives according to my text. There is a way of knowing, and it is this: "Therefore, with loving-kindness have I drawn thee." Were you ever drawn? *Have you been drawn with loving-kindness?* If so, then there is evidence that the Lord·loved you with an everlasting love. Be ready, therefore, to judge yourselves. You are challenged with this pointed question: Were you ever divinely drawn? Say now, beloved, have you experienced this sacred attraction that made you willing in the day of his power? Were you ever *drawn from sin to holiness?* You loved sin once; in it you found much pleasure; there were some forms and fashions of vice and folly which were very dear to your heart. Have your tastes been changed and your track been turned by the sovereign charm of this divine loving-kindness? Can you say, "The things I once loved, I now hate; and what gave me pleasure, now causes me a pang"? Is it so? I do not ask you whether you are perfect and upright. Alas! who of us could answer this question otherwise than with blushes of shame? But I do ask, if thou dost hate sin in every shape, and desire holiness in every form? Wouldst thou be perfect if thou couldst be? If thou couldst live as thou wouldst list, how wouldst thou list to live? Is thy answer, "I would live as though it were possible for me to serve God day and night in his temple, without a wandering thought or a rebellious wish"? Ah! then, if you have been thus drawn from sin to holiness by the way of the cross, no doubt he loved you with an everlasting love, and you need not discredit it. You may be as sure of it as if an angel should come and drop a letter into your hands on which these words should be inscribed.

Hast thou ever been *drawn from self to Jesus*? There was a time when thou thought thyself as good as other men. Had the bottom of thine heart been searched, there would have been found written there, "I do not see that I am so great an offender as the most of my neighbours; I am respectable, upright, moral; I should hope it would speed well with me at the last, for if I am not now all that I should be, I shall try to be good, and by earnest endeavours, joined with fervent prayers and repentance, I hope to fit myself for heaven." Oh! that you may be drawn away from all such empty conceit, and led to rest your hope solely on that blessed Man who sits at the right hand of God, crowned with glory, though he was once fastened to the tree, despised and rejected of men, and made to suffer as a scapegoat for our sins. This, beloved, would be a sure sign that you had renounced yourself and closed in with Christ. You must have been loved with an everlasting love. It is as impossible for any of the elect of God to come to Christ and lay hold on him without divine drawing, as it would be for devils to feel tenderness of heart and repentance towards God.

Have you ever been *drawn from sight to faith,* from consulting your creature faculties to confidence in God? You used to depend only on what you called your common-sense. You walked by the judgment of your own mind. Do you now trust in him who truly is, though he is invisible; who speaks to you, though his voice is inaudible? Have you a sense, day by day, of the presence of One Supreme whom you cannot hear nor see? Does the unseen presence of God affect you in your actions? Do motives drawn from the next world influence you? Say whether do you, in the day of trouble, lean upon an arm of flesh, or cry, and pray, and make supplication to the Almighty? Have you learnt to walk in dependence upon the living God, even if his providence seem to fail you, and give a lie to his promises? Know, then, that a life of faith is a special gift of God; it is the fruit of divine protection; so as thou art enabled to walk with God, and he deigns to befriend thee, thou mayest humbly but safely conclude that, in the records of the chosen, thy name stands inscribed. To be drawn into a life of faith is a blessed evidence of Christ's love.

Are you, moreover, day by day *being drawn from earth to heaven*? Do you feel as if there were a magnet up there drawing your heart, so that when you are at work in your business, in your family with all its cares, you cannot help darting a prayer up to the Most High? Do you ever feel this onward impulse of something you do not understand, which impels you to have fellowship with God beyond the skies? Oh! if this be so, rest thou assured that it is Christ that draws. There is a link between thee and heaven, and Christ is drawing that link, and lifting thy soul forward towards himself. If your heart is here below, then your treasure is here; but if your heart is up there—if your brightest hopes, your fondest wishes be in the heavenly places, your treasure is manifestly there, and the title-deeds of that treasure will be found in the eternal purpose of God, whereby he ordained you unto himself that you might show forth his praise.

Some people are frightened into religion. Beware of any religion that depends upon exciting your terror. Some people's religion consists entirely in doing what they think they must do, though they do not like it. They are afraid of punishment, or they are anxious for a reward. Such is not the religion of Jesus Christ. It is said that the soldiers of Persia were driven into battle, and that the sound of the whips of the generals could be heard even while the battle was raging, lashing on the unwilling ranks to fulfil their part in the fray. Not so went the Greeks to battle. They rushed like lions amidst a flock of sheep to tear their prey. They fought for their country, for their temples, for their lives, for all that they held dear, and right cheerily from such an impulse within did they engage in the war. The difference between the Greeks and the Persians is just the difference I want to describe among the professed followers of our Lord. The genuine Christian serves God because he loves him; not that he fears hell, for he knows that he has been delivered from condemnation, being washed in Jesus' blood; not that he expects to earn heaven; he scorns the idea. Heaven is not to be merited by our poor paltry works. And besides, heaven is his inheritance, since Christ has given it to him, having made his title sure. But *he serves God because he loves him*. He is drawn by a sense of the love of God towards him to love God in return.

What a lovely word this "loving-kindness" is! "Kindness" seems to be like some huge opal or some sparkling diamond, a Koh-i-noor; and love seems to be like fine gold to encircle it. Methinks I could stand and look at that word "loving-kindness" till with sacred enchantment I burst into a song. There is such a charming sweetness, and yet such an immutable stability in the grace of God which it reveals, that our rapture is kindled as often as we review it. Of that loving-kindess I have tasted here below, and of that loving-kindness I hope to sing in yonder skies in worthier notes than this weak voice can compass now.

Thus clearly and thus surely may ye judge for yourselves whether ye are God's chosen or not. Are you drawn, and how are you drawn? Is it with loving-kindness? These are the two points that melt and fuse in experience. As before that God whose eyes of fire search you through and through, I do conjure you to judge, and righteously judge, now as to your own condition. Be not satisfied to rest peacefully until you can say, "Thanks and praise to God's eternal love, I am drawn; by grace, by grace divine, I am constrained. Henceforth, I freely yield myself up to Christ to be his servant, his disciple, his friend, his brother, for ever and for ever. The Lord hath appeared unto me, saying, 'Yea, I have loved thee with an everlasting love.'"

Do I hear a sigh come up from some; a sigh which, being interpreted, would say, "Alas! for me, this sacred solace was never mine; I never was drawn; I feel no love, no such melting favours as your description of loving-kindness ever dawned on me; but, ah! I wish I were drawn; that I had a part amongst that blessed throng who shall for ever see his face. Oh! that I could believe that I, though the meanest of them all, should find my name written in the Lamb's book of life!" Why, friend, with thee, it would seem, the drawing has begun. Surely God's loving-kindness hath made thy mouth water.

I rejoice exceedingly over those who hunger after the bread of life, for they shall speedily be filled. Right well I know my Master will give it to them. If thou desirest Christ, depend upon it, Christ desireth thee. No sinner ever was beforehand with Christ. When you are willing to have him, he is evidently willing to have you. You had not put out one hand towards him, if he had not put two hands on you already. Oh! if thou wilt but trust the bleeding Lamb; believe that he can save thee, and trust in him to save thee with unfeigned confidence, then thou art already drawn. This is proof positive that God has loved thee from before the world's beginning. May the Holy Spirit attract you! May you feel in your heart the wish to belong to Christ; the desire to be counted among them when he maketh up his jewels. Turn that wish into a prayer. He does not reject sincere prayers, however badly they may be worded. If you can get no further than a sigh, it has its value in his kind esteem. God will accept thee if thou wilt accept Christ. If thou trusted Jesus now, 'tis done! Thou art saved —saved for ever.

> "'Tis done, the great transaction's done;
> I am my Lord's, and he is mine;
> He drew me, and I followed on,
> Glad to obey the voice divine."

XIV

THE BEST STRENGTHENING MEDICINE

"Out of weakness were made strong."—Heb. 11: 34.

THOSE who out of weakness were made strong are written among the heroes of faith, and are by no means the least of them. Believers "quenched the violence of fire, escaped the edge of the sword, out of weakness were made strong." Who shall tell which of the three grand deeds of faith is the greatest? Many of us may never have to brave the fiery stake, nor to bow our necks upon the block, to die as Paul did; but if we have grace enough to be out of weakness made strong, we shall not be left out of the roll of the nobles of faith, and God's name shall not fail to be glorified in our persons.

As believers in the Lord Jesus, *we are called to two things*, namely, to do and to suffer for his name's sake. Certain saints are summoned to active marching duty, and others are ordered to keep watch on the walls. There are warriors on the field of conflict, and sentries in the box of patience.

Both in doing and in suffering, if we are earnest and observant, *we soon discover our own weakness.* "Weakness" is all we possess. "Weakness" meets us everywhere. If we have to work for the Lord, we are soon compelled to cry, "Who is sufficient for these things?" and if we are called to suffer for him, our weakness, in the case of most of us, is even greater: many who can labour without weariness cannot suffer without impatience. Men are seldom equally skilled in the use of the two hands of doing and bearing. Patience is a grace which is rarer and harder to come at than activity and zeal. It is one of the choicest fruits of the Spirit, and is seldom found on newly-planted trees. The fact soon comes home to us that we are weak where we most of all desire to be strong.

Our longing is to be able both to do and to suffer for our Lord, and to do this *we must have strength from above, and that strength can only come to us through faith.* This glorious eleventh of Hebrews describes the mighty men of faith, the men of renown. They accomplished all their feats by a power which was not in them by nature. They were not naturally strong either to do or to suffer. If they had been, they would not have required faith in God; but being men of like passions with ourselves, they needed to trust in the Lord, and they did so. They were quite as weak as the weakest of us; but by their faith they laid hold on heavenly strength until they could do all things. There was nothing in the range of possibility, or, I might say, nothing within the lines of impossibility, which they could not have performed. They achieved everything that was necessary in the form of service, and they bore up gloriously under the most fearful pressure of suffering, simply and only by faith in God, who became their Helper. We are all in heavenly things so weak, that the idea of being made strong should be very attractive to us.

To begin with: FAITH MAKES MEN STRONG FOR HOLY DOING. Here, indeed, all our strength must come to us by faith in the thrice-holy God.

The first duty of a Christian man is *to obey God.* Obedience is hard work to proud flesh and blood; indeed, these ingrained rebels will never obey through our own efforts. By nature we love our own will and way; and it goes against the grain for us to bring ourselves into such complete subjection as the law of the Lord requires. "Thou shalt love the Lord thy God with all thy heart, and with all thy soul, and with all thy mind." Who among us has done this? Who among us can do this, unless a power outside of himself shall come to his aid? Faith alone takes hold of the divine strength; and only by that strength can we obey. Hence faith is the essential point of holiness. If you start on the voyage of life, by divine grace, with the resolve that you will follow the track marked down on the chart by the Lord your God, you will find that you have chosen a course to which the Lord's hand alone can keep you true. The current does not run that way. Before long you will find that the wind is dead against you, and the course to be followed is hard to keep. What will you do then if you have not faith? When duty is contrary to your temperament, what will you do without faith? When it involves loss of money, or ease, or honour, what will you do then if you have no faith? If you believe that God is the Rewarder of them that diligently seek him, you will persevere; but not else.

Suppose the right course should expose you to ridicule, cause you to be spoken of as a fanatic, or mocked at as a hypocrite, or despised as a fool, what can you do without faith? If you trust the living God, you will do the right, and bear the loss or the shame; but if your faith fail you, self-love will create such respect for your own good name, such fear of ridicule, such unwillingness to be singular, that you will slide from your integrity, and choose a smooth and pleasing road. Though you may think it a very ordinary thing to obey God in all things, you will find that a man had need to set his face like a flint in order to keep the right road; and the only way in which he will be able to hold on his way will be by having faith in God. Let him say, "God commands, and therefore I must do it"; and he will be strong. Let him feel, "God commands, and therefore he will bear me through"; and he will be strong. Let him say, "God commands, and he will recompense me"; and he will be strong. Faith in God made the cripple at the temple gate stand, and walk, and leap, and praise God; and even so does faith make our sin-crippled manhood obey the will of the Lord with exultation.

Taking another view, we would remark that faith makes us strong *to fulfil the relationships of life*. We are not alone by ourselves, and we can neither live nor die apart, for God has linked us with others. We either curse or bless those around us. If we have faith in God, we shall bless our children, as Isaac and Jacob blessed their sons. Faith leaves a legacy of benediction to its heirs. If you have faith in God, you may bless your brothers while you live, as Joseph did: faith has housed many a family which else had starved. If you have faith in God, you can lead others out of the bondage of sin, and through the wilderness world, as Moses led the children of Israel; for faith is a great guide. But you can do nothing aright for others without faith in God for yourself and them. Do I address a wife who has a godless husband? Have faith in God about him. Do not try to deal with your husband otherwise than by faith in God. If you attempt his conversion apart from heavenly power, you might as well try to take leviathan with a hook! Dear father, have you children who are unruly, irreligious, defiant? Do the young men refuse to be advised? Are your girls light and trifling? Go to God in prayer and faith. He that knows the care of a household knows how easily a parent can do serious mischief with his children by his very efforts to do them good. One parent is too indulgent, another is too severe. Take the children to God, take them to God, I pray you. It is here that your strength lies.

Do I speak to a youth who fears God, and who lives in an ungodly family? Do you feel bewildered as to how to behave yourself? Orders are given you which cause you great searchings of heart. You have to question in your inmost soul whether you can conscientiously do as your employer requires. I beseech you, have faith in God that he will direct you, and have faith also to follow that direction when you receive it. It is a very perilous spot, that beginning of life, when the youth first leaves the home of piety, and finds himself where the fear of God is not in the place. If, as a decided believer, he takes his stand, and if he is firm and steadfast for his God, he will make a man, and his after years will be bright and useful; but if he begins to give way a little, and if he tries to trim his sail to the wind, he will never attain to a holy character. That which begins with shamefacedness, equivocation, hesitation, and compromise will ripen into apostasy. Such a wretched faith has no influence on the man's self, and it will have no influence upon others.

There is a high and blessed duty and privilege—I will call it both—which is to every Christian the necessity of his life, and that is *to pray*. Can you pray, my brother? If you know how to pray, you can move heaven and earth. Can you pray, my brother? Then you can set almighty forces in operation. You can suffer no need, for everlasting supplies await the hand of prayer: "Ask, and it shall be given you." You cannot miss your way, for you shall be guided in answer to prayer. You shall hear a voice behind you, saying, "This is the way, walk ye in it."

"O sir," you say, "I cannot pray prevailingly." Then you are not like Jacob, good at wrestling. You cannot take hold upon the angel, and win the victory. Do you feel in prayer as if the sinew of your strength were shrunk, and your knee out of joint? Well, then, let me bring the text before you. Out of this weakness in prayer you can only be made strong *by faith*. Believe in God, and you will prevail with God. Believe in his promise, and plead it. Believe in his Spirit, and pray by his help. Believe in Jesus, who makes intercession; for through him you may come boldly to the throne of grace. He who knows how to pray has his hand on a leverage which moves the universe. But there is no praying without believing. If thou believest not, thou mayest be heard—it is more than I can promise thee; but if thou believest, *thou shalt* be heard, for God refuses no believing prayer. To refuse to keep his own promise when it is pleaded would be to falsify his word, and change his character; and neither of these things can ever be. Jesus said, "If ye then, being evil, know how to give good gifts unto your children, how much more shall your Father which is in heaven give good things to them that ask him?" Believe in prayer, and you will pray believingly. Some do not think that there is much in prayer. Poor souls! The Lord teach them better!

It may be that some feel that they cannot attain to the matters I have mentioned, for they are as yet battling to reach the position of servants and pleaders. Faith is the great force which is needed by those whose principal work is *to overcome sin*. When God began with many of us, he found us very low down beneath the flood of evil. It may be that an awful temper broke over us in surging waves. We have to rise superior to it. Possibly he found us plunged in the great deeps of an evil habit. Was it drunkenness? Was it gambling? What was it? It had to be left beneath; we were called to rise out of it. Some are permitted to sink a long way down in sin; and when God begins with them, they have a desperate ascent even to reach common morality; what must the conflict be before they attain to spirituality and holiness? It is hard for those to rise to the surface who have been plunged in the deeps. If a man has been sunk down in black waters full of filth, a thousand fathoms deep, and if he has been long imprisoned in dark caves where no light has come, what a wondrous power would that be which should raise him to the sunlight! The Spirit of God comes to many when they are in much the same condition; and what a work it is to bring up from the horrible midnight, and to give strength to rise out of the inky waters!

Dear struggler, you will never overcome sin except by faith in Jesus Christ. Trust him! Trust in the precious blood: that is the great sin-killer. Trust his pierced hands to pierce the hands of your lusts. Trust his wounded side to smite through the heart of your evil desires. Your hope lies there: where Jesus died, where Jesus rose again, where Jesus has gone into the glory. You may resolve to overcome a sin, and, perhaps, any one sin you may conquer for a time; but sin itself, as a force, in all its armies, is never to be overcome, save through the blood of the Lamb.

I have often met with persons awakened by divine grace to see the evil of a certain act, and they have said, "I do not know how I shall ever break off the habit"; yet they have very easily escaped from it. I remember one who was very foul-mouthed, and used oaths habitually. I hardly think that, for years, he had spoken without ill language; and yet, from the moment he turned unto the Lord, he never used an oath, and he also noted that he never had a temptation so to do. I remark that the particular form of sin known as blasphemy is one of the first to die, and to be buried out of sight. Other sins die hard, but this is shot through the head by true repentance and faith in Jesus. Some sins cling to a man like the fabled tunic of Hercules, which could not be torn away, but burned into his flesh and bone, whatever he might do. How long a well-beloved habit lingers at the door after the heart has given it a bill of divorce! How weak we are in this matter! How slow to cut off right hands, and pluck out right eyes! But yet it must be done; and only faith can do it, by calling in the aid of the Almighty One. In him we shall find succour, and by faith out of weakness we shall be made strong.

I change the run of my discourse altogether by remarking that there is another thing that falls to the lot of Christian men, a matter of the very first importance: namely, *to spread the Gospel*. "Yes," says one, "I own that it is an urgent service to make known to others what the Lord has done for me: but, somehow, I cannot discharge my conscience by fully doing as I would. I tried the other day to say a good word, and I am afraid that I made a failure of it. I stammered a good deal, and I said little that I thought to say, and some things which seemed to weaken what I did say. I resolved, the other day, that I would see a man whom I had known, and tell him that I was a changed character; but when I reached his house, I drifted into other talk, and went the way in which he led me. I could not come to the point." Many would make a similar confession if they made a clean breast of it. Many of the truest children of God are at first possessed by a dumb spirit; and it needs the Lord Jesus to cast it out. But do you not think that we are too apt to attempt to spread the gospel in our own strength; and need we wonder if we break down? If we were by faith to begin, humbly waiting upon the Lord for words, and taking hold upon divine strength, might we not accomplish far more than we now do?

I have heard of one brought to Christ, who was a very great sinner—of so stiff a neck that he never would be approached by anybody who aimed at his conversion. He hated the very mention of religion. He answered all appeals very coarsely. But one of his neighbours felt forced to go to him very early in the morning, and to say to him, "I beg your pardon for intruding so early, but I lay awake all last night thinking about you; and I cannot rest till I tell you something." He answered, "What were you thinking about me for? I don't want any of your thoughts." "Oh," said the other, "I felt so sorry to think that, if you were to die, you would die without hope, that I was obliged to come to you." The bearish man grumbled, "Mind your own business." "But," said the other, "it is my own business. I think my heart will break unless I see you saved." All the answer was, "Go away with you. Don't come here with your cant." The brother went home weeping; but he was not the only one who felt his heart breaking. The bearish one went away from his forge, and said to his wife, "I can always answer these religious fellows. I do not care for your parsons a bit; but that neighbour of ours has been in here, and he says he shall break his heart unless I am converted; *and that beats me.*"

"But," says one, "I know if I were to try to speak to any of my neighbours, I should break down." Friend, I am not careful in that matter, nor need you be. If you are in real earnest, you might possibly do more by a break-down than by anything else. Only break the ice, and begin; and you shall find my text to be true in your case also, and out of weakness you,

too, shall be made strong. Will you not yield your weakness
to him, and receive his strength?

Permit me to speak to some aspiring spirit and say—Dear
friend, would you like *to do something great for God*? Have
you heard the motto of our early missionaries: "Attempt great
things for God"? Does that thought burn within your heart?
Do you long to be of some use? "Oh, yes," says one, "I would
attempt great things for God, but I am terribly weak." If you
feel incapable, throw yourself upon the infinite capacity of
God. So long as you are willing to be used, so long as God
has given you an anxiety and travail of spirit for the souls of
others, you need not fear; but may with faith get to work in
all your feebleness, for as your day your strength shall be.

I would make one more application of my text, which is
capable of being used in a thousand directions. "Out of weakness were made strong:" this will be experienced *in bearing
witness for the truth of God*. Suppose that you are called to
testify for truth in the midst of those who doubt, disbelieve, or
even deride it. You look to those who agree with you, and
they are lukewarm; you turn to old associates, and they do
not share your concern. Friends tell you that you are making
much ado about nothing, or that you are uncharitable, narrow-
minded, and bigoted. I need not repeat the accusations ; they
have been so often hurled at myself that I know them by
heart. They say, "The man was born too late; he is behind
the age; he fights for a worn-out creed; he is out of place in
a world of progress." What then? Is there anything galling
to you in all this? Indeed there is, unless faith is strong ; and
then the bullets turn to pellets, and the stones are soft as
sponges. When they talk to you like that, do not begin bristling
up, and declaring that, after all, you are as wise and as strong
as your opponents though that may readily be the case ; but
accept all their remarks upon your folly and weakness, and
say to yourself, "Out of weakness were made strong." Hold
you to God's Word by faith, and you will be strong. God will
vindicate his own cause; but it may be his way to let error
prevail for a while. Bide your time when the cause is an eternal
one, for you can afford to do so.

In the conflict with evil, we would overcome it early, and
put it to the rout at the first attack ; but it may be that God

will allow error to proceed further, and let it seem to triumph, so that by its own presumption it may place itself where it may be the more effectually crushed, never again to afflict the Church. It is for us in our weakness to go forward as the Lord leads us; and the day of the resounding timbrels and the twinkling feet will come in due time, and Jehovah will be magnified when even humble maidens "sing unto the Lord, for he hath triumphed gloriously." Be steadfast, unmovable. Never mind the craft, policy, and number of the foe. God's time is best. He knows better than we do when to strike for victory.

Now, suffer me a few words upon the other cheering fact, namely, that FAITH MAKES MEN STRONG FOR PATIENT SUFFERING. The patience of hope is a very important part of Christian life, and faith is the essence of it.

Many are called to suffer much *in daily life*. Ah me! what a world of misery there is in this great city, among even good and gracious people! A man might study London till he turned his brain. The poverty and the suffering of even godly people in London would be a subject too harrowing for those of you who have specially tender hearts. Let us not forget those members of Christ's mystical body that are in the fire: "his feet are like unto fine brass, as if they burned in a furnace." Few, if any, are without sorrow, and many saints have a double portion of grief in their pilgrimage. I may be addressing those whose life is one protracted struggle for existence. Assuredly, you will not hold out without true faith, and much of it. You must endure, "as seeing him who is invisible." Earthly comforts are not yours; but if you grasp the spiritual and the eternal you will not repine. If in this life only you had hope, you would be of all men most miserable; but having that hope, you are among men most happy. Commend me to firm faith for power to bear the daily cross. Trust thou in thy God, in his love to thee, in his care of thee, and then thou shalt be as the lilies, which toil not, and spin not, and yet are clothed; or as the ravens, which have no store, and yet are fed.

Certain saintly ones are called to bear *great physical pain,* and I commend to them, from practical experience, the power of faith in God under acute agony. This is the sweetest support in the presence of a threatened operation. How grim those surgeon's lancets seem! Ah me! I knew a patient once—I know her still—who, when the lancets had been used upon her, caused the doctor's case of instruments to be filled up with roses! God alone can help you to fill up with roses that grim memory of danger and suffering. Oh, how sweet to feel that, if God has sent diseases to your house, he has made them a chariot in which benedictions have been brought to you! Go not to wine for comfort in the hour of depression. Above all things, dread the intoxicating cup in all its forms. You need not even appeal to friends for consolation. What do they know about your inward sorrow? There are seas of suffering which the sufferer must navigate alone. He knows thy poor body, and he permits it to be frail, and permits thy heart to be trembling, because he will glorify himself in his tenderness to thy weakness, wherein he will make thee strong. JEHOVAH ROPHI is his name: "The Lord that healeth thee."

But there are other forms of suffering than these of daily life and of bodily pain. Possibly I speak to some who are suffering the evils of *persecution*. No cruel tyrant can burn believers now, nor even cast them into prison for Christ's sake; but there are ways enough for the seed of the serpent to show its enmity to the seed of the woman. "Trials of cruel mockings" are common yet. There are many ways in which the devil's whip can reach the back of the child of God. Persecution is still abundant, and many a man's foes are of his own household. I will rehearse no stories of Christian women with jeering husbands, nor of godly youths who endure scoffing, and far worse; but many a house is still a place of martyrdom. Gracious sufferers, may the Lord keep you from anger and unkindness! By faith alone can you bear persecution, and turn it to account for the good of others. Do not attempt to escape by yielding what is right and true; but ask the Lord to help you to stand fast for him. If it be true that the Lord has his martyrs still, let it be seen that they are as brave as ever.

Not now do they gather in the great amphitheatre, where sits the emperor in state, with all the proud citizens of Rome in the nearer gallery, tier on tier, and the multitude up yonder, gazing with their cruel eyes into the vast arena below. Not now do I see them lift up the great iron door, and let loose the monsters that come forth roaring, hungry for their prey. Not now do I see, standing in the middle, a man and his wife and

children, all unarmed. Not now do I hear the shouts of the
mob, as they exult that Christians are given to the lions. This
is all over. Christ, in his suffering members, has conquered
Cæsar and pagan Rome; for out of weakness believers were
made strong. A softer spirit has come over the human mind;
but there is as much enmity against God as ever; and now it
finds a less public arena, and a meaner mode of torture.
To-day, the tried one suffers alone, and misses the encouragement of Christian eyes. Have faith in God in your hidden
sorrow! Cry to him in the secret of your soul, and you will
bear your load. Of your secret martyrdom angels will be
spectators, and Christ will suffer in you—wherefore, fear not.

We have among us those who are not exposed to persecution,
but have to stand against *assaults of unbelief*. That which
believers in past ages have accepted as truth, is not believed
in many places nowadays; and so it comes to pass that one
brings to us a bit of sceptical science which he has picked
up from Huxley or Tyndall; another comes with a criticism
that he has found in some of the modern divines, who are the
devil's instruments for spreading infidelity; and a third appears
with a vile blasphemy from one of the coarser assailants of
religion, and each one demands an immediate answer to his
quibble, or his difficulty. Do they really expect that we are
to answer, on the spur of the moment, every objection that
they are pleased to raise? Do not try to answer cavillers; but
if you do, mind that faith is your weapon. If you take the
wooden sword of your own reasoning, you may easily be
beaten. Believe for yourself, because God has said it; and
speak as the Lord guides you. Fix it in your mind, "This is
God's Book. This is his infallible revelation, and I believe it
against every argument that can possibly be urged against it.
Let God be true, but every man a liar." For an offensive
weapon, take "the sword of the Spirit, which is the word of
God"; and if this does not serve your turn, nothing will.

Again, it may be that I am speaking to sad ones who suffer
under *mental depression*. Some of us are by constitution inclined to that condition. I have sometimes envied those good
people who are never excited with joy, and consequently
seldom or never despond. "Along the cool, sequestered vale
of life they hold the even tenor of their way." Happy people!

At the same time, when I rise, as upon eagle's wings, in joyous rapture, I feel right glad to be capable of the blissful excitement. Yet if you soar to the skies, you are very apt to drop below the sea-level. He that can fly, can faint. Elijah, after he had slain the prophets of Baal, was found fleeing into the wilderness from the face of Jezebel. If you are so constituted that you rise and fall; if you are a creature that can be excited, and that can be depressed; and, worse still, if you happen to have been born on a foggy day, and to have swallowed so much of that fog that you have found it shading your spirit many a time ever since; then you can only be strong by faith. If you are never mirthful, and seldom able to call yourself joyful—the only cure for depression is faith. Settle this in your heart: "Whether I am up or down, the Lord Jesus Christ is the same. Whether I sing, or whether I sigh, the promise is true, and the Promiser is faithful. Whether I stand on Tabor's summit, or am hidden in the vale of Baca, the covenant standeth fast, and everlasting love abideth." Believe in the Lord Jesus, though you see no flashes of delight nor sparkles of joy.

It may be that certain of you are called to suffer in your minds, not because of any wrong thing in yourselves, but *for the sake of others*. Some years ago, I preached a sermon to you from the text, "My God, my God, why hast thou forsaken me?" and in a mournful degree I felt what I preached, as my own cry. I felt an agony of spirit, for I was under an awful sense of being forsaken of God, and yet I could not understand why I was surrounded by such thick darkness. I wished to clear myself if any sin remained upon me, but I could not discover any evil which I was tolerating. When I went back into the vestry, I learned the secret of my personal distress, for there was an elderly man in a horror of great darkness, who said to me, "I have never before met with any person who has been where I am. I trust there is hope for me." I bade him sit down, and I talked with him. I saw him afterwards, and I hope I conducted him from the verge of insanity into the open, healthy place of peace through believing. I fear I should never have touched his case if I had not been in the miry clay myself. Then I understood why I must feel like one forsaken. The Lord was leading me where I should be taught to know my man, and should be made willing to sit side by side with him in the dark prison-house, and lend him a hand to escape. Since then, in presenting myself to my Lord for service, I have said to him, "Make me useful to the doubting and the feeble-minded. I do not bargain for comfort, and peace, and joy, if I can be more helpful to thy poor, weary children without them. Place me where I can best answer thy purpose by being made to sympathize with thy troubled people. I only want to bring them to heaven, to the praise of the glory of thy grace ; and as for me, let me rejoice or suffer, as best suits their case." For this a man must have faith in God ; and he must be sure that his trials, endured through his office, will have great recompense of reward. If you are chosen to be a leader and a helper, or a mother in Israel, be satisfied to endure hardness with the full belief that it is all right, and that God will not only bring you through, but will also bless somebody else by the means of your tribulations.

If I should never again have the pleasure of speaking for my Lord upon the face of this earth, I should like to deliver, as my last confession of faith, this testimony—that nothing but faith can save old England: nothing but faith can save the present unbelieving Church: nothing but firm faith in the grand old doctrines of grace, and in the ever-living and unchanging God can bring back to the Church again a full tide of prosperity, and make her to be the deliverer of the nations for Christ: nothing but faith in the Lord Jesus can save you or me.

XV

LIGHT AT EVENING TIME

"And it shall come to pass in that day, that the light shall
not be clear nor dark: But it shall be one day which shall be
known to the Lord, not day, nor night; but it shall come to
pass, that at evening time it shall be light."—Zech. 14 : 6, 7.

OUR text reveals to us in a remarkable manner the pene-
tration, the discernment, the clear-sightedness of God.
To our weak vision the current of human affairs is like twilight.
It is not altogether dark, for it is broken with some gleams of
hope. Nor is it altogether bright, for heavy masses of darkness
intervene. It is neither day nor night. There is a mingle-
mangle of good and evil, a strange confused mixture, wherein
the powers of darkness contend with the powers of light. But
it is not so with God. With him, it is one clear day. What we
think to be confusion, is order before his eye. Where we see
advance and retrogression, he sees perpetual progress. We full
often bemoan our circumstances as altogether disastrous, while
God, who seeth the end from the beginning, is working out his
ordained purpose. Our God maketh the clouds to be the dust
of his feet, and the winds to be his chariot. He sees order in the
tempest and the whirlwind.

"Things are not what they seem." Oh! how good it is for us
to know that this world's history is not so black and bad as to
our dim senses it would appear. God is writing it out, sometimes with a heavy pen; but when complete, it will read like
one great poem, magnificent in its plan, and perfect in all its
details. At the present hour there may be much in the condition
of our country to cause anxiety, or even to create alarm. And
it is not hard to point certainly to many things that seem to
augur no good. But there always were evil prophets. There
always have been times and crises when dark portents favoured
unwelcome predictions. But thus far the fury of every tempest
has been mitigated; a sweet calm has followed each perilous
swell of the ocean. We thank God that the history of our

deliverances supplies us with fair omens of an ever-gracious Providence. Then let each man brace up his sinews for the fight, and struggle for the right. Bright days are assuredly in store for those who lift the standard and unfurl the flag of righteousness and truth. "At evening time it shall be light."

I mean to confine your attention to one clause of the text, "At evening time it shall be light." It seems to be a rule in God's dispensations that his light should break upon men gradually; and when it appears about to suffer an eclipse it will brighten up and shine with extraordinary lustre. "At evening time it shall be light." Of this mode of God's procedure we will take five illustrations.

LET REVELATION SUPPLY US WITH THE FIRST.

When God first revealed himself to the sons of men, he did not come to them in a blazing chariot of fire, manifesting all his glorious attributes. The sun in the Tropics, we are told, rises on a sudden. The inhabitants of those regions know none of our delightful twilight at dawn or evening, but the curtain rises and falls abruptly. This is not the way in which God has revealed himself to us. By degrees, softly, slowly, he lifts the veil. Thus has God been pleased to make himself known. He took in his hand a flaming torch, when the world was dark, without a single ray of comfort, and he lit up the first star that ever shone over the wild waste of the world's wilderness. That star was the promise that the Seed of the woman should bruise the serpent's head. In the light of that promise our first parents and their immediate descendants were cheered in their daily toil. Seth and Enoch walked with no other light that we know of but that. There is no record of any promise beside, which they had received from the Lord. By-and-bye, as years revolved, God lit up another star, and then another and another, till at last Holy Scripture became like our sky at midnight—studded all over with greater and lesser luminaries, all brightly manifesting the glory of God.

Still it was night. Though there was a little light, there was a prevalence of darkness. All through the Jewish dispensation, the sun did not shine. There was only cold, but beauteous in its season, silver moonlight. Heavenly truths were reflected in shadows; the substance was not visible. It was an economy of cloud and smoke, of type and symbol, but not of light and day of life, and immortality. For all the light that "o'er the dark her silver mantle threw," the saints of those times were glad and grateful; but how much more cause for joy and gratitude have we on whom the golden sun has shone! Star after star had been lit up in the heavens by the inspiration of Moses, and Samuel, and David, and all the prophets, till dark and deep the night began to fall, till sable clouds gathered dense with direful auguries, and at length a wild tempest was heard thundering in the sky.

Isaiah had completed the long roll of his prophecy; Jeremiah had uttered all his lamentations. The eagle wing of Ezekiel soared no longer. Daniel had recorded his visions and entered into rest. Zechariah and Haggai had fulfilled their mission, and at last Malachi, foreseeing the day that should burn as an oven, and beyond it the day when the Sun of righteousness should arise with healing in his wings, closed that volume of testimony. That was midnight. The stars seemed to be dying out, like as withered fig-leaves fall from the tree. There was no open vision; the Word of God was scarce; there was a famine of the bread of life in those days. And what then? Why, you all know. At evening time it was light. He who had long been promised suddenly came into his temple, a light to lighten the Gentiles, and to be the glory of his people Israel. The world's darkest hour had come, when there was born in Bethlehem, of the house of David, Jesus, the King of the Jews, and the Saviour of men. Then the day dawned, and the day-spring from on high visited us, precisely at that darkest hour, when men said, "God has forsaken the world, and left it to pine away in everlasting gloom." Let that serve for a first illustration of light at evening time, notable as a fact, and worthy to be recollected.

This, too, is precisely the way in which God acts IN THE CONVERSION OF INDIVIDUALS.

God's laws on a great scale are always the same as his laws on a little scale. A pretty little rhyme, that many of you are familiar with, endorses this statement.

> "The very law that moulds a tear,
>   And bids it trickle from its source;
> That law preserves the world a sphere,
>   And guides the planets in their course."

The same law which controls a planet affects a grain of dust. As God caused revelation to arise gradually, and, growing clearer and clearer, to become clearest when it seemed about to expire, so in the experience of each individual, the dawn precedes the day. When the light of divine grace first visits a man, it shines with feeble beam. Man by nature is like a house shut up, the windows of which are all boarded over. Grace does not open every window at once and bid the sun stream in upon weak eyes accustomed to darkness. It rather takes down a part of a shutter at a time, removes some obstruction, and so lets in, through chinks, a little light, that one may be able to bear it by degrees. The window of man's soul is so thickly encrusted with dirt, so thoroughly begrimed, that no light at all can penetrate it, till one layer is taken off, and a little yellow light is seen; and then another is removed, and then another, still admitting more light, and clearer.

Was it not so with you who are now walking in the light of God's countenance? Did not your light come to you by little and little? Your experience, I know, confirms my statement, and as the light came, and you discovered your sin, and began to see the suitability of Christ to meet your case, you hoped that all was going on well. Then peradventure, on a sudden, the light seemed altogether to depart. You were cast into the thick darkness, into the Valley of the Shadow of Death, and you said, "Oh! now my lamp is put out for ever! I am cast out from God's presence! I am doomed beyond the hope of mercy! I shall be lost for ever and ever!" Well now, Christian, ask yourself what came of this? When you were thus broken, sore broken in the place of dragons, and your soul suffered the wreck of all its carnal confidences, what then? At that evening time the light shone clearer with you than it had ever before. When darkness veiled your mind, you looked to Christ, and were lightened with the true light. Despairing of yourself, you cast yourself into the arms of Christ, and you had that peace of God which passeth all understanding, and still keeps your heart and mind through Jesus Christ.

May be I am addressing some who have been for a long while the subjects of such humbling influences, breaking them down. You had hoped things were going pretty fairly with you, and you trusted that at the last you would come out into clear sunshine. But oh! how disappointed you feel! You never felt so wicked, never knew that you were so desperately rebellious. Your heart is hard and stubborn; you feel as if there was a mutiny in your breast. "Surely," you say, "such an one as I am never can be saved; it is a hopeless case." Oh! my brother, very hopeful to our view is that which appears so hopeless to you.

Are you emptied of all merit, goodness, and hope in yourselves? Then your redemption draweth nigh. When you are cleared out and turned upside down, then eternal mercy greets you. Trust Christ. If you cannot stand, give yourself up to him, and he will bear you as on eagle's wings. Give up *yourself*. There, let it die; it is the worst enemy you ever had. Though you relied upon it, it has been a delusion and a snare to you. Now, therefore, throw the whole weight and burden of your life of sin and folly upon Jesus Christ, the Sin-bearer, and this shall be the time of your deliverance, so the darkest hour you ever knew shall give place to the brightest you have ever experienced.

A third illustration may be found in THE DELIVERANCES WHICH A COVENANT GOD WORKS FOR AN AFFLICTED PEOPLE.

The same rule which we have already observed will hold good here—at evening time it shall be light. No child of God can be very long without trouble of some kind or other, for sure it is that the road to heaven will always be rough. Some visionaries have been talking of making a railroad to the Celestial City. With this view, they would fill up the Slough of Despond, run a tramway right through the middle of it, and construct a tunnel through the hill Difficulty. I would not advise any of you to be shareholders in the company, for it will never answer. It will bring thousands to the river of Death, and swamp them there, but at the gates of the Celestial City not a passenger will ever arrive by that route. There is a pilgrimage, and a weary pilgrimage too, which must be taken before you can obtain entrance into those gates. Still, in all their trials, God's people always find it true that at evening time it shall be light.

Are you suffering from temporal troubles? You cannot expect to be without these. They are hard to bear. This, however, should cheer you, that God is as much engaged to succour and support you in your temporal, as he is in your spiritual interests. Beloved, the very hairs of your head are all numbered. Not a sparrow falls on the ground without your Father knowing it. Well, now, taking quite *a material view of the question,* you are of more value than many sparrows. You may be very poor, yet be very, very dear to your Father in heaven. Your poverty may reduce you to the utmost pinch, but that will be the time of your sweetest relief. The widow woman at the gates of Zarepta could hardly have been more wretched than when she had gone out to gather a few sticks—she says two—enough, I suppose, to cook the handful of meal and the few drops of oil, with which to make the last morsel for herself and for her son. Aye, poor soul! At that very moment the prophet of God came in—not while there was much meal or much oil, but just as they were all spent. He came to tell her that the barrel of meal should not waste, nor the cruse of oil fail, till the Lord sent rain, and famine ceased in the land.

God's people in Egypt were not brought out until the rigour of their bondage had become too bitter to bear. When it was intolerable, the Lord redeemed them with a strong arm and a high hand. You may be so tried that you think nobody ever had such a trial. Well, then, your faith may look out for such a deliverance as nobody else ever experienced. If you have an excess of grief, you shall have the more abundant relief. If you have been alone in sorrow, you shall, by-and-bye, have a joy unspeakable, with which no stranger can intermeddle. You shall lead the song of praise, as chief musicians, whose wailings were most bitter in the abodes of woe. Do cast your burden on God. Let me beseech those of you who love him, not to be shy of him. Disclose to him your temporal griefs. For you, young people, you remember I have just prayed that you might early in life learn to cast your burden upon God. Your trials and troubles, while you are at home under your father's roof, are not so heavy as those that will come when you begin to shift for yourselves. Still, you may think them heavier, because your older friends make light of them. Well, while you yet remain at the home of your childhood, acquire the habit of carrying your daily troubles and griefs to God. Whisper them into your Heavenly Father's ear, and he will help you.

And why should you men of business try to weather the storm without your God? 'Tis well to have *industry, shrewdness,* and what is called *self-reliance*—a disposition to meet difficulties with determination, not with despondency:

> *"To take arms against a sea of troubles,*
> *And by opposing end them."*

Still, the only safe, the only happy course for merchant or tradesman is to commit his way unto God, with a simple, child-like faith, taking counsel at the Scriptures, and seeking guidance in prayer. You will find it to be a blessed way of passing through the ordinary routine of daily anxieties, and the extraordinary pressure of occasional alarms and panics, if you can but realise your sacred privileges as disciples of Christ in the midst of all your secular duties.

Or are our trials of a *spiritual character*? Here full often our trials abound, and here, too, we may expect that at evening time it shall be light. Perhaps some of you pursue the road to heaven with very few soul-conflicts. Certainly there are some who do not often get through a week without being troubled on every side—fighting without, and fears within. Ah! brethren, when some of you tell me of your doubts and fears, I can well sympathise with you, if I cannot succour you. Is there anywhere a soul more vexed with doubts, and fears, and soul-conflicts than mine? I know not one. With heights of joy in serving my Master, I am happily familiar, but into very depths of despair—such an inward sinking as I cannot describe—I have likewise sunk. A more frequent, or a more fearful wretchedness of heart than I have suffered it is not likely any of you ever felt. Yet do I know that my Redeemer liveth, that the battle is sure, that the victory is safe.

If my testimony be worth aught, I have always found that when I am most distressed about circumstances that I cannot control, when my hope seems to flicker where it ought to flare, when the worthlessness and wretchedness of my nature obscure the evidences of any goodness and virtue imparted to me or wrought in me, just then it is that a sweet spring of cool consolation bubbles up to quench my thirst, and a sweet voice greets my ear, "It is I; be not afraid." My witness is for the Master, that, though he may leave us for a little, it is not for long. "For a small moment have I forsaken thee, but with great mercy have I gathered thee; in a little wrath I hid my face from thee for a moment, but with everlasting mercy will I have pity upon thee, saith the Lord, thy Redeemer." Oh! believer, stay yourself upon God when you have nothing else to stay upon. Do not rely upon appearances; above all, do not listen to the suggestions of a murmuring, hardened spirit; do not credit the insinuations of the infernal fiend who, when he finds you downhearted, be it from sickness of body or anxiety of mind, is sure then to whisper some disparaging thoughts of God. What though the suggestion strikes your heart that the Lord has forsaken you, that your sins cannot be forgiven, that you will fall by the hand of the enemy, hurl it back. You know whence it came.

Depend upon it, though heaven and earth go to wreck, God's promise will stand. Should hell break loose, and demons innumerable invade this earth, they shall not go one inch beyond their tether. The chain that God has cast about them shall restrain them. Not an heir of heaven shall be left to the clutches of the destroyer. Nay, his head shall not lose a hair without divine permission. You shall come out of the furnace with not a smell of fire upon you.

And now may I not appeal for a fourth illustration of the same truth to some of our friends who have come to THE EVENING TIME OF HUMAN LIFE?

This is often a delightful time, when the shadows are drawn out, and the air is still, and there is a season of preparation for the last undressing, and of anticipation for the appearing before the King in his beauty. I envy some of our brethren, the more advanced saints. Although old age brings its infirmities and its sorrows, yet they have found that it brings with it the mellow joys of a matured experience, and a near prospect of the coming glory so near, so very near to their actual realisation.

John Bunyan's picture of the Land Beulah was no dream, though he calls it so. Some of our aged brethren and sisters have come to a place of very peaceful repose, where they do hear the songs of angels from the other side of the stream, and the bundles of myrrh from the mountains of Bethen they bear in their bosoms. I know you find that at evening time it is light to you, very light. You were called by grace when you were young. Bright was your day-dawn; a precious dew from the

Lord fell upon you in the morning. You have borne the burden and heat of the day. You feel like a child that has grown tired. You are ready to say, "Let us go to sleep, mother; let us go to sleep." But meanwhile, before you close your eyes you are conscious of such divine refreshment, of such love and such joy shed abroad in your hearts, that you find the last stage of the journey to be blessed indeed, waiting and watching for the trumpet-call that shall bid you come up higher. Your light is brighter now than ever it was before.

When you come at length to depart, though it will be "evening time" in very truth, it will be "light." You have watched the sun go down sometimes. How glorious he is at his setting! He looks twice as large as he did when he was high up in the sky, and if the clouds gather round him, how he tints them all with glory! Is there anything in all the world so magnificent as the setting sun, when all the colours of heaven seem poured out upon earth's sky? It does not fill you with gloom, for it is so radiant with glory. Such, now, shall your dying bed be. To those who watch you, you shall be an object of more sacred interest than ever you were before. If there be some pains that distress you, and some temptations that harass you, they shall be but the clouds which your Master's grace and your Saviour's presence shall gild with splendour. Oh! how light, how very light, it has been at evening time with some of our beloved friends! We have envied them as we have beheld the brightness .gleaming from their brows in their last expiring moments. Oh! their songs! You cannot sing like them. Oh! their notes of ecstasy! You cannot understand the bliss unspeakable, as though the spray of the waves of heaven dashed into their faces, as though the light of the unclouded land had begun to stream upon their visage, and they were transfigured upon their Tabor before they passed into their rest!

Never fear dying, beloved. Dying is the last, but the least, matter that a Christian has to be anxious about. Fear living— that is a hard battle to fight; a stern discipline to endure; a rough voyage to undergo. You may well invoke God's omnipotence to your aid. But to die, that is to end the strife, to finish your course, to enter the calm heaven. What a light, oh! what a transparent light it must be when the spirit immediately passes through the veil into the glory-land! In vain the fancy strives to paint the vision of angels and of disembodied spirits, and, above all, the brightness of the glory of Christ the Lamb in the midst of the throne! Oh! the joy of that first bowing before the Mercy-seat! Oh! the rapture of that first casting the crown at his feet who loved us and redeemed us! Oh! the transport of that first folding in Immanuel's bosom, that first kiss with the kisses of his mouth, face to face! Do you not long for it?

We seek our last illustration in the mysterious unfolding of destiny, for it is our firm belief that IN THE HISTORY OF THE WORLD AT LARGE this saying shall be verified, and it shall come to pass that "at evening time it shall be light."

Darkness has prevailed for a long time, nor does the prospect grow much brighter at present. The noble enterprise of our great missionary societies is not altogether unrequited. The prayers and efforts of a long succession of godly men are not to be accounted vain and fruitless, but we commonly feel more cause to lament than to exult. How little is the world lit up with the light of God yet! Are there more saved souls in the world now than there were a hundred years after Christ's death? I do not know that there are. A greater surface is covered with the profession of Christianity now, but at that time the light was bright where it did shine. I am afraid to say what I think of the gloom that is hanging in thick folds of cloud and scud, over the nations of the earth. Still the oracle cheers my heart, "At evening time it shall be light." Some men prophesy that it will not be so. Long ages of delay make them grow impatient. This impatience provokes questioning. Those questions invariably tend to unbelief. But who shall make void the promises of God? Are not nations to be born in a day? Will the wild Arab never bow before the King of Zion? Shall not Ethiopia stretch out her arms to God? As Children of the day, doth it not behove us to walk in the light of the Lord? Divine testimony has more weight with us than the conjectures of benighted men! Christ has bought this world, and he will have it in possession from the river even to the ends of the earth. He has redeemed it, and he will claim it for his own. You may rest assured that whatever is contained in the scroll of prophecy shall be fulfilled according to the determinate counsel and foreknowledge of God. Notwithstanding any difficulties you may have in interpreting the seals or the trumpets of the Apocalypse, you have no room to doubt that Jesus Christ will be acknowledged King of kings and Lord of lords over this whole world, and that in every corner and nook of it his name will be famous. To him every knee shall bow, and every tongue shall confess that he is Lord, to the glory of God the Father. Do not be troubled by seers or soothsayers. Rest patiently. "Of the times and seasons, brethren, ye have no need that I write unto you, for ye yourselves know perfectly that the day of the Lord so cometh as a thief in the night." As for you, your business is to work for the spreading of his kingdom, to be continually scattering the light you have, and praying for more; to be waiting upon God for more of the tongue of fire, for more of the baptism of the Eternal Spirit, for more vital quickening power. When the whole Church shall be wakened up to a spirit of earnestness and enterprise, the conversion of this world will be speedily accomplished; the idols will then be cast to the moles and the bats; anti-Christ shall sink like a millstone in the flood, and the glory of the Lord shall be revealed, and all flesh shall see it together, for the mouth of the Lord hath spoken it.

"At evening time it shall be light." Accept this as a prophecy. Believe it on the highest warranty. Hope for it with the liveliest anticipation. So may ye live to see it. And unto God shall be the praise, world without end.

XVI

SERMONS FROM SAINTLY DEATH-BEDS

"And when Jacob had made an end of commanding his sons, he gathered up his feet into the bed, and yielded up the ghost, and was gathered unto his people."—Gen. 49: 33.

JACOB did not yield up the ghost until he had delivered the last sentence of admonition and benediction to his twelve sons. He was immortal till his work was done. So long as God had another sentence to speak by him, death could not paralyse his tongue. Yet, after all, the strong man was bowed down, and he who had journeyed with unwearied foot full many a mile, was now obliged to gather up his feet into the bed to die. His life had been eventful in the highest degree, but that dread event now came upon him which is common to us all. He had deceived his blind father in his youth, but no craftiness of Jacob could deceive the grave. He had fled from Esau, his angry brother, but a swifter and surer foot was now in pursuit from which there was no escape. He had slept with a stone for his pillow, and had seen heaven opened, but he was to find that it was only to be entered by the ordinary gate. He had wrestled with the angel at the brook Jabbok, and he had prevailed: at this time he was to wrestle with an angel against whom there was no prevalence. He had dwelt in Canaan in tents, in the midst of enemies, and the Lord had said, "Touch not mine anointed, and do my prophets no harm," and therefore he had been secure in the midst of a thousand ills; but now he must fall by the hand of the last enemy, and feel the great avenger's sword. It was appointed to the patriarch to die as meaner men must do.

From the wording of the text, it appears very clearly that Israel did not dispute the irrevocable decree, nor did his soul murmur against it. He had long before learned that few and evil were his days, and now that they came to an end, he joyfully accepted their conclusion. He was not like a bullock dragged to the slaughter, but he gathered up his feet by a voluntary act of submission, and then, bowing his head, he yielded up the ghost; like a man weary with a long day's toil, he was glad to rest, and therefore most cheerfully he attended to the great Father's summons, and was peacefully gathered unto his people and his God.

As this is to be our lot by-and-by, we may contemplate in our meditations the departure of this mighty man, and ask that our death may be like his, that we also may finish our course with joy.

It is remarkable, my brethren, that the Holy Spirit has given us very few death-bed scenes in the book of God. We have very few in the Old Testament, fewer still in the New, and I take it that the reason may be, because the Holy Ghost would have us take more account of how we live than how we die, for life is the main business. He who learns to die daily while he lives, will find it no difficulty to breathe out his soul for the last time into the hands of his faithful Creator. If we fight well the battle, we may rest assured of the victory. If, enlisted under the banner of truth, resting in Jesus Christ, we finish our fight and keep the faith, we need not fear but that our entering into rest will be a blessed one.

Peradventure, the Holy Spirit would also show us that it is not so much to our profit to have our feelings harrowed by recitals of dying experiences. Certain preachers in their sermons are very fond of extorting tears from their hearers by dragging before them the funerals of friends, painting the death-bed scenes of parents, unwrapping the winding sheets of little infants, and exhibiting the skeletons of buried relatives. This may be of some avail: preachers may have used these scenes to work through the natural affections to something deeper; but this is not the way the Holy Spirit has selected. If the teachers of the Gospel will study the Holy Spirit's model, they will learn that we are to strike at conscience rather than at the natural affections, and teach men holy principles rather than remind them of their sorrows. From the great reticence of the Holy Spirit in this matter, I learn that he would not have us be abundant to superfluity in such things.

It may be suggested that the Holy Ghost has given us few of these death-bed scenes on paper, because being present with us, he presents them to us frequently in actual flesh and blood, visible to our eyes and audible to our ears. We are to look upon the presence of the Holy Spirit in the witness of dying men, as in some sense the continuance of the Holy Spirit's instructive authorship. He has finished yonder book written with paper and ink, but he is writing fresh stanzas to the glory of God in the deaths of departing saints, who one by one are taken from the evil to come singing the Lord's praises as they depart.

First, THE DEPARTURES OF GOD'S SAINTS, AND ESPECIALLY OF HIS MINISTERS—WHAT ARE THEIR LESSONS?

The first that lies upon the surface, is this, *"Be ye also ready: for in such an hour as ye think not the Son of man cometh."* When in the forest there is heard the crash of a falling oak, it is a sign that the woodman is abroad, and every tree in the whole company may tremble lest soon the sharp edge of the axe should find it out. We are all mortal, and the death of one should remind us that death lurks hard by us all. I trust we do not, by often hearing of death, become callous to it. In the old wars of the Danish kings, there is a legend that, when Harold was contending with his brother Harequin, an arrow was seen flying in the air, quivering as if it scarcely knew its way, and was searching for its victim; then on a sudden it pierced the leader's forehead. A little imagination may picture us as being in the same position as the Danish lordling: the arrow of death is flying for awhile above us, but its descent is sure and its wound is fatal. It ill behoves us to laugh and sport while life hangs on a thread. He who does not prepare for death is more than an ordinary fool, he is a madman. When the voice of God is calling to us through the departures of others, if we do not listen to the warning, we may expect him to follow the rejected word of counsel with a blow of wrath; for he often strikes down right terribly those who would not listen to his reproving messages. Be ready, minister, see to it that thy church be in good order, for the grave shall soon be digged for thee; be ready, parent, see that your children are brought up in the fear of God, for they must soon be orphans; be ready, men of business, you that are busy in the world, see that your affairs are correct, see that you serve God with all your heart, for the days of your terrestrial service will soon be ended, and you will be called to give account for the deeds done in the body, whether they be good or whether they be evil. O may we all prepare for the tribunal of the great King with a care which shall be rewarded with the commendation, "Well done, good and faithful servant."

Secondly, *the deaths of righteous men should teach us their value.* According to the old saying, we never know the value of things till we lose them. I am sure it is so with holy men. Let me urge young people here to prize their aged godly parents, to treat them kindly, to make their last days happy, because they cannot expect to have them long on earth to receive their tokens of affectionate gratitude. Those who have Christian parents, little know how great is the privilege they enjoy until they become parents themselves, and learn the cares and sorrows of the mother's office and the father's state. Are any of you favoured with friends who have given you instruction in faith, whose goodly words and holy examples have helped you on the way to heaven? Thank God much for such good company; be much with them, treasure up the pearls which drop from their lips. They must soon be gone, value them to-day as you will do when they are departed.

Are you privileged with an earnest, faithful ministry? Do you hear the Gospel lovingly and honestly proclaimed? Then bless God every day of your life for that faithful ministry. All ministry is not such—all people are not in such a case. Be grateful, then, and show your gratitude by giving earnest heed to the things that are spoken, lest by any means you should let them slip, and so should miss the great salvation through want of earnestness. I do beseech you, value the Christian ministry. I ask no honour for men, but I do ask honour for the office which Paul said he would magnify; and wherever you see that God has sent an ambassador, and that his ambassador is praying you in Christ's stead to be reconciled to God, turn not away from his entreaties, close not your ear to his persuasions, but honour the man's office, pay homage to the King who sent him, by yielding up your heart in obedience to the word which is delivered to you.

Furthermore, I think the departures of great saints and those who have been eminent, teach *us to pray earnestly to God to send us more of such*—a lesson which, I am quite certain, needs to be inculcated often. There is sadly little prayer in the church for the rising ministry. You pray for those who are your pastors, and rightly so. "Brethren, pray for us," you cannot do us a better favour. But there is so little prayer that God would raise up ministers! Know ye not that, as surely as the blood of Christ bought the redemption of his people, as surely as the resurrection of Christ was for the justification of the saints, so surely the ascension of Christ was for the distribution of ministry among the sons of men? Know ye not the passage, "He ascended up on high, he led captivity captive, and gave gifts unto men . . . and he gave [these were the gifts] some, apostles; and some, prophets; and some, evangelists; and some, pastors and teachers"?

Now, you plead the precious blood when you would obtain pardon; you plead the resurrection, and you receive justification; but how seldom do you plead the ascension, so as to obtain a faithful ministry! Parts of Christendom are becoming terribly deficient in ministry. "Lord, send forth labourers into the harvest." I see a dreadful lethargy in the hearts of many of God's people as to the work of praying for preachers, and assisting in training them. In olden times, if any men showed the slightest ability in speech, the saints sought such out and tried to instruct them, as Aquila and Priscilla; when they found Apollos a man eloquent and mighty in the Scriptures, they took him and instructed him further; and Paul, when he saw that Timothy was an apt scholar, instructed him further in the faith; while our blessed Lord not only preached the Gospel, but founded a college in which he had twelve students (and more than that), who constantly went about with him, learning from his example and ministry how themselves to become teachers of others. But now, forsooth, there are wiseacres who talk about "man-made ministers," and depise all attempts to assist our youth to become qualified in the testimony of the truth. The Lord teach them reason and give them common sense, but let no Christian give one single particle of heeding to their prattling. Let it be our earnest endeavour, both by prayer and every other means, to seek to obtain from God a succession of earnest, faithful, qualified ministers, for, say what you will, it is upon the ministry that God shall send you that much of the success of the Church must depend.

Those sects which pretend to do without a special ministry

(for it is usually a transparent pretence), may prosper for a little while: their setting up every disciple to be a teacher suits the natural pride of the human heart, and Christian men, being grossly deceived, yield to it for a little while, but I wot that not one single one of these communities can endure throughout a generation in vigorous existence. With a spasm of excitement, and a flush of zeal, they grow awhile, and then they dwindle away to nothing, or divide into little knots, each one agreed in hating the other most fervently. What is everybody's business is nobody's business; and since there is no man set to see after souls, no man does see after them; and the flock become scattered for want of a shepherd, who, in God's hand, might have kept them together. Faithful servants of the living God, as ye prize the Church and its ordinances, strive with God that as he takes one by one of his servants away, he would send us others, that the Church may never lack her standard-bearers, and the flock of God never be destitute of pastors after God's own heart. Pray ye seven times each day that God may keep alive the name and glory of Christ in the land by faithful teachers of the truth.

Yet there is a valuable truth on the other side. We desire always to look at both sides of a question. *The taking away of eminent saints from among us should teach us to depend more upon God, and less upon human instrumentality.* I was reading, yesterday, the dying prayer of Oliver Cromwell, and one sentence in that man of God's last breathings pleased me exceedingly. It was to this effect, I think, I have copied out the words, "Teach those who look too much on thy instruments to depend more upon thyself." Brave old Oliver was a man upon whom the whole nation rested; he could say with David, "The earth and all the inhabitants thereof are dissolved: I bear up the pillars of it." In a time of terrible anarchy, when men had become fierce with fanatical prophesyings, and wild with political passions, Oliver Cromwell's iron hand restored peace, and kept a tumultuous land in order; and now, when he would be worst missed, and could very ill be spared, he must depart, and this is his prayer, "Teach them to depend less upon thy instrument, and more upon thyself." You may have observed that frequently when a man is in the zenith of his power, and people have said, "That is the man who of all others we could least afford to lose," that very man has been taken away, that special light has been quenched, that particular pillar has been removed. The Lord would have all the glory given unto his own name. He will honour and bless an instrumentality, for that is his mode of working, but he will not divide the crown with the most honoured agency, he will have all the glory redound unto himself; and by frequently breaking up his battle axes and weapons of war, he teaches his Church that he can fight with his own bare arm, and win the victory to himself without an instrument of warfare.

Coming back, however, to the old thought, do you not think that the departure of eminent saints should teach *each one of us to work with more earnestness and perseverance while we are spared?* One soldier the less in the battle, my brethren: then you must fill up the vacancy; you who stand next in the ranks must close up, shoulder to shoulder, that there be no gap. Here is one servant the less in the house: the other servants must do the more work. It is but natural for us so to argue, because we wish the Master's work to be done, and it will not be done without hands. If *we* do not preach the Gospel, angels will not preach it. If *we* do not win souls for God, we must not expect cherubim and seraphim to engage in this divine employment. Somebody must do it, and, since we would have all done that can be done, you and I must do the more when helpers are removed. If there be fewer labourers, we must ask the Master to give those labourers the more strength, that the work may still be done, and nothing be marred for want of effort.

I have sought before the Lord that he would teach me to live an active, earnest, laborious, heavenly life. Very few of us understand what *life* is. Baxter at Kidderminster, from morning to night spending and being spent for the Master's service: Whitefield, all over England and America, toiling and labouring without the thought of rest, instant in season and out of season: these are the men we should emulate. But, alas! we do a little, and then we fold our hands, with ridiculous self-satisfaction. Now and then we arouse ourselves to something like zeal, and then we fall back into a state of carelessness.

Come with me to the second part of my discourse. Much may be learned from the MODES OF DEPARTURE of God's servants.

All believers fall asleep in Jesus, and in him they are all saved; the precious blood hath washed them, the hand of Christ keeps them, the earnest of the Spirit is with them, and the ever-lasting gates are opened to receive them; but unto them all there is not ministered the same abundant entrance in the kingdom, neither do all their faces shine with those gleams of glory which rest upon the highly favoured. To some of God's own children the dying bed is *a Bochim*, a place of weeping. It is melancholy when such is the case, and yet it is often so with those who have been negligent servants: they are saved, but so as by fire: they struggle into the port of peace, but their entrance is like that of a weather-beaten vessel which has barely escaped the storm, and enters into harbour so terribly leaking as to be ready to founder, without her cargo, for she has thrown that overboard to escape the waves, sails rent to ribands, masts gone by the board, barely able to keep afloat. Thousands enter into glory as Paul and his companions in peril landed at Melita, some on boards, and some on broken pieces of the ship; all come safe to land, but it is as it were by the skin of their teeth. In the dying beds of some believers that text is sadly illustrated, "If the righteous scarcely be saved." We have known them lying on the brink of eternity, bemoaning themselves after this fashion: "God has forgiven me, but how can I forgive myself? I am saved; but, oh! that I had made a profession of religion more plainly and boldly! Would God that I had not been so dilatory in serving my Master! I have prayed so little, given so little, done so little, I am a most unprofitable servant. Woe is me, for I have been busy here and there, and have forgotten my life's work; I have made money, but have won no jewels for Christ; I have taken care of my family, but alas! I have done next to nothing for the cause of Christ. I shall have no means of serving the cause of God when I enter heaven; I cannot then succour the poor, feed the hungry, or clothe the naked, or send the gospel to the ignorant. I might have done much when I was in health and strength, but now I can do little or nothing, for I am weak, and languishing upon this bed. Would to God that my Sabbaths had profited me more, and that I had walked more in nearness to God." Such dolorous heart-breaking confessions have we heard, varied occasionally by the lament, "Would to God I had brought up my children better, for now I am obliged to say with David, 'My house is not so with God,' though I know that he hath made with me an everlasting covenant, ordered in all things and sure." Many a dying pillow has been wet with the penitential tears of saints.

Brethren, it is beautiful to see the repentance of a dying saint: travel far as you may, you will not readily behold a more comely spectacle. I have seen it, and have breathed the prayer, "Lord, give me a humble and contrite spirit, like that which I see before me, and help me now to feel the like brokenness of heart." Yet at the sight of such instances it has struck me that the fruit though precious was scarcely seasonable: it must be acceptable to God, for he never rejects repentance anywhere, but yet a brighter state of soul would have glorified him more in dying moments. We are glad to see contrition anywhere, because it is evermore a lovely work of the Spirit; but we should have preferred to see it sooner, when regrets would not have been unavailing, when the repentance would have brought forth practical fruit in a change of life. I say, thank God if there be a deep repentance on the dying bed, but this is not the highest or best thing: to enter into life halt or maimed is not the grandest or most comely mode of departing out of this life into another. To die in the dark with Jesus is safe, but to have light at the last is better.

It has not unfrequently occurred that the dying scene has been to the Lord's departing champions a *battle*, not perhaps by reason of any slips or shortcomings—far from it, for in some cases the conflict appeared to arise by very reason of their valour in the Lord's service. Who among us would assert that Martin Luther failed to live up to the light and knowledge which he had received? So far as he knew the truth, I believe he most diligently followed it; beyond most men he was true to conscience, he knew comparatively little of the truth, but what he did know he maintained with all his heart, and soul, and strength; and yet it is exceedingly painful to read the record of Luther's last few days. Darkness was round about him, thick clouds and tempest enveloped his soul. At the last the sky cleared, but it is very evident that, among all the grim battles in which that mighty German fought and conquered, probably the most tremendous conflict of his life was at its close. Can we not guess the reason? Was it not because the devil knew him to be his worst enemy then upon the earth, and therefore hating him with the utmost power of infernal hate, and feeling that this was his last opportunity for assaulting him, he gathered up all his diabolical powers, and came in against him like a flood, thinking that mayhap he might at the last overcome the stout heart, and cow the valiant spirit! Only by divine assistance did Luther win the victory, but win it he did.

Is this form of departure to be altogether deprecated? I think not. It is to be dreaded in some aspects, though not in others, for is it not a noble thing for the knight of the cross to die in harness? a blessed thing for the Christian soldier to proceed at once from the battle field to his eternal rest? The like was the case with John Knox, the Scottish Luther, whose bold spirit feared the face of no man; he was beset with a temptation which seemed a strange one to trouble *him,* namely, a temptation to self-righteousness. He had always denounced all trust in works, and yet that error assaulted him at last, and he had a long and bitter conflict, though it ended in joyful victory. It has been quaintly said that, "Sometimes God puts his children to bed in the dark." When our heavenly Father sends the rider upon the pale horse to fetch us home from the school of this life's tribulation, he comes riding down the street making such a clangour with his horse hoofs that we are alarmed, until we come to know that he is sent by our Father, and then we are glad. God permits the Jordan to overflow its banks when some of his best children are passing through, for he designs to magnify his grace in the last trial of their faith, and thus to show to men, and angels, and devils, who are looking on, how he can triumph in his servants when flesh and heart are failing.

Beloved, I think these instances are rare compared with others which I am now to mention. To many saints their departure has been a peaceful entrance into the fair haven of repose. The very weakest of God's servants have frequently been happiest in their departing moments. John Bunyan, who had observed this fact, in the description of Mr. Feeble-mind's passage of the river, "Here also I took notice of what was very remarkable; the water of that river was lower at this time than ever I saw it all my life. So he went over at last not much above wet-shod." Heaven's mercy tempers the wind to the shorn lamb, and gives to babes no battle, because they have no strength for it: the lambs calmly rest on the bosom of Jesus, and breathe out their lives in the Shepherd's arms. What encouragement this ought to be to you who are the tender ones among us! what cheering tidings for you who are weak in faith! Like Mr. Ready-to-halt, you shall cry, "Now, I shall have no more need of these crutches, since yonder are chariots and horses for me to ride on."

Many of the saints have gone farther than this, for their death-beds have been *pulpits*. Not to all of them was it so given, for Mr. Whitefield desired to bear a dying testimony for Christ, but did not do so, somebody remarking to him, "You have borne so many living testimonies to so many thousands, that your Master wants no dying testimony of you." If you have read Brainerd's Journal, what wonderful things he speaks of there, when all his last thoughts were delighfully fixed upon eternity and the world to come! Thus he wrote in his diary, "Oh! how sweet were the thoughts of death to me at this time! Oh! how I longed to be with Christ, to be employed in the glorious work of angels, and with an angel's freedom, vigour, and delight." At another time he wrote, "'Tis sweet to me to think of eternity; but oh! what shall I say to the eternity of the wicked! I cannot mention it or think of it. The thought is too dreadful!" His thoughts, however, were all taken up with the joyful eternity belonging to believers, into which he entered with holy triumph.

Then there was that dear man of God, Mr. Payson. His last expressions were weighty sermons. He says, "I suppose, speaking within bounds, I have suffered twenty times as much as any martyr that was ever burnt at the stake, through the painfulness of my disease, and yet frequently, day after day, my joy in God has so abounded as to render my sufferings not only tolerable but welcome." When Matthew Henry was dying, Mr. Illidge came to him, and he said, "You have been used to take notice of the sayings of dying men: this is mine, 'A life spent in the service of God and in communion with him, is the most pleasant life that any one can live in the world.'" Well spoken! Our pulpits often lack force and power; men suppose that we speak but out of form and custom, but they do not suspect dying men of hypocrisy, nor think that they are driving a trade and following a profession. Hence the witness of dying saints has often become powerful to those who have stood around their couch: careless hearts have been impressed, slumbering consciences have been awakened, and children of God quickened to greater diligence by what they have heard.

Brethren, do you never find dying beds become *thrones of judgment*? Have you never seen the hoary saint stayed upon the pillows, prophesying like a seer concerning the things of this world and of the world to come? Have you never heard him deliver sentences as weighty as the verdict of a judge? "What," says he, "what are all these earthly things to me now, now that I am about to leave them? They are all bubbles and emptiness. Solomon in his life could not moralize with such force as holy men do in their deaths: and then, as they point the finger to eternity, and tell of worlds to come, and of the need of being prepared for the tremendous day of the great assize, they appear as if, clothed in their white raiment, they were performing a rehearsal of the last dread judgment. Many who care not for the voice of the ministry, nor even for the witness of God's written word, have felt the power of the speeches of men standing on the borders of eternity.

And brethren, we have known not unfrequent cases (nay, commonly this is the case), when the dying bed has become *a Pisgah*, from the top of which the saint has viewed his inheritance, while anon his couch has glowed on a sudden into the chariot of Amminadib, a flaming chariot such as that in which Elias was borne away to dwell with God. Saints have frequently been in such triumphant conditions of mind, that rapture and ecstasy are the only fit words in which to describe their state. "If this be dying," said one, "it is worth while living for the mere sake of dying." Dr. Payson, in his dying hours, wrote to his sister, "Were I to adopt the figurative language of Bunyan, I should date this letter from the land of Beulah, of which I have been for some weeks a happy inhabitant. The celestial city is full in my view. Its glories beam upon me, its odours are wafted to me, its sounds strike upon my ears, and its spirit is breathed into my heart. Nothing separates me from it but the river of death, which now appears but as an insignificant rill, that may be crossed at a single step, whenever God shall give permission. The Sun of Righteousness has gradually been drawing nearer and nearer, appearing larger and brighter as he approached; and now he fills the whole hemisphere, pouring forth a flood of glory, in which I seem to float as an insect in the beams of the sun; exulting, yet almost trembling, while I gaze on this excessive brightness, and wondering, with unutterable wonder, that God should deign thus to shine upon a sinful worm. A single heart and a single tongue seem altogether inadequate to my wants: I want a whole heart for every separate emotion, and a whole tongue to express that emotion."

It has been sometimes said these excitements are produced by delirium or caused by drugs, yet there are multitudes of clear cases in which men have had no delirium, and have been altogether untouched by drugs, as in the case of Halyburton, who said, "I know that a great deal from a dying man will go for canting and raving; but I bless God, he has kept the judgment I had, that I have been able to reflect with composure on his dealings with me. *I am sober and composed, if ever I was so.* . . . You may believe a man venturing on eternity. I have weighed eternity this last night—I have looked on death as stripped of all things pleasant to nature; . . . and under the view of all these, I have found *that* in the way of God that gave satisfaction, a rational satisfaction, that makes me rejoice."

Halyburton, indeed, broke forth into such ecstatic expressions, that I fear to quote them, lest I should spoil them; among his words were these, "If ever I was distinct in my judgment and memory in my life, it is since he laid his hands upon me. My bones are riving through my skin, and yet all my bones are praising him. O death, where is thy sting? O grave, where is thy victory? . . . I am now a witness for Christ, and for the reality of religion. . . . I have peace in the midst of pain; and oh! how much of that I have had for a time past!—my peace has been like a river—not a discomposed thought. . . . Strange that this body is going away to corruption, and yet my intellectuals are so lively, that I cannot say there is the least alteration, the least decay of judgment or memory; such vigorous actings of my spirit towards God and things that are not seen." When drawing near his end, one remarked to him, "Blessed are they that die in the Lord." He replied, "When I fall so low that I cannot speak, I'll show you a sign of triumph if I am able." And when he could no longer speak, he lifted up his hands, clapped them as in token of victory, and in a little while departed to the land where the weary are at rest.

Oh, it is grand to die thus, to get heaven here below in fore-tastes; to partake of dainty dishes brought from off the tables of immortals, to stay our souls while lingering here! This shall be your portion, and this shall be my portion, if we be faithful unto death, continuing diligent in service. I have already told you, if we believe in Christ, we shall die safely, but we may not necessarily die in this triumph: this blessing is given to those who are faithful, earnest and diligent, a special reward which God reserveth to some men who, like Daniel, are greatly beloved, or who, like John, are indulged with special visions of the New Jerusalem, before entering upon the scene!

XVII

LIFE IN CHRIST

"Because I live, ye shall live also."—John 14: 19.

THIS world saw our Lord Jesus for a very little time, but now it seeth him no more. It only saw him with the outward eye and after a carnal sort, so that when the clouds received him and concealed him from bodily vision, this spiritually blind world lost sight of him altogether. Here and there, however, among the crowds of the sightless there were a few chosen men who had received spiritual sight; Christ had been light to them, he had opened their blind eyes, and they had seen him as the world had not seen him. In a high and full sense they could say, "We have seen the Lord," for they had in some degree perceived his Godhead, discerned his mission, and learned his spiritual character. Since spiritual sight does not depend upon the bodily presence of its object, those persons who had seen Jesus spiritually, saw him after he had gone out of the world unto the Father.

We who have the same sight still see him. Read carefully the words of the verse before us: "Yet a little while, and the world seeth me no more; but ye see me." It is a distinguishing mark of a true follower of Jesus that he sees his Lord and Master when he is not to be seen by the bodily eye; he sees him intelligently and spiritually; he knows his Lord, discerns his character, apprehends him by faith, gazes upon him with admiration, and looks to him for all he needs. Now, my brethren, remember that as our first sight of Christ brought us into spiritual life, for we looked unto him and were saved, so it is by the continuance of this spiritual sight of Christ that our spiritual life is consciously maintained. We lived by looking, we live still by looking. Faith is still the medium by which life comes to us from the life-giving Lord. Let us ever remember the intimate connection between faith and spiritual life. Faith

is the life-look. We must never think that we live by works,
by feelings, or by ceremonies. "The just shall live by faith."
We dare not preach to the ungodly sinner a way of obtaining
life by the works of the law, neither dare we hold up to the
most advanced believer a way of sustaining life by legal means.
We should in such a case expect to hear the Apostle's expostu-
lation, "Are ye so foolish? having begun in the Spirit, are ye
now made perfect by the flesh?" Our glorying is that our life
is not dependent on ourselves, but is safe in our Lord, as saith
the Apostle, "I am crucified with Christ: nevertheless I live;
yet not I, but Christ liveth in me: and the life which I now
live in the flesh I live by the faith of the Son of God, who loved
me, and gave himself for me." Because he lives, we live, and
shall live for ever. God grant that our eye may ever be clear
towards Jesus, our life.

First, we have LIFE here spoken of. We must not confound
this with existence. It were indeed to reduce a very rich text
to a poverty-stricken sentence if we read it, "Because I exist,
ye shall exist also." Before the disciples believed in Jesus they
existed, and altogether apart from him as their spiritual life
their existence would have been continued; it was something
far other and higher than immortal existence which our Lord
was here dealing with.

Life, what is it? We know practically, but we cannot tell
in words. We know it, however, to be a mystery of different
degrees. As all flesh is not the same flesh, so all life is not the
same life. There is the life of the vegetable, the cedar of
Lebanon, the hyssop on the wall. There is a considerable
advance when we come to animal life—the eagle or the ox.
Animal life moves in quite a different world from that in which
the plant vegetates—sensation, appetite, instinct, are things to
which plants are dead, though they may possess some imitation
of them, for one life mimics another. Animal life rises far above
the experience and apprehension of the flower of the field. Then
there is mental life, which we all of us possess, which introduces
us into quite another realm from that which is inhabited by
the mere beast. To judge, to foresee, to imagine, to invent, to
perform moral acts, are not these new functions which the
ox hath not? Now, let it be clear to you, that far above mental
life there is another form of life of which the mere carnal man

can form no more idea than the plant of the animal, or the animal of the poet. The carnal mind knoweth not spiritual things, because it has no spiritual capacities. As the beast cannot comprehend the pursuits of the philosopher, so the man who is but a natural man cannot comprehend the experience of the spiritually minded. Thus saith the Scripture: "The natural man receiveth not the things of the Spirit of God: for they are foolish unto him: neither can he know them, because they are spiritually discerned. But he that is spiritual judgeth all things, yet he himself is judged of no man." There is in believers a life which is not to be found in other men—nobler, diviner far; education cannot raise the natural man into it, neither can refinement reach it; for at its best, "that which is born of the flesh is flesh," and to all must the humbling truth be spoken, "Ye must be born again."

It is to be remarked concerning our life in Christ, that it is the removal of the penalty which fell upon our race for Adam's sin. "In the day that thou eatest thereof thou shalt surely die," was the Lord's threatening to our first parent, who was the representative of the race. He did eat of that fruit, and since God is true, and his word never fails, we may be sure of this, that in that selfsame day Adam died. It is true that he did not cease to exist, but that is quite another thing from dying. The threatening was not that he should ultimately die, but "In the day thou eatest thereof thou shalt surely die"; and it is beyond all doubt that the Lord kept his word to the letter. If the first threatening was not carried out we might take liberty to trifle with all others. Rest assured, then, that the threat was on the spot fulfilled. The spiritual life departed from Adam; he was no longer at one with God, no more able to live and breathe in the same sphere as the Lord. He fell from his first estate; he had need if he should enter into spiritual life to be born again, even as you and I must be. As he hides himself from his Maker, and utters vain excuses before his God, you see that he is dead to the life of God, dead in trespasses and sins.

We also, being heirs of wrath even as others, are through the fall dead, dead in trespasses and sins; and if ever we are to possess spiritual life, it must be said of us, "And you hath he quickened." We must be as "those that are alive from the dead." The world is the valley of dry bones, and grace raises the chosen into newness of life. The fall brought universal death, in the deep spiritual sense of that word, over all mankind; and Jesus delivers us from the consequences of the fall by implanting in us a spiritual life. By no other means can this death be removed: "He that believeth on the Son hath everlasting life: and he that believeth not the Son shall not see life; but the wrath of God abideth on him." The work of regeneration, in which the new life is implanted, effectually restores the ruin of the fall, for we are born again "not of corruptible seed, but of incorruptible, by the word of God, which liveth and abideth for ever."

But you remind me that still sin remains in us after we have received the divine life. I know it does, and it is called "the body of this death"; and this it is which the new life has to struggle with. There is a contention which rages within, between the power of the death in the first Adam, and the power of the life of the second Adam; but the heavenly life will ultimately overcome the deadly energy of sin. Even to-day our inner life groans after deliverance, but with its groan of "O wretched man that I am! who shall deliver me from the body of this death?" it mingles the thankful song, "I thank God through Jesus Christ our Lord."

This life is of a purely spiritual kind. We find analogies and resemblances of it in the common mental life, but they are only analogies, the spiritual life is far and high above the carnal life, and altogether out of sight of the fleshy mind. Scarce are there words in which it can be described. To know this life you must have it; it must pulsate within your own bosom, for no explanations of others can tell you what this life is; it is one of the secrets of the Lord. It would not be possible for us with the greatest skill to communicate to a horse any conception of what imagination is; neither could we by the most diligent use of words, communicate to carnal minds what it is to be joined unto the Lord so as to be one spirit. One thing we know of it, namely, that the spiritual life is intimately connected with the indwelling of the Holy Spirit in the soul. When he comes we are "born again from above," "born of the Spirit." While he works in us mightily our life is active and powerful; if he

withdraws his active operations our new life becomes faint and
sickly. Christ is our life, but he works in us through his Holy
Spirit, who dwelleth in us evermore.

Further, we know that this life very much consists in union
with God. "For to be carnally minded is death; but to be
spiritually minded is life and peace. Because the carnal mind
is enmity against God: for it is not subject to the law of God,
neither indeed can be. So then they that are in the flesh cannot please God." Death as to the body consists in the body
being separated from the soul; the death of the soul lies mainly
in the soul's being separated from its God. For the soul to be
in union with God is the soul's highest life; in his presence it
unfolds itself like an opening flower; away from him it pines,
and loses all its beauty and excellence, till it is as a thing
destroyed. The new life brings us near to God, makes us think
of him, makes us love him, and ultimately makes us like him.
It is in proportion as you get near to God that you enter into
the full enjoyment of life—that life which Jesus Christ gives
you, and which Jesus Christ preserves in you. "In his favour
is life." Psalm 30: 5. "The fear of the Lord is a fountain of
life." Prov. 14: 27. To turn to God is "repentance unto life."
To forget God is for a man to be "dead whilst he liveth." To
believe the witness of God is to possess the faith which over-
cometh the world.

This life within the soul bears fruit on earth in righteousness
and true holiness. It blooms with sweetest flowers of fellowship
with God below, and it is made perfect in the presence of God
in heaven. The life of glorified spirits above is but the life of
justified men here below; it is the same life, only it is delivered
from encumbrances, and has come to the fulness of its strength.
The life of heaven is in every believer even now. The moment
a sinner believes in Jesus he receives from God that selfsame
life which shall look down serenely upon the conflagration of
earth, and the passing away of these lower skies. Blessed is
that man who hath everlasting life, who is made a partaker of
the divine nature, who is born again from above, who is born
of God by a seed which remaineth in him, for he is the man
upon whom the second death hath no power, who shall enjoy
life eternal when the wicked go away into everlasting
punishment.

Thus much concerning this life. We have now to ask each of you whether you have received it. Have you been born, not of blood, nor of the will of the flesh, nor of the will of man, but of God? Was there a time with you when you passed from death unto life, or are you abiding in death? Have you the witness in yourself that you have been operated upon by a divinely spiritual power? Is there something in you which was not once there, not a faculty developed by education, but a life implanted by God himself? Do you feel an inward craving unknown to carnal minds, a longing desire which this world could neither excite nor gratify? Can you say, with the favoured apostle, "We know that the Son of God is come, and hath given us an understanding, that we may know him that is true, and we are in him that is true, even in his Son Jesus Christ. This is the true God, and eternal life."

Our second head treats of LIFE PRESERVED. "Because I live, ye shall live also." There stands the promise, "Ye shall live also." This heavenly life of yours which ye have received shall be preserved to you.

Concerning this sentence let me draw your attention, first of all, to its *fulness*: "Ye shall live." I think I see in that much more than lies upon the surface. Whatever is meant by living shall be ours. All the degree of life which is secured in the covenant of grace, believers shall have. Moreover, all your new nature shall live, shall thoroughly live, shall eternally live. By this word it is secured that the eternal life implanted at regeneration shall never die out. As our Lord said so shall it be. "Whosoever drinketh of the water that I shall give him shall never thirst; but the water that I shall give him shall be in him a well of water springing up into everlasting life." We may be tempted, but we shall not be so led astray as to cease to live in Christ. It may be that we shall decline in grace, a thousand sorrows that it should be so! but we shall not so decline as to become utter apostates, or sons of perdition. "He that is begotten of God keepeth himself, and that evil one touched him not." Thus said the Redeemer unto you, ye trembling children of God, "Ye shall live," ye shall never perish, neither shall any pluck you out of his hands. May I not view this precious word as referring to all the essential spiritual graces which make up the new man? Not even, in part, shall the new man die. "Ye shall live," applies to all the parts of our new-born nature. If there be any believer here who has not lived to the full extent he might have done, let him lay hold upon this promise; and seeing that it secures the preservation of all his new nature, let him have courage to seek a higher degree of health.

"I am come," said Christ, "that ye might have life, and have it more abundantly." There is no reason, Christian, why your love to Jesus should not become flaming, ardent, conquering; for it lives, and ever must live. As to your faith, it also has immortal vitality in it, and though it be just now weak, and staggering, lift up the hands that hang down and confirm the feeble knees, for your faith shall not die out. Here in your Lord's promise the abiding nature of the vital faculties of your spirit is guaranteed. There is no stint to the fulness of life which is given you in Christ Jesus. I know not who shall tell me what it must be to live in all the fulness of Christian life. As surely as I have this day eternal life by reason of faith in Christ Jesus, so surely shall I reach its fulness when Christ who is my life shall appear. Even here on earth I have the permit to seek for the fullest development of this life; nay, I have a precept in this promise bidding me to seek after it. "Ye shall live," means that the new life shall not be destroyed— no, not as to any of its essentials. The shield of Christ's own life covers all the faculties of our spiritual nature. We shall not enter into life halt or maimed; but he will present us faultless before the presence of his glory, not having spot or wrinkle, or any such thing, much less any dead limbs or decayed faculties. It is a grand promise, and covers the spiritual nature as with the wings of God.

The text secures that the death-penalty of the law shall never fall upon believers. The quickened man shall never fall back into the old death from which he has escaped; he shall not be numbered with the dead, and condemned either in this life or the next. Never shall the spiritually living become dead in sin. As Jesus being raised from the dead dieth no more, death hath no more dominion over him; even so sin shall not have dominion over us again. "For if, when we were enemies, we were reconciled to God by the death of his Son,

much more, being reconciled, we shall be saved by his life."
Rom. 5: 10.

We are united to Christ this day by bands of spiritual life
which neither things present nor things to come can separate.
Our union to Jesus is eternal. It may be assailed; but it
shall never be destroyed. The old body of this death may for
awhile prevail, and like Herod it may seek the young child's
life, but it cannot die. Even as sin reigned unto death, even
so must grace reign unto eternal life, by Jesus Christ our
Lord.

Remark carefully *the continuance* insisted upon in this verse.
Continuance is indeed the main element of this promise—"Ye
shall live." It means certainly that during our abode in this
body we shall live. We shall not be again reduced to our
death-state during our sojourn here. Ten thousand attempts
will be made to bring us under dominion to the law of sin and
death, but this one word baffles all. Your soul may be so
assailed that it shall seem as if you could not keep your hold
on Christ, but Christ shall keep his hold on you. The incorruptible seed may be crushed, bruised, buried, but the life
within it shall not be extinguished, it shall yet arise. "Ye shall
live." When ye see all around you ten thousand elements of
death, think ye, believers, how grand is this word, "Ye shall
live." No falling from grace for you, no being cast out of the
covenant, no being driven from the Father's house and left
to perish. "Ye shall live."

Nor is this all, for when the natural death comes, which
indeed to us is no longer death, our inner life shall suffer no
hurt whatever; it will not even be suspended for a moment. It
is not a thing which can be touched by death. The shafts of
the last enemy can have no more effect upon the spiritual,
than a javelin upon a cloud. Even in the very crisis, when the
soul is separated from the body, no damage shall be done to
the spiritual nature. And in the awful future, when the judgment comes, when the thrones are set, and the multitudes are
gathered, and to the right the righteous, and to the left the
wicked, let what may of terror and of horror come forth, the
begotten of God shall live. Onward through eternity, whatever may be the changes which yet are to be disclosed, nothing
shall affect our God-given life. Like the life of God himself—

eternal, and ever-blessed, it shall continue. Should all things else be swept away, the righteous must live on; I mean not merely that they shall exist, but they shall live in all the fulness of that far-reaching, much-comprehending word "life." Bearing the nature of God as far as the creature can participate in it, the begotten from the dead shall prove the sureness of the promise, "Ye shall live."

Let me further call to your notice that the fact here stated is *universal*, in application to all spiritual life. The promise is, "Ye shall live," that is to say, every child of God shall live. Every one who see Christ, as the world sees him not, is living and shall live. I can understand such a promise given to eminent saints who live near to God, but my soul would prostrate herself before the throne in reverent loving wonder when she hears this word spoken to the very least and meanest of the saints, "Ye shall live." If it had been said, "Because your faith is strong, ye shall live," then weak faith would have perished; but when it is written, "Because I live," the argument is as powerful in the one case as in the other.

Our third point is, THE REASON FOR THE SECURITY OF THE SPIRITUAL LIFE.

The reason assigned is this, "Because I live, ye shall live also." Christ has life essentially as God. Christ, as man, having fulfilled his life-work, having offered full atonement for human sin, dieth no more, death hath no more dominion over him. His life is communicated to us, and becomes the guarantee to us that we shall live also.

Observe first, that this is *the sole* reason of the believer's spiritual life. "Because I live, ye shall live also." The means by which the soul is pardoned is found in the precious blood of Jesus; the cause of its obtaining spiritual life at first is found in Christ's finished work; and the only reason why the Christian continues still to live after he is quickened, lies in Jesus Christ, who liveth and was dead and is alive for evermore. When I first come to Christ, I know I must find all in him, for I feel I have nothing of my own; but all my life long I am to acknowledge the same absolute dependence; I am still to look for everything to him. "I am the vine, ye are the branches: he that abideth in me, and I in him, the same bringeth forth much fruit: for without me ye can do nothing."

The temptation is after we have looked to Jesus and found life there, to fancy that in future time we are to sustain ourselves in spiritual existance by some means within ourselves, or by supplies extra and apart from Christ. But it must not be so; all for the future as well as all for the past is wrapped up in the person and the work of the Lord Jesus. Because he died, ye are pardoned; because he lives, ye live; all your life still lies in him who is the way, the truth, and the life.

Does not the Christian's life depend upon his prayerfulness? Could he be a Christian if he ceased to pray? We reply, the Christian's spiritual health depends upon his prayerfulness, but that prayerfulness depends on something else. The reason why the hands of the clock move may be found first in a certain wheel which operates upon them, but if you go to the primary cause of all, you reach the main-spring, or the weight, which is the source of all the motion. Many secondary causes tend to sustain spiritual life; but the primary cause, the first and foremost, is because Jesus Christ lives. While Jesus lives, he sends the Spirit; the Spirit being sent, we pray; our prayer becomes the evidence of our spiritual life.

"But are not good works essential to the maintenance of the spiritual life?" Certainly, if there be no good works, we have no evidence of spiritual life. In its season the tree must bring forth its fruit and its leaves; if there be no outward sign we suspect that there is no motion of the sap within. Still, to the tree the fruit is not the cause of life, but the result of it, and to the life of the Christian, good works bear the same relationship, they are its outgrowth, not its root.

Secondly, it is a *sufficient* cause for our life. "Because I live, ye shall live also." It must be enough to make believers live that Christ lives; for first, Christ's life is a proof that his work has accomplished the absolution of his people from their sins. He would have been in the tomb to this hour had he not made a complete satisfaction for their sins, but his rising again from the dead is the testimony of God that he has accepted the atonement of his dear Son; his resurrection is our full acquittal. Then if the living Christ be our acquittal, how can God condemn us to die for sins which he has by the fact of

Christ's resurrection declared to be for ever blotted out? If Jesus lives, how can we die? Shall there be two deaths for one sin, the death of Christ and the death of those for whom he died?

Moreover, he is the surety for his people, under bonds and pledges to bring his redeemed safely home. His own declaration is, "I give unto my sheep eternal life, and they shall never perish, neither shall any pluck them out of my hands." Will he break his covenant bonds? Shall his suretyship be cast to the winds? It cannot be. The fact that Jesus lives guarantees our life to all eternity. Remember, that if any of his people for whom he died, to whom he has given spiritual life, should after all die, Christ would be disappointed of his intent, which supposition involves the grossest blasphemy. What he came to do he will do. As many as his Father gave him, so many shall he have for his reward. The purchase-price shall not be given in vain; a redemption so marvellous as that which he has presented upon the tree, shall never in any degree become a failure.

Recollect, and this perhaps will cheer you most of all, that all who have spiritual life are one with Christ Jesus. Jesus is the head of the mystical body, they are the members. Suppose one of the members of the mystical body of Christ should die, then from that moment, with reverence be it spoken, Christ is not a complete Christ. What were the head without the body? A most ghastly sight. What were the head with only a part of the members? Certainly not perfect. There must be every member present to make a complete body. Therefore we gather that you, brother, though you think yourself the meanest part of the body, are nevertheless essential to its perfection; and you, sister, though you fancy yourself to be one of the uncomely portions of the body, yet you must be there, or else the body cannot be perfect, and Christ cannot be a complete Christ. From him, the head, the life streams into all the members, and while that head lives as a perfect head of a perfect body, all the members must live also.

And be it remembered, that this reason is an *abiding* reason —"Because I live, ye shall live also"—a reason which has as much force at one time as another. From causes variable the effects are variable; but remaining causes produce permanent effects. Now Jesus always lives. Yesterday, dear brother, you were exalted in fellowship with him, and stood upon the mountain top; then your heart was glad, and your spirit rejoiced, and you could say, "I live in Christ." To-day darkness has intervened, you do not feel the motions of the inner life as you did yesterday, but do not therefore conclude that the life is not there. What is to be your sign; what is to be the rainbow of the covenant to you? Why, that Jesus lives. Do you doubt that he lives? You dare not. You trust him, doubt not then that you live, for your life is as sure as his. Believe also that you *shall* live, for that also is as sure as the fact that he lives. God gave to Noah a token that he would not destroy the earth—it was the rainbow: but then the rainbow is not often seen; there are peculiar circumstances before the bow is placed in the cloud. You, brother, you have a token of God's covenant given you in the text which can always be seen, neither sun nor shower are needful to its appearance. The living Christ is the token that you live too.

And lastly, it is a most *instructive* cause. It instructs us in many ways: let us hint at three. It instructs us to admire the condescension of Christ. Look at the two pronouns, "ye" and "I"; shall they ever come into contact? Yes, here they stand in close connection with each other. "I"—the I AM, the Infinite; "ye" the creatures of an hour; yet I, the Infinite, come into union with you, the finite; I, the Eternal, take up you, the fleeting, and I make you live because I live. What? Is there such a bond between me and Christ? Is there such a link between his life and mine? Blessed be his name!

It demands of us next abundance of gratitude. Apart from Christ we are dead in trespasses and sins; look at the depth of our degradation! But in Christ we live, live with his own life. Look at the height of our exaltation, and let our thankfulness be proportioned to this infinity of mercy.

Let the last lesson be, see the all-importance of close communion with Jesus. Union with Christ makes you live; keep up your enjoyment of that union, that you may clearly perceive and enjoy your life. Think much of the spiritual life and less of this poor carnal life, which will so soon be over. Go to the source of life for an increase of spiritual life. Go to Jesus. Think of him more than you have done, pray to him more; use his name more believingly in your supplications. Serve him better, and seek to grow up into his likeness in all things.

XVIII

LIFE MORE ABUNDANT

"I am come that they might have life, and that they might have it more abundantly."—John 10 : 10.

" THE thief cometh not but for to steal, and to kill, and to destroy." False teachers, whatever their professions, seriously injure and emperil the souls of men, and in the end cause their destruction; their selfish ends can only be answered by the ruin of their dupes. The Lord Jesus, the true teacher of men, causes injury to none, and brings death to no man's door. His teaching is full of goodness, kindness, and love, and it works most effectually for human happiness and benefit. Error is deadly; truth is life-giving. The coming of the old serpent wrought our death; the advent of the woman's seed has brought us life.

The first truth is that JESUS CHRIST HAS COME THAT MEN MAY HAVE LIFE.

I will not dwell upon the thought that even the prolonged natural life of the sinner is due, in a large measure, to the coming of Christ. The interposition of the Mediator accounts for the lengthened lives of gross offenders, whose crimes tax the long-suffering of heaven. If the prayers of our great Intercessor should cease for a single hour, the ungodly among mankind would, perhaps, sink down quick into hell, as Korah, Dathan, and Abiram did, when the Lord's anger broke forth upon them. That, however, is not the drift of the text.

Life in the sense of pardon, and deliverance from the death penalty, is the great result of Christ's coming. All men in their natural condition are under sentence of death, for they have sinned, and shortly they must be taken to the place of execution, there to suffer the full penalty of the second death. If any of us are delivered at this time from the sentence of death, and have now the promise of the crown of life, we owe the change to the coming of the Redeemer to be a sacrifice for our sins. Every man among us must go down to the endless death unless, through him who came to earth and hung upon the tree as the sinner's substitute, we obtain full remission for all offences, and the verdict of *life* instead of *death*. Life there is in a look at Jesus, but apart from him the sons of Adam are under sentence of death.

Moreover, we are all by nature "dead in trespasses and sins." In the day when our first parents broke the law they died spiritually, and all of us died in them; and now to-day, apart from Christ, we are all dead to spiritual things, being devoid of that living Spirit which enables us to have communion with God and to understand and enjoy spiritual things. All men are by nature without the Spirit which quickeneth to the highest form of life. Unregenerate men have physical life and mental life, but spiritual life they have not; nor will they ever have it except as Jesus gives it to them. The Spirit of God goes forth according to the divine will, and implants in us a living and incorruptible seed which is akin to the divine nature, and confers on us a new life, by virtue of which we live in the realm of spiritual things, comprehend spiritual teachings, seek spiritual objects, and are alive unto God, who is a Spirit. No one among us has any life of this kind by birth, neither can it be bestowed upon us by ceremonial rites, nor obtained by human merit. The dead cannot rise to life except by miracle, neither can man rise to spiritual life except by the working of the Spirit of God upon him, for he it is who alone can quicken us. Christ Jesus has come to call us from the graves of sin.

This spiritual life is the same life which will be continued and perfected in heaven. We shall not, when we rise again from the grave, obtain a life which we do not possess on earth; we must be alive unto God here, or take our place among those whose worm dieth not and whose fire is not quenched. There beats within the believer's heart this day the selfsame life which shall enjoy the fulness of joy in the divine presence. If you have only looked to Jesus a few minutes ago, yet is there in your heart now the blessed life; the incorruptible seed is sown in you which liveth and abideth for ever. The heavenly life is within you, and this Jesus Christ came to bestow upon us.

The truth that Jesus is the life-giver is clear enough in the text, and it leads to the following practical reflections. Life for your souls is only to be had in Jesus. If, then, you are this day seeking salvation, you are instructed as to the only source of it. Spiritual life is not the result of working; how can the dead work *for* life? Must they not be quickened first, and then will they not rather work *from* life than *for* life? Life is a gift, and its bestowal upon any man must be the act of God. The Gospel preaches life by Jesus Christ. Sinner, see where you must look! You are wholly dependent upon the quickening voice of him who is the resurrection and the life. "This," saith one, "is very discouraging to us." It is intended so to be. It is kindness to discourage men when they are acting upon wrong principles. As long as you think that your salvation can be effected by your own efforts, or merits, or anything else that can arise out of yourself, you are on the wrong track, and it is our duty to discourage you. The way to life lies in the opposite direction. You must look right away from yourself to the Lord Jesus Christ, you must rely upon what he has done and not upon what you can do, and you must have respect not to what you can work in yourself, but to what he can work in you. Remember that God's declaration is that "Whosoever believeth in Jesus *hath* everlasting life." If, therefore, you are enabled to come and cast yourselves upon the blood and righteousness of Jesus Christ, you have immediately that eternal life, which all your prayers and tears, repentance, and church-goings, and chapel-goings, and sacraments, could never bring to you. Jesus can give it you freely at this moment, but you cannot work it in yourself.

Thou mayest imitate it and deceive thyself, thou mayest garnish the corpse and make it seem as though it were alive, and thou canst galvanise it into a spasmodic motion, but life is a divine fire, and thou canst not steal the flame, or kindle it for thyself; it belongs to God alone to make alive, and therefore I charge thee look alone to God in Christ Jesus. Christ has come that we may have life; if we could have obtained life without his coming, why need he come? If life could come to sinners apart from the cross, why nail the Lord of Glory to the shameful tree? Why thy bleeding wounds, Immanuel, if life could come by some other door? Yet, further, why did the Spirit of God descend at Pentecost, and why does he still abide among men if they can be quickened without him? If life is to be obtained apart from the Holy Spirit, to what end does he work in the human heart? The bleeding Saviour and the indwelling Spirit are convincing proofs that our life is not from ourselves, but from above.

But we intend to spend the most of our time at this time upon the second truth, namely, that JESUS HAS COME THAT THOSE TO WHOM HE HAS GIVEN LIFE MAY HAVE IT MORE ABUNDANTLY.

Life is a matter of degrees. Some have life, but it flickers like a dying candle, and is indistinct as the fire in the smoking flax; others are full of life, and are bright and vehement, like the fire upon the blacksmith's forge when the bellows are in full blast. Christ has come that his people may have life in all its fulness.

Increase of life may be seen in several ways. It may be seen in healing. A man lies sick upon his bed: he is alive, but he can hardly move a limb; he is helplessly dependent upon those around him. His life is in him, but how little is its power! Now, if that man recovers, and rises from his bed, and takes his place in the world's battle, it is evident that he has life more abundantly than in his illness. Even thus there are sick Christians of whom we need to say, "Strengthen ye the weak hands and confirm the feeble knees." Their spiritual constitution is weak, they do but little. When the Lord Jesus restores them, strengthens their faith, brightens their hope, and makes them healthy, then they not only have life, but they have it yet more abundantly. Our Lord desires to have us in spiritual health, he has for that end become the physician of our souls; he healeth all our diseases, and is the health of our countenance.

A person may, however, be in health, and yet you may desire for him more life. Yonder little child, for instance, is in perfect health, but as yet it cannot run alone. Put it upon the ground, it totters a little way, and is ready to fall. Those bones must harden, those muscles must gather strength. When the boy becomes a man, he will have life more abundantly than when he was a babe. We grow in grace, we advance in knowledge, in experience, in confidence, and in conformity to the image of our Lord. From babes in Christ Jesus we advance to young men, and from young men we become fathers in the church. So Jesus would have us grow; this is one of the designs of his coming; thus do we possess life more abundantly.

A person might, however, have both health and growth, and yet enjoy a stinted measure of life. Suppose him to be confined as a prisoner in a narrow cell, where chains and granite walls perpetually bound his motions: can you call his existence life? Might it not be accurate to speak of him as dead while he lives, and to describe his dungeon as a living tomb? Can that be life which is forbidden the pure air, which is the poorest man's estate? denied the sun which shines for all that breathe? He lives, for he consumes that piece of dry bread, and empties the pitcher, daily placed upon the stone floor, but in the truest sense he is shut out from life, for liberty is denied him. When the poor prisoner once more climbs the hill, crosses the ocean's wave, and wanders at his own sweet will, he will gratefully know what it is to have life more abundantly. Now, mark well that if the Son of God shall make you free, you shall be free indeed, and in that freedom find life sparkling, flashing, and overflowing like the streams of a fountain. To be under bondage through fear of death is scarcely life; to be continually fretted with mistrusts, and receive the spirit of bondage again to fear, gendereth unto death; but it is truly life to be able to cry, "Thou hast loosed my bonds!"

Yet I can suppose a man at liberty, and in health, who might have still more abundant life. He is extremely poor, he may wander where he wills, it is true, but no foot of ground can he call his own. He may live where he chooses, if he can live, but he has scarcely bread for his body, covering for his limbs, or shelter from the night-dews; penury pinches him sorely. The poor man works from before the sun proclaims the morning, till far into the night, to earn a miserable pittance. His toil is exacting to the last degree, and his remuneration insufficient to provide necessaries; he can scarcely keep body and soul together. Is this life? It is almost a sarcasm so to name it. When we have met with persons compelled to sleep upon the bare floor, or who have for many hours been without a morsel to eat, we have said, "These poor creatures exist, but they do not live." This saying is true. So sometimes there are believers who rather exist than live; they are starving, they do not feed upon the promises; they do not enjoy the rich things which Christ has stored up in the covenant of grace. When the Lord Jesus enables them to partake of the "fat things full of marrow," and the wines on the lees well refined, then they not only have life, but they have it "more abundantly."

I can still suppose a person who is free, in health, and in the enjoyment of abundance, who needs more life. He is mean and despised, a Pariah, and a castaway. He has none to love him, or look up to him with respect, he does not even respect himself. He slinks along as if the mark of Cain were upon him, he has forgotten hope and bidden farewell to love. You pity such a man every time you think of him. To possess the love and esteem of our fellows is needful if we would live. When under conviction of sin a man has felt himself to be less than nothing, a sinner unworthy to lift his eyes to heaven, a leper fit to be shut up among the unclean, or as a dead man, forgotten and out of mind; then I tell you, by experience, he finds it a mighty addition to his life when the Lord Jesus lifts him up from the dunghill and puts him among princes, even the princes of his people.

I will now set forth the same subject in another way. I would lay before you seven particulars in which Christians should seek after more abundant life.

First, let them desire more *stamina*. An embankment is to be thrown up, or a cutting to be dug out. You want labourers. Here are your spades, and your picks, and your wheelbarrows, and the men are required. See, a number of persons offer themselves for hire. They are very thin, they have singularly bright eyes, sunken cheeks, and hollow churchyard coughs—they are a choice company from the Consumptive Hospital. Will you hire them? Why do you look so dubious? These men have life. "Oh, yes," say you, "but I wish they had it more abundantly: they cannot do such work as I have to offer them." We must send these poor men away, they must go to the doctor, and be taken care of. See yonder another band of rough, stalwart fellows! These men will suit your purpose. Look at their ruddy faces, their broad shoulders, their mighty limbs; hand them the picks and the spades and the barrows, and you will see what British navvies can do. What is the difference between the two sets of men, these navvies and those consumptives? Why the difference lies in the presence or absence of stamina in their constitutions. There is a something, we cannot exactly say what it is, perhaps the physician himself cannot put his

finger upon it, but the one set of men without it are weak, and
the others with it are full of force.

Our Lord Jesus has come that, in a spiritual sense, we may
have stamina, may have well-founded, well-furnished, well-
established, confirmed, and vigorous life, so that we may be
capable of arduous service and powerful action. He would have
us walk without weariness, and run without fainting. He would
have us quit ourselves like men, and be strong. Beloved, do
you not see how great a difference there is between some
Christian men and others? Are not some of them spiritual
invalids? They believe, but their favourite prayer is, "Lord,
help our unbelief!" They hope, but fear is almost as fully in
possession of their hearts. They want medicine and nursing.
Give them any work to do for the Lord, and how soon they
grow weary; discourage them a little, and they are in despair.
Oh that the Spirit of God would give them life more abundantly!
I am afraid that a very large proportion of Christian men in
this day are on the sick list, and are in a decline, from want of
deep-seated principle, and sound vitality of godliness, which
is what I mean by stamina. It is sad to see how some professing
Christians are led astray by any error which is plausibly put
before them. They believe, but they know not why or wherefore, and cannot give a reason for the hope which is in them.
It is to be feared that they profess the truth because others go
that way, and some eloquent preacher has won their affection,
and become their oracle. They have not the stuff in them of
which martyrs are made, they have no grit in their nature, no
decision, no tenacity of belief, no firmness of grip.

Those who have life more abundantly are good soldiers of
Jesus Christ, they have learned to stand fast in the truth, and
by the blessing of God they are more than a match for the
teachers of error, for they know what they know, and are able
to put to silence the fair speeches of deceivers; they are not
carried away with every wind of doctrine, but abide in the truth
as they have been taught. They cry, "O God, my heart is
fixed!" They are "strong in the Lord and in the power of his
might." I compared such strong believers to navigators, and
I shall not withdraw the comparison, for we want men who can
say to the mountains, "Be ye removed," and to the valleys,
"Be ye exalted"; and it is by such agents that the Lord will

make straight in the wilderness a highway for his march of mercy.

In a second sense we have life more abundantly by *the enlargement of the sphere of our life.* To some forms of human life the range is very narrow. Our streets swarm with men in broadcloth of the same race, to whom "the music of the spheres" means the chink of sovereigns, and whose choice quotations relate to the price of stocks, and changes of the market. Over the Exchange we read, "The earth is the Lord's and the fulness thereof," but they read it, "This earth is our God, and the fulness thereof is our all." The souls of such men live like squirrels in cages, and each day their wheel revolves; it is all the world they know. Jesus Christ has come to give his people a wider, broader life than this. True, there are many men upon whom Christ has never looked, whose life traverses wider areas than those which content the baser sort. Such men map out the stars, and fathom the sea; they read the mysterious story of the rocks, and con the ages past; they are deep in philosophy, and force their way into the secret chambers, where the callow principles of things are nestling; they have a life which is bounded only by time and space.

But, beloved, when Jesus comes, he enlarges the sphere of the most capacious mind, and makes the greatest intellect to feel that it was but "cabin'd, cribb'd, confined," until he set it free. What a blessed thing it is to be forgiven, to be dear to the Father's heart, and to feel the Father's kiss! This is a new world to us—to live as they live who live at home with God, and see his smile, and feast upon his love! This is a life of no mean dimensions, for we dwell in God, and are in fellowship with the Infinite. We are no longer shut up to self, but we hold converse with the spirits before the throne, and commune with all the saints redeemed by blood. We have entered into the mysteries of the invisible, and have stood within the veil. In this sense we have life more abundantly.

Thirdly, our life in Christ becomes more abundant as *our powers are brought into exercise.* I suppose all the powers of the man are in the child, but many of them are dormant, and will only be exercised when life is more abundant. None of us know what we may be, we are but in our infancy yet. Christ has come to give us a fuller life than we have yet attained.

Look at the Apostles! Before Pentecost they were mere junior scholars, only fit to occupy the lower forms; they were often ambitious, and contentious among themselves; but when Jesus had given them the Spirit, what different men they were! Would you believe that the Peter of the gospels could be the same person as the Peter of the Acts? Yet he was the selfsame man; Pentecost had developed in him new powers. When I hear him saying, "I know not the man," and a few weeks after see him standing up in the midst of the Parthians, Medes, and Elamites, and boldly preaching Christ, I ask, What has happened to this man? and the reply is, Christ has given him life more abundantly, and he has developed in himself powers which were concealed before.

Beloved, you pray; yes, but if God gives you more life, you will pray as prevalently as Elias. Even now you seek after holiness; but if you have life more abundantly, you will walk before the Lord in glorious uprightness as Abraham did. I know that you praise the Lord; but if the more abundant life fills you, you will rival the angels in their songs. I repeat what I have already said to you—we do not know what we may become. Fain would I fire you with a holy ambition. Pray to Jesus to make you all you can be. Say to him, "Lord, nurture in me all the graces, powers, and faculties by which I can glorify thee. To the fulness of my manhood use me. Send a full stream of life upon me that all my soul may wake up, and all that is within me may magnify thee. Get all out of me that can possibly come out of such a poor thing as I am. Let thy Spirit work in me to the praise of the glory of thy grace." Some Christians are alive only in parts, and in some it must be some very hidden part which is quickened, for little or nothing is to be seen of practical love or zeal. Oh for men who are alive from head to feet, whose entire existence is full of consecration to Jesus and zeal for the divine glory; these have life "more abundantly."

Fourthly, *an increased degree of energy* is intended in the text. We may have the powers, but may not exercise them, and no doubt many men have great spiritual capacities, but they lie still for lack of intensity of purpose. Now, when is a man most alive? Some are so alive when they are in determined pursuit of a favourite purpose. They have formed a resolution, and they mean to carry it out, and you can see their whole man pressing forward upon the track, all aroused and full of eagerness. Now, the Lord Jesus has furnished us with a purpose which is sure to stimulate us to energetic life, for "the love of Christ constraineth us." He has given us a motive and an impulse which we cannot resist, and we are in covenant with him that we will glorify his name so long as we have any being. We are solemnly resolved, and earnestly set to seek his honour. This gives an intensity to life which increases its abundance by arousing it all. A man is said to be full of life when he is worked up into excitement and fired with passion. Enthusiasm is life effervescing, life in volcanic eruption. Where there is determined resolve, if you arouse the man by opposition, you will see his whole life come into action. A heart which is wholly surrendered to the love of Jesus is capable of thoughts and deeds to which colder souls must for ever be strangers. Energetic, forceful, triumphant life belongs to souls enamoured with the cross, and espoused in ardent love to the heavenly Bridegroom.

We will change the line of our thought, and coming to the fifth point, we will say that abundance of life is often seen in *the overflow of enjoyment*. On a spring morning, when you walk in the field, and see the lambs frisking so merrily, you have said, "There is life for you." You see a company of little children, all in excellent health, how they amuse themselves, and what pranks they play! You say, "What life there is in those children!" Catch one of the little urchins, and see if he does not wriggle out of your arms, and you say, "Why, he is all life." Just so, and hence his mirth. In youth there is much life and overflow of spirits. When Israel came out of Egypt, she was young Israel, and how merrily did she smite her timbrels and dance before Jehovah. When churches are revived, what life there is in them, and then what singing! Never comes a revival of religion without a revival of singing. As soon as Luther's Reformation comes, the Psalms are translated and sung in all languages; and when Whitefield and Wesley are preaching, then Charles Wesley and Toplady must be making hymns for the people to sing, for they must show their joy, a joy born of life. When the Lord gives you more life, you also will have more joy. I should not wonder but what you will get into the habit of singing at your work, and humming over tunes in your walks. I should not wonder if persons ask, "What makes So-and-so so happy? what makes his eyes twinkle as with some strange delight? He is poor, he is sick, but how blissful he appears to be!" This will be seen, brother, when you not only have life, but when you have it more abundantly.

Now, sixthly, this is a somewhat peculiar fact, but I think it should not be omitted. The abundance of life will be seen in *delicacy of feeling*. No doubt there is a very great deal of difference as to the amount of pain which persons suffer under the same operation. There are persons so constituted that you might cut off an arm and they would scarcely feel more than another person would suffer during the drawing of a tooth; there are some, on the other hand, to whom the slightest pain involves a thrill of horror, they are so sensitive. Whether it is an advantage or a disadvantage I cannot tell, but it has certainly been observed by skilful physicians that those persons who have strong mental constitutions, who use their brains much, and have a fine mental organisation, are usually those who suffer most when subject to pain; there is more life in them of a certain sort, and they are more sensitive for that reason.

Now, when the Lord Jesus Christ gives his people life in its higher forms, they become more capable of pain. The same sin will pain them a hundred times more than it used to do, and they will shrink from it with greater anxiety to avoid it. If you are only just a Christian, you may do wrong, and you will be penitent; but if you have much life and you do wrong, ah, then your heart will be wrung with anguish, and you will loathe yourself before God. The man full of delicate life will not only suffer more, but he has probably more pleasure; he is sensitive to joys unknown to others, and his whole constitution thrills with a pleasure which another but faintly perceives. The name of Jesus is inexpressibly sweet to those who have abundant life. It is precious if you only have life, but it is beyond all price to those who have very tender hearts, which swell with exuberant life. I have met with some Christians who say they cannot understand Solomon's Song, and I have not wondered at it, for that is a test book for sensitive souls, and when men have much of the life of love, that sacred canticle suits their feelings better than any other book in the Bible, because it is a tender book of sacred love, and glows like altar coals.

Nor is this all I mean by delicacy. I mean this. There is a delicacy of hand which a man may acquire by long practice, which renders that wonderful member a great worker of feats. The fingers and palm are all life, and can execute manipulations of a most surprising kind. Even so the hand of educated faith can not only grasp but handle the good word of life. When gifted with this faculty, we pry into the mysteries of the heart of Jesus as others cannot. So the Lord would have his people enjoy a sensitively discerning life, which shall reveal to them what else they would never have felt and known.

Once more this delicacy shows itself in a marvellous apprehensiveness and keenness of perception which had not been there before. The Indian will put his ear to the ground, and say, "There is an enemy on the way," while you cannot hear a sound. When he comes to a turn in the forest, "There is the trail," says he, "to the right," though you cannot see that a stick has been moved, or that a single blade of grass has been bent. His faculties are full of life, and therefore he has a better ear and a better eye than you. Remember the story of the Siege of Lucknow. When the Highland woman said, "Dinna ye hear it?—dinna ye hear it?" she could hear the sound of the Highland music, when it was far away. I do not doubt she heard it, though others did not; her ear was quicker than theirs. Jesus would have us quick of understanding in the fear of the Lord, so that we shall say, "He is coming—he is coming! I can hear his footfall!" And the world will say, "You are mad; let us eat, and drink, and be married and given in marriage." We want to be able to say, "I can hear the Bridegroom's voice," when others will say, "Not so, it is mere imagination."

The seventh point is this—life, when it is in abundance, becomes *supreme*. Some races of men have physical life, but have it not abundantly; for instance, the Red Indian and the Australian races have life, but after a while they perish and die from off the face of the earth, while other races of more vigorous life battle with their surroundings and survive. Christians should have such abundant life that their circumstances should not be able to overcome them; such abundant life that in poverty they are rich, in sickness they are in spiritual health, in contempt they are full of triumph, and in death full of glory. Glorious is that life which defies circumstances. Christ has given to us, brethren, a supreme life, supreme in its tenacity; it cannot be destroyed, none can cut its thread. "Who shall separate us from the love of God which is in Christ Jesus our Lord?" Neither things present, nor things to come, shall ever avail to do this; we have life so abundantly that it triumphs over all. What I desire beyond everything is to have this life so abundant that it may be supreme over my entire self. There is death within us, and that death struggles with our life. Our life has dashed death down, and holds it beneath its feet; but tremendous is the struggle of death to rise again and get the mastery. Brethren, we must hold death down, we must grip him as with bands of iron, and hold him down, and plant the knee of prayer upon his bosom, and press him to the earth. We must not suffer sin to have dominion over us, but life more abundant must, through grace, triumph over inward corruption.

Christ has come that you might have more life. Come to him by faith. Do not look to ceremonies or outward services or anything else for growth in grace, apart from Jesus, but fly to him and he will give it you, and you shall be rich to all intents of bliss.